FRANCE DAVIS

Rev. France Davis, relaxing in front of new church, summer 2002

FRANCE DAVIS

An American Story Told

Rev. France A. Davis and Nayra Atiya

THE UNIVERSITY OF UTAH PRESS
Salt Lake City

16 15 14 13 12   1 2 3 4 5

The Defiance House Man colophon is a registered trademark of the
University of Utah Press. It is based upon a four-foot-tall, Ancient
Puebloan pictograph (late PIII) near Glen Canyon, Utah.

LIBRARY OF CONGRESS CATALOGING-IN-PUBLICATION DATA
Davis, France.
  France Davis : an American story told / France A. Davis and Nayra Atiya.
      p. cm.
  ISBN-13: 978-1-60781-183-1 (pbk : alk. paper)
  1. Davis, France. 2. African American Baptists—Utah—Salt Lake City—
Clergy—Biography. I. Atiya, Nayra. II. Title.
  BX6495.D365A3 2006
  286'.1092—dc22
  [B]
                                    2006020550

To the Cooper and Davis families
and to Lola Atiya (1917–2002)

CONTENTS

1 | I Am Born and Later Burned | 1

2 | The Coopers and Cooper's Town | 8

3 | The Good Book and Our Goodly Heritage | 12

4 | Magazines, Books, and Stories | 17

5 | Lifelong Student | 20

6 | Calvary's Saturday School | 25

7 | Schools and Teachers | 28

8 | Two Institutions | 32

9 | What Mom and Dad Expected of Their Children | 35

10 | Death | 40

11 | Educational Opportunities | 51

12 | Church Homes | 55

13 | I Am Off to Tuskegee | 58

14 | Florida and the Call to Preach | 63

15 | Common Sense and Honoring Personal Needs | 67

16 | A Full-Time Obligation with My Family's Arms Around Me | 70

17 | A Good Name | 75

18 | Mrs. E. Louise DeBies | 77

19 | Destiny | 82

20 | The Visible Church |85

21 | Sermons | 88

22 | The Pastor and His Family | 94

23 | Willene, Pastor's Wife | 100

24 | The Military and Elsewhere | 104

25 | A Student and His Ministry | 110

26 | Installation | 121

27 | Glass House | 124

28 | Time and Tasks | 128

29 | Ministers | 130

30 | Lessons | 135

31 | Basic Training | 139

32 | Texas | 141

33 | Las Vegas, Nevada | 143

34 | Southeast Asia | 148

35 | Dreaming and Sharing | 183

36 | Some Siblings and Our Old House | 190

37 Educate the Head and the Heart | 192

38 | A Minister's Reputation | 194

39 | Sharecropping Neighbors | 196

40 | Responsibilities and Roles | 199

41 | Crafts | 202

42 | Mom | 204

43 | Dad | 207

44 | The Fruits of Summer | 209

45 | Body and the Soul | 212

46 | Born Again | 216

47 | It Takes a Village | 219

48 | Neighbors and Mutual-Aid Societies | 224

49 | The Little Store | 226

50 | Andrew Cooper and Family | 228

51 | Games | 230

52 | Money | 233

53 | Let Your Word Be Your Bond | 235

54 | Aunt Rena, Folklore, and Home Remedies | 238

55 | Medical Care | 241

56 | Peddlers and Storekeepers | 243

57 | Goldberg's | 246

58 | Company | 248

59 | Be Still, God Is at Work | 251

60 | Medicine for the Soul | 253

61 | Home | 258

62 | Burns: My Side of the Story | 260

63 | Burns: Willene's Side of the Story | 267

64 | Utah | 270

65 | Going Somewhere! | 274

Acknowledgments | 277

About Nayra Atiya | 278

I Am Born and Later Burned

I was born in 1946 in Burke County, Georgia, in a little place called Cooper's Town, named after my mother's family—three miles from Gough, 14 miles from Waynesboro (the county seat), and 100 miles from Atlanta. My wife says that if you blink while driving through Gough, you'll miss it, that's how small it is. Cooper's Town is even smaller than that. My brother Clarence (two years my junior), my cousin Allie Mae Cooper Turner, and my nephew Earl are the only immediate family members living nearby. They check on property and activities in Cooper's Town on a weekly basis. To my knowledge only one family (tenants of my cousin Allie Mae, not family) currently lives in Cooper's Town, or as we say in Georgia, *on* Cooper's Town. There was a time, however, when this tiny place was bursting with life. When my parents were raising their nine children, every house in Cooper's Town was occupied. There were neighbors down the road a piece, folks passing through, coming and going, schools and churches were active, certainly the spirit of community was alive and well. Families generally lived on the land they farmed, whether they were sharecroppers, plantation owners, or landowners who, like us, farmed their own ground.

Like all of my parents' children I was born at home, delivered by Mrs. Mattie Warren, a self-taught practitioner, I would guess in her 60s when I came along. Everyone called her Mrs. Mattie Warren, never using her first name alone, a custom among African Americans by which we signal respect for elders. In fact, it is still true in our communities that the name one uses in relationship to one's friends ofttimes signifies the level of high regard one holds them in. To call one's friend by a first name is to emphatically suggest that this person is somebody special, that the two of you are on great talking terms, that you have an understanding that works when all is well and likewise when all is not well. Such a friend is the Reverend Lafayette Moseley. I can call him by his first name, and he can call me by

mine because we have been and still are close friends. However, as an indication of my respect for him, I would never presume to refer to him as
Lafayette in a public setting.

Lafayette Moseley and I were colleagues in the gospel ministry. He
pastored another Baptist church in town before moving to Las Vegas,
Nevada. We did a lot together and still keep in touch. We visited each other's churches. We preached for each other. We took our congregations to
support each other's projects. But more than that, before he moved, we set
aside a regular time each week when we could get together informally, go
to lunch, sit down and talk about the challenges that we were facing. We
started with a good working relationship that mushroomed into a very
personal one. We helped each other, we studied in seminary for our ministerial training together, we worked as pastors in the larger community, and
whatever projects I had, he considered them his projects. The same went
for me. We also shared meals at holidays with Reverend Isaac Brantley
and Reverend T. P. Fields and their families. There was just a group of us
who became fast and good friends, but Moseley and I in a very special way.
He had the flexibility as well as the personal commitment to me during
the time of my burns (summer of 1980) to make the sacrifices needed to be
helpful in a way I can never forget. For a full year, he took time off from
work, driving from the west side to pick me up and take me to and from
the hospital for therapies. At such times, both he and my wife, Willene,
uncomplainingly endured a 10-mile automobile ride in the heart of summer, the heat cranked up. As I was burned over 30 percent of my body, I
could not get warm and thus could not stand the windows being open, let
alone air conditioning. Tough days! I remembered the verses from Proverbs that talk about the spirit of man being the candle of the Lord that
searches the inward patches of the belly.

To watch a person who is burned and not be able to touch them, to
want to be close…it was very difficult for the entire family. I now visit
burn centers knowing that there is a natural kind of empathy that comes
to the person who has been burned when he sees another. At the airport
once, traveling with my wife to Nashville, I encountered a young man who
had been burned some four months earlier. He was with his grandmother.
He sat with his head downcast. I stopped and talked to him, showed him
the results of my burns, pointed out the healing of my face.

To walk with others as I had people walk with me on my burns journey, to talk to them, to spend time talking to their families, is a critical

facet of successful healing. There are so many things one agonizes over when one is burned! One wonders: How am I going to look? Will I ever heal? Will the pain subside? Will I ever be warm again? To be able to share my experiences with others in similar distress, to be able to show a stranger how I have healed, makes a difference. This, too, is ministry.

While I was at the hospital, I took the opportunity to minister in another sense. I shared what I believed with the nursing staff and encouraged the doctors. Many who came to visit me left reporting that while they came to cheer me, they found cheer themselves. I communicated to those I was interacting with that there is something greater than intellect, power, and position at work in our lives. My unfailing mantra was: Faith and love will get you through when nothing else will do. The Bible says, "Now abides faith, hope, and love, these three. The greatest of these is love....Faith is the substance of things hoped for and the evidence of things not seen." So, as my body struggled to heal, I took seriously the opportunity to interact positively with those around me and to share my personal testimony. It was helpful to them, even more so to me. "It is more blessed to give than to receive," the Bible teaches in Acts chapter 20, verse 35. Interestingly, as I lay in a hospital bed in Augusta, Georgia, the only pastor in the whole area who came to visit me was the Reverend Jerry Smith.

When I got home after being burned, our children looked on with a sense of awe, not being able anymore to sit on their father's lap, to play, to have me throw them up in the air, to have me participate in events. We had to find another way to be a family, if you will. That other way was to talk more, to explain things, to give answers to questions raised about why I looked as I did. I told the story not only to my family but to different people, told it hundreds of times. It was both a way of self-therapy and a way of teaching about the dangers of fire.

Today, as we look back at the time of the burns, we see it as a growth process. Then, however, I was in bed for six months, except when going to therapies or spending hours sitting under a gentle shower of water to keep warm. I had to lie on my back; my arms were a different color, and pressure on them had to be limited and minimal; my head and ears were parched by the fire; my face was completely without skin. Getting dressed was a chore and staying warm an even greater one. Anything that touched me stuck and pulled away the flesh. When I sat up, it was across the room from anyone. I made no personal contact. In the hospital there were occupational and other therapies; the physical therapy was gut-wrenching. Wherever there were joints in the body, we had to be careful that these did not tighten up, that as the skin returned it did not draw the arms so that they would close and the elbows fold. We had to insure that joints in the hands were stretched. I literally walked around with a ball in my hand, pumping it to keep my fingers operating. I held a weight in my other hand at various times to insure that my arm was fully stretched. When on one occasion the arm did clench up, the therapists while stretching it tore the skin and blood spurted. I insisted they continue though they were ready to quit. Whatever else one goes through (except childbirth, perhaps) is no match for the pain that comes with having no skin, having nerve endings that are titillated and burned by fire. Having burned flesh removed is excruciating. This debriding process was so painful that I eventually insisted the doctor put me to sleep.

The whole body responds to having no skin: the kidneys are affected, along with the heart and all internal organs. I remembered the verse in Romans 12 and I Corinthians 12 which says that the hand cannot say to the eyes, "I don't need you," because as members of the same body every part needs every other part to be fully functional. Eventually, whenever I went out, a skin-tight stocking (TED) was used to cover the bandages dressing the burns. These TED hose were designed to reduce the swelling but made me look like a masked man with only my nose and eyes and the ends of my fingers showing. When bandages were removed, new, light-weight skin sometimes came off with them. The back of my hand was almost an inch thick at one point. The excess skin had to be shaved, and was eventually replaced with a skin graft. It was grueling, but a number of personal things kept me going. One was my faith in God, my belief that whatever tragedy came about was a way of bringing me to understand some of the lessons of life. The other was my sense of responsibility toward my young family and my church family. Both had me saying, "You can make it. It may be difficult. Nobody promised you that it was going to be easy, but continue to go. You can do it!"

The expressions of concern from other people of faith made all the difference. People prayed. Along with Willene, some, like Mrs. Gladys Hesleph, hand-fed me when I could not feed myself. Every now and then she and I talk about those days and laugh. Laughter is, after all, medicine for the soul. I think Mrs. Hesleph remembers fondly our interactions. As for Lafayette Moseley, when he and I get together one of his first comments is, "Remember how we spent all of that time with those windows rolled up and the heat going?!" He watched the therapies and wondered how I survived. His faith was made stronger, I believe. He saw new possibilities in terms of where faith can take you. Perhaps he remembered the passages from the Bible, from Isaiah and the writings of Peter and Paul, about being tried in the fire and coming out "as pure as gold." These made sense to me when I later talked and wrote of my experience. I can count Moseley as a best friend, one who over the long haul went the extra mile. Whatever I have, he knows he can get. Whatever he has, I know I can get. Somebody said that to find one good friend in all of a lifetime may be the best you can do. I have been blessed with more than one.

So fire, faith, friendship…

But let me get back to names and titles.

Titles in our communities are ofttimes used with first names, especially when speaking of older females to distinguish between several ladies with the same last name. Thus, when I was growing up, it was considered appropriate to say "Miss Lucy," "Miss Willie," "Miss Annie Mae," or "Miss Julia," as in the case of my mother. But if there was only one person in the community with a given last name, they would be referred to as Mrs. Cooper or Mrs. Davis. It is interesting to note that for ministers in the African American tradition it is a common practice to use their initials and their last names by way of avoiding familiarity and to signal regard and respect.

Mattie Warren was always referred to as Mrs. Warren and was known as one who had never lost a baby. She was highly sought after even though she was not the only midwife in the area. I am told she was the one with the best reputation, however. My mother would let Mrs. Warren know about when a baby was due, and Dad would go to Gough by whatever means of transportation he had to fetch her when the time came. Either he drove her back home after Mom was safely delivered, or a member of her own family came out to get her after she had spent a few days attending to mother and child. At the time of my own birth, however, my father was laid up and had been bedridden for many months. I am not certain how Mrs. Warren got to our house.

Midwives ofttimes acted as godparents to the children they delivered. Mrs. Mattie Warren was no different. She was always there. As children, we knew her and could point to her house in Gough. I remember we took vegetables, fruits, nuts, and other food items to her by way of showing appreciation and also because my parents paid for her services in goods, not money. We paid special attention to her. She came to visit "her" children in the community and was a cherished personality. I for one am convinced that we were the better for having had so many parents!

My first cousin Lula Hatcher named me after her husband, France Hatcher, but it was the responsibility of the midwife to report and register births. I would venture to guess that because Mrs. Warren was either illiterate or minimally able to read and write, she recorded my name as Francis instead of France. Later, around the time I was 12 years old, my parents corrected the error on my birth certificate. My name is certainly an odd one and sets me apart. In fact, I had never encountered the name France outside of our family until I ran across it in an obituary in a Salt Lake City newspaper not long ago.

In our community most people had nicknames and these were used as a way of affectionately referring to someone, sometimes to emphasize a character trait. I never was given one. I was called either France, Albert, or Davis. Some called me Francie, Francis, or Frank, but these were not really nicknames. It is noteworthy that even today I know some people I grew up with only by their nicknames. That's how important nicknames were to us!

Reminiscing about his childhood, the African American author Arna Bomptemps explains it well: "I had already become aware of nicknames among the people we regarded as members of the family. I got the impression that to be loved intensely one needed a nickname." I remember Dad calling Mom "J" and Mom calling Dad "H" or "Hay" when she was being more tender. One of my brothers was called "Boo" because he liked to go around scaring people. A neighbor was called "Sly" because he was conniving. A sister was nicknamed "Walker" because she walked everywhere. As I was coming up, I was pained not to have one; it made me feel different, or rather that I was being treated differently. I wondered why everybody else was spoken to in terms of their identity, their character, their behavior, terms of endearment in a sense, and I was simply identified by my given name, the tag! In high school and even later, I signed F. Albert Davis because I felt ashamed of my name. However, in 1965, at Tuskegee, as I experienced a greater sense of personal awareness, I saw the potential the name France provided for being an individual, for being different (I was now prepared for this), for being me. Although this took time, I came to believe my name spoke for itself and I stopped caring about not having a nickname. I even began to feel a thrill when introducing myself and thoroughly warmed to it when one day I read that France meant free. I imagined that my given name could energize and define me, even infuse and suffuse me with a sense of movement, of flight. From that day forward I used none other and named my only son France.

The Coopers and Cooper's Town

OUR HOUSE, THE HOUSE IN WHICH I WAS BORN, sat on a piece of property originally owned by the Coopers—not purchased by my grandfather, July Cooper, but by his wife, Scoatney, my mother's mother. I am told that while my grandmother, Scoatney, was out working in the fields, doing things to provide for the family, my grandfather was out riding around having a good time. He called himself Reverend, and was known as a jackleg preacher. In fact, July Cooper had the reputation of one who went around in a buggy and wore a white shirt and a necktie every day of the week, leaving my grandmother and their 14 children to work in the fields, at first as sharecroppers. My grandmother was a good manager—so frugal, it would seem, that some called her stingy. It was she, however, who was able to purchase 180 acres of agricultural land in Cooper's Town as well as a house and lot in Gough, thus enhancing her life and leaving a legacy for the rest of us. When she died, her property was divided among her children. My mother's portion was 21 acres. Uncle James Cooper, who earlier ran away from home, sent word back that he wanted his youngest sister, my mother, Julia Cooper Davis, to have his share of the Cooper land. Uncle James was the last of Mom's siblings to die. He passed away in the 1990s a few years after his sister. I visited him some months prior, the two of us sitting on his bed. He was then a blind man.

My mother was the youngest girl in her family and her brothers somewhat looked after her all of her life. When Uncle James deeded his share of the Cooper land to her, she was already married (1927), and she and Dad had started their first crop of children, my five older siblings. There were four of us in the second crop. Because my parents worked hard farming, planting cotton, corn, wheat, oats, peanuts, and a little sugar cane, they talked about their children as crops, also. I was the next to the youngest of my parents' second crop of children, December 5, 1946.

Over time, in addition to what they inherited, my parents were able to purchase 41 acres of Cooper land from my mother's siblings, raising us children on the earnings from their labors on the dirt farm. By the time I was born they had acquired 83 acres in total, some of it orchards. I now own almost half of this land, having inherited 10 acres and purchased from my siblings another 24 acres along with farmland my father inherited from his mother, some seven miles away.

I am told that my father's mother, Grandmama Lula, had been a single parent who raised her nine children, farming at first as a sharecropper. She was known for her industry and thus had earned the respect of all who knew her, blacks and whites alike. Saving her money, she gradually was able to buy her own land, farm it, live on it, and after her death leave it for her children.

Grandmama Lula also worked for an elderly white lady. Dad told the following story about his mother being asked by her employer to go to the post office to check on and bring back the mail. "One day the lady came to Mama," Dad recounted. "She said, 'Lula, go check on the mail for me.' Your grandmama answered: 'If I go I will have to put on some more clothes. I'll be back in just a minute or two.' She went home, put on her good dress and came back. 'Okay, Miss, I'm ready to go.' The old lady was so outdone, all she could say was, 'Oh! You proud little thing, you!'"

When Grandmama Lula died, each of her descendants inherited 14 acres of land from her. In addition, my father and his sister, Aunt Annie, received the two houses on their mother's property in exchange for cash payments made to their siblings, some of whom no longer lived in the area. My father got the smaller house as we already lived on land from Grandmama Scoatney Cooper. Aunt Annie Mae Braswell, her husband, and their nine children got the larger house. My father and Aunt Annie Mae got the houses as they had the greatest number of children and could also afford to buy the family members out.

I did not hear my dad speak more than a couple of times about his father, or in fact about his father's side of the family. Of course, we as a people were numbered like chattel when we were brought to this country, and what my grandparents knew about their origins and heritage is not preserved in any more than a sketchy way, at least not that I am aware of. I do know that we can go back to my great grandfather, July, so to the late 1700s or early 1800s, and to his son, also named July, my mother's father.

We can trace my grandparents to Georgia, though there seem to be links to North and South Carolina as well.

Because my parents and the older generation exercised great discretion in what they brought into conversation (especially when children were present), we only got a whiff of what they may have known. If we asked Dad about his father, he usually dismissed us by saying, "We'll talk about that another time," or even, "Today's not the time to talk about that." We did hear, however, that Dad's father was from South Carolina, perhaps a slave. As I think about it, had we been told more about him, his behavior, where he was and what he did, I am not sure what we might have done with the knowledge. While I feel shortchanged, I understand that the discretion Dad exercised was perhaps his way of protecting us from details that may not have been in any way constructive or helpful to us.

Like the older generation, Dad shielded his candle to keep it burning. He knew that a word misplaced, an incautious disclosure could prove fatal. No doubt, his prudence grew out of a history of slavery, a time of great pain and hurt when a group of people were treated as less than human. As an oppressed people, African Americans learned to hold their tongues to screen themselves as much as possible from harmful exposure or abuse. Clearly, their silence did not always offer the protection they sought, but within it they sustained an abundant and vivid oral tradition of story and song, which in turn sustained them.

Gwendolin Sims Warren writes in her book *Ev'ry Time I Feel the Spirit: 101 Best Loved Psalms, Gospel Hymns, and Spiritual Songs of the African-American Church*: "In much the same way that our music sustained our forefathers and mothers as they struggled for release from physical and spiritual bondage, it continues to sustain and encourage each new generation."

As to conversation, in my father's world it was conducted by and large on a need-to-know basis. Dad never said any more than he had to. He went to his grave lamenting that the younger generation was talking too much. Had my grandparents said the same?!

I never had the opportunity of meeting any of my grandparents. My parents and older sisters told me, however, that our grandmothers were the centering force of the family. They were the ones who gave us some hope for the future by the example they set, providing firm values and a legacy rooted in the land. They left us property they had labored and endured to acquire and maintain along with lessons about hard work, saving, and using resources wisely.

My father certainly lived accordingly. I heard him say more than once, "Buy you a piece of land because ain't nobody makin' any more. Buy it and you'll always have some place to go, stand on your ground, be your own person."

I have tried to follow in his footsteps.

3

THE GOOD BOOK AND OUR GOODLY HERITAGE

As I MENTIONED, THERE WERE ABOUT SEVEN MILES between the Davis and the Cooper lands. We drove or walked between these properties to visit one another, principally on Sundays as farm life was a life of great demand every day of the week. On Sundays we did chores but did not work in the fields. We spent the day in church, with family or friends, playing, reading the Bible with our father in the afternoon. One of my earliest memories is of Dad gathering us around him, and with his third-grade education stumbling through Psalm 23, First Corinthians, chapter 13, on love, or Galatians 5, on the fruits of the Spirit. He also told Biblical stories about David and Goliath, illustrating how the strongest person does not always win. He told the story of Daniel in the lion's den, of Adam and Eve and their sons, Cain and Abel. He also tried to show us that one who is wisest achieved peace of mind by having his spiritual life working for him as well as his physical and economic houses in order. He used to say, "Balance these and you'll have peace."

As small children, if there was a ball game on Sunday, we would have preferred to play with the kids next door, but Dad was the head of his house. He was guided in thought and deed by the teachings of the Bible, by the wisdom gleaned from his elders, and by what he learned through trial and error. He took seriously the values handed down to him (especially by his mother) and passed them on. No doubt some of his wisdom was simply carried in his genes. Like my father, imbedded in me, in my nature, in my being is that which came from the motherland of Africa and that which is American. The teachings that came down to me, our family's history (what we knew of it and even perhaps what we didn't know) as well as our life experiences were and are indeed shaped by a world view emerging from these two perspectives.

I don't remember my parents mentioning Africa in any but a geographical sense. They had very little to say about our African origins, but their behavior, how they carried themselves, bespoke their roots. When I traveled in Africa, when I heard the music and stories, noted the way conversation was conducted, looked at physical features, experienced the rhythmic lifestyles that occur, I felt a physical and emotional connection. Having felt it, having gotten a taste, I suspect I'll search for more. When a couple of Ghanaians came to share with us at Calvary, I couldn't help thinking, "My, how familiar that look is that they have!" And, the first time I set foot on African soil there was a burning on the inside, an urging that said, Here is where it all got started from. Since then, I have thought with higher regard about what for years I had been taught was called the Dark Continent. I am convinced that much of what we learned about how the people who came here as my ancestors were unlearned, is only half the story. They had going for them lots of things, different ways of expressing that were rarely recognized.

Twice (February 1996 and again in 1999) I was invited to southern Africa to join Dr. William Harvey as a member of the National Baptist Missionary Preaching Team. We visited workers and sites of our sponsored work in South Africa, Lesotho, Swaziland, Zambia, and Malawi. We lived and learned about the extreme conditions of those who have everything and those with nothing. The National Baptist Convention USA Incorporated, through her Foreign Mission Board, of which Calvary Baptist Church is an active member, provides support for South African churches—most often known simply as preaching points—schools, medical facilities, and a 1,000-acre farm. Perhaps the most meaningful thing for me was being able to give clothing and medical supplies to people with unimaginable needs and to learn not to complain. I came home with the clothes on my back and empty suitcases.

Inspired by my African journey, I wrote a poem reflecting my feelings and impressions.

Half the Story

Nobody told us how beautiful
The motherland could be.
Not just bush, jungle, beast, and vine alone

But green grass, sandy beaches and sea shores
Sunrise over the Indian cloud forms rolling in
And fresh, clean air to breathe,
'Tis a spirit of joy just being home.
The people are my family
We share a common song.
It speaks of hope with joy
And brings us back together, again.
If we only knew the whole story
We would hold our heads up high
And bid despair goodbye
For we are Nubian sons and daughters.

My parents adapted to their own lifestyles what they heard passed down through stories as well as what was being preached in their churches. They did not adopt what they heard, but adapted it. They were keenly aware of the coded meanings in such spirituals as "Go Down Moses," which the freedom fighter Harriet Tubman used as a rallying cry when helping slaves to freedom by way of the underground railroad. The story of Moses and the children of Israel living in Egyptian bondage became my parents and their parents' story. It meant something to them, it motivated them, and they passed it on. Perhaps never to be downgraded, they also passed on the power of their dreams and imagination.

"If you can dream it, you can reach it," my father and mother repeated more times than I can count!

The Bible was Dad's chief beacon, his guidebook. Its importance and its teachings were passed down to him as such through his mother, who apparently did not read very well. She had memorized many passages from the Scriptures, ofttimes reciting them to her children. The Good Book became his manual, one he read all of his life. It provided him with the operating instructions by which he lived, telling him what to do and what not to do. As superintendent of our Sunday school he urged his fellow church members to depend on the Bible, not just on a preacher or pastor, for their knowledge of the Word of God. When we children got beyond the third grade, we became the readers and he listened. In fact, that same Bible, with its light-and-dark-brown cover, originally belonging to Grandmama Scoatney Scott Cooper, along with my father's hymn book, are in my possession today. Although the pages of this Bible are now tattered, the Book of Genesis missing, the binding in need of restoration, I treasure it. Also, what makes this Bible so valuable is that in the middle of it my mother has set down in her slanted, halting script the names of 25 family members (Coopers, Lovetts, and Davises), recording their birth, marriage, and death dates. On a page decorated with leaves and flowers, she noted when family members joined the church, were perfected in hope—meaning when they turned their lives over to Jesus—and were baptized or born again. For herself she wrote: "Jullia Cooper, was Bone Burke County, Sept 4. 1907, Married Nov 27, 1927." And on the next page: "Miss Julia Cooper was perfect to hope July the 20, 1927, Baptice Aug. 14, 1927 on the second Sunday At Robison Grove Baptist Church Rev W. M. Lovett pastor." Later, I added, "Died July 4, 1989."

My grandparents' marriage certificate is on a page decorated with leaves, dogwood blossoms, roses, lilies of the valley, forget-me-nots, and the picture of an old-fashioned wedding ceremony set in an oval. This document certifies that "July Cooper and Scoatney Cooper was married Mar. 1, 1879, at Second Menterl Spring Baptist Church By Rev. William Raford and outhers." A banner at the bottom of the page declares: "Therefore shall a man leave his father and his mother and shall cleave unto his wife and they shall be one flesh," a quotation from Genesis, chapter 2, verse 24.

When I was born mother recorded: "France Albert Davis, Burke County, Dec. 5, 1946." She had later added: "1st Sermon, April, 1967," and "Married September 1, 1973." My first sermon was in fact delivered in April of 1966.

Mother's spelling and use of language do not take away from the impact of these few pages in the middle of her Bible. They are a treasure of family history that I have copied and given to all of my siblings and other family members at recent family reunions. When I first read these entries, I understood how the Bible had many uses for us. It was a major part of who we were, of what our family was. The Good Book sustained us spiritually and served us practically. When I went to college, it was where I kept my money. In fact, I left my Bible in full view and never lost anything. Was this because of the sacred nature of the book or because no one ever bothered to read it? I rather suspected the latter!

The Bible was our first book. My parents used it to teach us to read, to spell, to count. Because it is divided into chapters and verses, we had to know how to recite up to 150 in order to get through the Book of Psalms, for example. We also learned to distinguish Arabic and Roman numerals.

Mom and Dad encouraged us to memorize and say whole passages of scripture. We were excited to identify words and spell them: "That's what that word is! The Lord is my S-H-E-P-H-E-RD!" The Bible was certainly a family workbook, if you will, used to guide us as we practiced the steps of daily life.

As for my father's hymn book, it was packed with words without musical score. Dad would line the hymn, indicating its number and whether it was short meter, common meter, long meter, or irregular beat.

The hymn book and our family Bible are today my most cherished and precious possessions.

4

Magazines, Books, and Stories

My parents subscribed to *Ebony* and *JET* magazines. Once a year they received the Sears Roebuck Catalogue. All these came by general delivery to our post office in Gough where we picked up our mail on Saturday afternoons or whatever other times Dad had to go to Gough for business. *Ebony* said to us, Here's what's possible. It portrayed people of color who had risen to the top, showing them with their families, in their homes, displaying their lifestyles. *JET* was more of a gossip, news-in-brief sort of magazine. Its focus on African Americans and their achievements gave us a glimpse of worlds beyond Burke County and our rural communities. Both magazines, the Sears Roebuck Catalogue, and, of course, the Bible were the books we learned from. The Bible was our first reader, our principal source of spiritual and practical guidance. The magazines were full of possible role models. The Sears Roebuck Catalogue was a book for dreaming about things we would like to have. It also served a more practical purpose in the outhouse where it was retired after a new copy arrived.

While books were for us one source of information and inspiration, stories were more vehicles for wisdom. This story about a two-headed man (a fortune teller, a shaman, or a Munti Man as I heard him called in Southern Africa) was told to my father by his mother and to her by her mother, it would seem.

During slavery time, a man went to a two-headed man so he could go out at night without Master's permission. That two-headed man gave him a hand. The man used it the very next night, but as he left, Master and the bloodhounds were out. They chased him but he got away. The next day the man took the hand he'd been given and went to see the two-headed man. "I thought you gave me this to keep my secret safe," he said. "I had to run mighty hard to get away!" The two-headed man looked down and said, "They didn't catch you, did they?" The runaway said, "No, I'm here before you." The two-headed man said, "That's because the hand I gave you is a running hand!"

Whether it is a running, walking, or sitting hand, you have to know what hand you have!

Another story related by one of my older siblings was meant to teach that if you ask too many questions, somebody is bound to get messed up.

Once upon a time a lady walking against traffic was stopped by a policeman. He said, "Don't you know you're walking on the wrong side of the street?" She said, "No, Sir." The officer then asked her, "Which is your right hand?" She raised up her left. "You sure don't know which side you're on!" the officer declared.

I can still hear my father's chuckle as he told another story. "An old man and an old woman decided that they would get married to each other. Somebody told them they must have a blood test. They said, 'Why's that? The only thing we gonna raise is chickens!'"

Perhaps the most famous of Dad's stories, however, is the one he told to a jury who then, I am told, returned a not-guilty verdict. In a matter of months, the accused was again arrested, tried, and this time convicted.

Two men went bird hunting one day. They walked and talked into the woods with guns ready to shoot the first bird they came upon. Soon they came to a beautiful red bird. The first man said to the second, "There he is, there he is, shoot 'im, shoot 'im!" The second man responded, "No, no, no, he's too pretty!" The two men walked on. They came upon a blue bird. The second man said to the first, "There he is, there he is, shoot 'im, shoot 'im!" The first man said, "Noooo, he's too pretty." Then, further into the woods they heard a pecking sound coming from the side of a green tree: Peck, peck, peck, peck, peck, peck, peck, peck, peck.... The men looked up and saw a pretty black and white woodpecker with a red crown. The first man said, "There, there he is, there he is! Shoot 'im, shoot 'im!" His companion answered, "Oh, just let 'im keep a peckin', he'll end up killing his self!"

Dad said if you give some people enough rope, they'll hang themselves.

Stories stand out as major sources of wisdom as I was growing up. Seldom did Dad come out straightforward to teach a long-lasting truth. Instead, he told a story that was then etched in our memories for all of life. He was a master storyteller and I spent the last months of his life talking to him with a tape recorder to capture a few.

5

Lifelong Student

I HAVE BEEN A LIFELONG STUDENT, A LIFELONG STUDENT...

When I finished my time in the United States Air Force, I went to Oakland, California, where I lived with my brother Joseph and his family. Soon, I enrolled at Laney College, Merritt College, and the University of California at Berkeley, using the G.I. Bill. I went full time during the day and received degrees in African American Studies, Arts and Letters, and Rhetoric. In the evening, I attended Bay Cities Bible Institute as a nonmatriculating student as I felt that each of these programs was foundational to my training and life in ministry. Later, in Salt Lake City, I earned a second bachelor's degree from Westminster College, a master's degree from the University of Utah, and another master's from Northwest Nazarene College in Nampa, Idaho. These graduate degrees (in ministry, religion, philosophy, and mass communication) were closely related to my work as pastor of the Calvary Baptist Church and in another way to my teaching work at the University of Utah. At Northwest Nazarene, assignments included developing church policies (how money should be handled, people employed, nuts and bolts issues) as well as sermon development and delivery. It was meaningful to deliver a sermon there, get feedback and grades, then turn around and preach that same sermon to the congregation at Calvary. The connection between school and practical life is valuable and all too frequently overlooked. At Northwest Nazarene assignments tended to be tailored to meet the needs of students and their congregations. The college, in fact, required that the congregation be willing to release its pastor for this period of training and also to participate in certain phases of the courses: surveys, and special projects that could not be completed by the pastor alone.

There were two or three from Calvary who had discussed the possibility of my going outside of Salt Lake City for further ministerial education. Brother Edward Miller, Brother L. C. Wynne, Brother Nelson Styles, and

Brother Willie Hesleph were keen. Brother Lawrence Wynne had attended a training session at the national level where he had heard about churches sponsoring their pastors. We discussed Northwest Nazarene in a small group and then again at the annual business meeting. A sum was proposed from the church's budget to cover this training, at first as an alternative to a salary raise. The second year, Calvary's congregation voted in a raise anyway and because Northwest Nazarene had a plan where the church paid a set amount every month, it was easy for Calvary to budget a couple hundred or so dollars a month for my training. Initially, my commitment to the congregation was that if we didn't raise the money (the pastor's responsibility), we would not do it. They were excited, however, voted unanimously in favor of sending me to Idaho, came up with the necessary funds, and launched me on a two-year program which culminated in my receiving the degree of Master of Ministry. The difference between this degree and the Master of Divinity, by the way, is that the former does not require the studying of a foreign language.

As I indicated earlier, the program at Nazarene was centered in and directed toward the specific work of ministry I was doing. I investigated new areas and topics in the classroom, then on Tuesday nights (in our Bible study class at Calvary) we would talk about them. The entire set of courses was passed on directly to the congregation.

Though the program was essentially a home study program, it required a scheduled week of intensive work on site at different intervals. My children were in high school then, or nearing the end of their high school years. Being away for a week at a time meant leaving my wife to carry on with family matters alone. It also meant planning more tightly the operations of the church. We felt the rewards for family and church family justified the sacrifices made.

I remember with a sense of exhilaration those days! They were good days when I could drive off for a week expecting to be rejuvenated, to be renewed, to learn something fresh, to explore subjects that I had not explored and be able to then share with the congregation. Ofttimes, on my way up to Idaho, I pondered the course that I was going to be taking. On the way back, my thoughts revolved around what I was going to do when I returned to the congregation and how we would work together to get the job done. I could stop at the rest stops and snack or buy a sandwich, get back on the road, eat, reflect. It was meaningful to have time alone to think and even to reason with myself about all sorts of issues and challenges—

everything from what to do about parking problems around the church, to graduating children at home.

I continued to attend four or five times each year until graduation in June of 1994, driving to Idaho on a Monday, returning home on a Friday, preaching and conducting Sunday school class at Calvary on Sunday. On the first Sunday of the month, in addition to the eight o'clock and 11 o'clock scheduled services, I preached (and still do, with few exceptions) an evening sermon for the Lord's Supper worship service, communion. I had been at Calvary about 18 years at the time. The Calvary congregation paid my tuition; I covered the expense of getting there and back. They saw the benefits and I believe they also were hoping to encourage my transition from a pastor who was about to leave to one who would stay on longer. We had gone past the years of my being just "the boy who is here to preach for us"!

As Calvary envisioned me as one who would help to lead them, a number of projects were realized. During this time we erected a housing complex for the elderly, we were able to purchase a vehicle to transport our young people to and from various training programs, and the church was now on stable financial ground, able to sponsor such a training program for their pastor. They encouraged me and were very supportive of their young minister in all sorts of ways. When I was burned, Calvary's congregation did everything they could to take care of my family, providing resources to fly me home, paying me and somebody else to do my work for a full year while I was recovering. All the while Calvary prayed more than at any time in my ministry before or since. I am told that at various times during the week the whole congregation gathered to pray about me and my welfare and that of my family. Likewise, when my parents died our Calvary family was there for us physically and spiritually, continuing to lend their support. Is it a wonder that we committed to stay and live in Salt Lake City?!

Over the years, when other opportunities came along, some with greater resources, I asked myself, "How would it be to start another family?" In Salt Lake City my family and I felt sincere demonstrations of love, care, concern, and support from Calvary, and appreciation both from the community at large and from the university, particularly those in the departments of Ethnic Studies and Communication. The support continues until now. On my end, I believed (still do) that I could bring positive influence to bear and that my service could make a difference in people's lives at Calvary and in the community. I committed to the role of servant, and to doing my utmost to help others become all that they could be. In the process I have become more of what I could be, more fulfilled. I remind people that it is in giving that we receive, and that you take with you what you give and lose what you keep. Some things money can't buy!

When I graduated from Northwest Nazarene everybody was excited and happy, having supported my belief that all would benefit from a more informed ministry. The degree I earned is the only one that hangs in my office at the church, where members of the congregation can look at it and say: "We helped! We participated in this degree that's hanging on the wall!" At Calvary, especially during the worship service, we lift up every kind of moving forward and urge all to be the best they can, be they a plumber, a ditch digger, a judge, a university professor…It is my goal and personal commitment not to have anybody feel slighted or "less than." All of us are significant and all of us are members of the same body. As the beautiful little passage in Romans reminds us, no one part of the body can say to the other, "I can get along without you." Everyone, whoever they may be, whether they be nine or 109, has something to contribute to the completeness of the community. Our goal is to try to make a way.

Personally, I give God credit and thank Him. If at times I walk on water, other times I am sidetracked by the storms. I may falter, but then I get up and make it to the shore. Making an impact on the community would have been impossible without Calvary's congregation! They provided the backing all along and minimized the distractions, encouraging my every step. While I am the one up front, they deal with the real stuff behind the scenes. When I took on the issue of the death penalty in Utah, for example, they allowed me the latitude and time to have meetings at their expense, at their facilities, to gather people to be publicly associated with what might have been a disruptive cause. They continued to hold my arms and did not complain. During times when I was away, traveling regularly, there were always those who filled in the gaps and kept things going until I returned. I recall when we were trying to get the Martin Luther King holiday bill passed, the whole congregation said: "Okay, Reverend, you go forth and we'll help you do it, march with you." They took care of the church's work while I was on the hill trying to educate legislators.

So, holding up my arms…

To be a lifelong student is truly the preparation for the work of ministry. Now that we finally have a theological seminary in Salt Lake City,

I have enrolled in a Doctor of Ministry program, hoping to earn my degree in the next three years. I started in January of 2005 and have since taken three classes—one on preaching, one on Psalms, the third on Revelation. The reading of assignments and books helps both me and the congregation because the more widely read I am the easier it is to prepare a sermon, enriching it with citations, images, and illustrations from one or more of the thousands of books I own. I sometimes will purchase a book for just one line! The Bible, of course, is the sermon's foundation, its heart.

So, lifelong learning...It began with learning to read...

6

CALVARY'S SATURDAY SCHOOL

READING HAS BEEN KEY TO MY LIFE. For as long as I can remember, I considered myself to be a good reader. With Calvary's Saturday school programs, I wanted to tell others of the importance of reading. I recall a poem I once wrote:

LEARNING TO READ

Most of my life I've spent in school
Learning to read from an early age.
But in the book I learned to read from
The stories stirred up a burning rage.
For they speak of Columbus sailing,
His finding of a people and their land.
They share misty dreams of plenty
Saying, "Everybody can join the band."
They speak of a booming nation
With riches and rest on the shore.
Oil flowing like streams of water
Diamonds in the backyard and more.
I learned how to read alright
Though the books were used before.
The stories they told left me out.
I missed the clothes I wore.
I wondered, "Are there people like me?"
"Are the only ones those in the fields?"
"Does anybody speak my language?"
"Has history tracked my yields?"
So, I take the reading I've learned
And find my own goodly heritage.

There I sense my own being and worth.
I'll pass on the wisdom of my age.
Those who read and walk life's pathway
Find the lessons easier to learn.
For the joy in learning to read
Inspires dreams and fans hope's urn.
Reading is the rock to hold the free
For Frederick, Mary, as well as me.
Sometimes in silence, sometimes aloud
Look for the sunshine through the cloud.

Under my leadership, the Calvary Baptist Church began to focus on the needs of children and young people. To that end we started a Saturday school where we brought youngsters in for three hours of tutoring, coaching them in cultural skills and offering them religious training as well. As time went on, a reading program blossomed and soon involved classes Monday through Thursday as well as Saturday. The Waterford Institute, which developed a music-based, state-of-the-art reading software, donated equipment and provided technical assistance in exchange for research statistics. Students enrolled in this program are both from the larger community and from the congregation. Parents are expected to assist their children both at the church facility and at home. Also, at one time, we taught youngsters not only how to use computers, but how to take them apart and put them together again.

We have all along encouraged young people (and parents or guardians) to develop a reading habit, watch educational videotapes, participate in science programs at the church, and take books home. We have started to assemble a library and have a room set aside for that purpose on the ground floor at Calvary, as well as many classrooms on the second floor. Adults have the opportunity to tutor and serve. Students who participate in these programs are then able to go to school, pass their courses, and at the same time be assured of who they are regardless of what anybody tells them.

France II developed an interest in the medical field and started a high school medical science program at Calvary. Young people sit down with doctors, nurses, and medical students to dissect a heart or a kidney. It offers hands-on experience and the students see real blood. They can then decide whether they are really interested in being doctors and nurses.

With the growing population of AIDS/HIV in our community, we operate a special education and testing program. We publish culturally relevant booklets, conduct clergy and community workshops, warn people of risky behavior, and encourage people to be tested for the disease.

All of these programs are part of our educational plan. And, with our new gym, we are developing physically with volleyball, baseball, basketball, and various martial arts. Thus, the church is not only a safe haven, a place for spiritual growth and cultural replenishment, it is also an educational institution.

7

SCHOOLS AND TEACHERS

MY SIBLINGS AND I WALKED THREE MILES to the Gough Elementary School, the nearest public school that was available to us. Most of the schools for African American children in our community had been little one-room schools, ofttimes attached to or beside one of the local African American churches. In our area, there were the Roberson Grove School, Noah's Ark Baptist Church School, and Bryant Grove School. For me, however, school was not a church school. It was a four-room schoolhouse built by members of our community to accommodate children within a certain radius of Gough. The principal served both as a teacher and as head of the school. They conducted their business out of their classroom. Teachers had more than one grade level in their classrooms.

In the beginning I was in what we called the primer school, the equivalent of kindergarten. The building had no electricity. Light came from the windows alone. Chores such as sweeping out the classrooms, washing down blackboards, and cleaning erasers were all done by students at the close of the day. We had no janitor. Students also went into the nearby forest to gather wood that was burned along with coal in potbellied stoves, our only source of heat in the classrooms. We also cut switches used for discipline, as corporal punishment was very much a part of that school experience. The teachers were indeed supported by our parents in that regard and if one of us caused a teacher to use a switch on us in class, we could count on getting another whipping at home. There was no question of parents going down to school to straighten out messes we made. Parents and teachers acted on one accord.

Our school day always started with a period of devotions. We sang Negro spirituals—"Swing Low Sweet Chariot," "Nobody Knows the Trouble I've Seen," "Steal Away," "We are Climbing Jacob's Ladder." We then read from the Bible (often from Psalms) and recited the Lord's Prayer, concluding with a time of personal prayer, the pledge of allegiance

to the flag, and a final song. Devotionals got us going, rhythms and routines prepared us for the work of learning, and a competitive spirit ener-
gized us. We vied with one another to see who could learn faster and better. This spirit was most vivid when our teachers led us in learning games
and spelling bees.

Having African American teachers was an advantage in many ways.
They were role models, showing us what we could become, giving us a special perspective on our history and heritage. They were by and large trained
at black colleges such as Tuskegee, Morehouse, Morris-Brown, Clark, Fisk,
and Howard. There they had been exposed to the African American experience, learning more about it than the textbooks normally covered. As we
read a chapter on President Abraham Lincoln and what he did in the
1850s the teachers pointed out how he had made a difference in terms of
the emancipation of African Americans, adding: "And you also ought to
know that Frederick Douglass did such and such during that same time
period." We thus received a broad-based education, one that also incorpo-
rated a system of values mirroring that of our parents. We were taught in a
variety of ways. One was through Biblical and other stories, frequently
repeated. Another was through example. Our role models were our teachers and elders. Lessons were meant to inculcate courage, integrity, perseverance. I learned about the courage to be truthful no matter what the
consequences. Mom and Dad instilled in us this lesson very early, as did
our teachers. I can still hear the echoes of their words: "If you make your
bed hard, you have to lie in it!" As I matured, I heard someone say, "I asked
for courage and God gave me challenge."

I believe that challenge does test our courage, as faith alleviates our
fears. In my adult life all of this translates into accepting responsibility and
paying the price. In 1973, for example, I made a snap decision that I no longer needed an automobile. I left the car parked in Reno, Nevada, while I
went on to Utah. Shortly after getting to Salt Lake City, I realized how far
things were and had to buy a bus ticket to reclaim the car. I didn't have the
money or the time, but had to find both. So, by going through the valleys,
by confronting life's difficulties, by determining to overcome fear (in my
case, of the invisible, the unexpected, the unknown) courage can emerge.

Courage is, I believe, a learned behavior. Courage, in simple terms, is
the ability to confront the unknown and to overcome fear. It is also, I
believe, being able to sense danger, look at the darkness, see beyond it, and
be able to say: "I'll make it anyway!" We were taught to see that there is

more to life than where one currently is and that education is the goal if you are going to be somebody, if you are going to make it in life.

Frederick Douglass said that when he discovered education, he also realized that freedom was possible. And, indeed, as I think of my own life experiences (many of which were racial and negative, many of which were economically challenged), it was courage that suggested a life beyond the farm, certainly beyond my fears. Of course, it was easy to have courage at home, surrounded by family and friends. Once I was out on my own, however, I quickly understood that I must stand on my own two feet, build a foundation to hold and sustain me, find courage from within, go through the tunnels, and press on toward the light.

One song says, "Time is filled with swift transition, Naught of earth unmoved can stand, Build your hopes on things eternal, Hold to God's unchanging hand!" And so it has been for me.

There is another, a beautiful little hymn we used to sing, which we referred to as "The Mountain Railroad Song," but which is actually entitled "Life's Railway to Heaven." It likens life to a mountain railroad:

> *Life is like a mountain railroad,*
> *With an engineer that's brave;*
> *We must make the run successful,*
> *From the cradle to the grave;*
> *Watch the curves, the fills, the tunnels;*
> *Never falter, never quail;*
> *Keep your hand upon the throttle,*
> *And your eye upon the rail.*

There is always something that points back to the impossible, but armed with faith and courage we can move on to become strong and free. Freedom and education—that was the dream! If you could get education, if you could get freedom from sharecropping, freedom to make your own way, to not be restricted in terms of the laws of the land, then you had it made. I might add that it didn't matter what kind of property you had, how much money you had, although these were important in a sense. Freedom and education were the high-water marks that we aimed for. School was one of the institutions giving us a hand up.

School for us was exciting. At the end of each day we participated in physical education, a class for which we were graded. Our teachers believed

in the concept of a healthy mind in a healthy body. We went outside, practiced side-straddle hop, an exercise where one jumps up in the air, legs
going one way and arms another. We also played basketball, baseball, and
softball, and did callisthenic exercises such as pushups. We then did our
assigned chores, preparing classrooms for the next day. When the bell
sounded, we rushed out the door with great excitement, ready to go
home.

The walk home was a time of play, of interacting with one another
without adults present, a time to smell our own musk, as Dad used to say.
Halfway between school and home was a stream, and in those days it was
safe to drink the water. We cupped our hands and drank, put our faces in
the water to cool off in the hot months. When we came to the last stand of
trees before the home stretch, we broke branches that bore little red fruits
the size of pearls, sweet. We called them apples because they tasted like
apples. We nibbled along the way, scavenging for peanuts as we got closer
to home, and in season picking fruit or pecans from our own trees. We
were fairly well satisfied by the time we walked into our kitchen, but were
glad to find bread and meat Mom had left for us under the tablecloth if
she had gone out to help Dad in our absence. We were expected to eat and
head out to the fields to help our parents. Mom usually returned to fix
supper.

8

Two Institutions

There have always been two primary institutions in the world of my childhood. One was the church and the other was the family. The church was talked about a great deal. The family, though equally significant, was less talked about as such. I should point out that among us family included members whose blood was the same as ours as well as extended family, other people we knew and interacted with regularly, people who had an impact on us. Ofttimes people who had the same blood and had done well professionally served as role models, but so did people not related by blood, people who were just in the neighborhood. Cousin Horace Cooper was a family member whom we looked up to and he and his family were an intimate part of our family life. Mrs. Sarah Harvey was not related but took care of us as if family. Still today, I never go to Georgia without visiting her home.

Although they lived quite a ways from us, on rented land, Cousin Horace, his wife Pearl, and their children were the family we interacted with most frequently, ones that had a lasting impact on us. Like my mother, Cousin Pearl was an excellent cook, although Mom's reputation as the best baker was never in question. The Horace Coopers were almost the only family with whom we ate meals. We felt that their house was ours and ours was theirs.

As I said earlier, my father was chairman of the deacons at Roberson Grove, a strong church member all of his life. Cousin Horace was the same at Portersville Baptist Church, about 20 miles south of Coopers Town. My father and mother were members of the Prince Hall Masonic Lodge. So was Cousin Horace. In fact, in high school, I was one of the few students to become a Junior Mason, which signaled that I was part of the leadership. The Masons helped to bring about much positive change in our community.

My parents and Cousin Horace were active participants and I am certain their shared faith and values, and the roles they played as pillars of their churches and their communities, contributed to the special bond between them. Cousin Horace was a peanut farmer who farmed with the help of hired hands and mules to do the plowing. Yet, he always seemed to have a new pickup. He seemed to enjoy life and live it to the fullest. He was also generous. When his young sister died leaving behind children, he raised them along with his own. We respected him, held him in high esteem, and felt at ease in his presence. As Cousin Pearl managed their resources wisely, when Cousin Horace retired, they were able to purchase a nice piece of land on the edge of Waynesboro and build a first-rate house where they lived until they died. Cousin Horace Cooper, like Dad, was a role model that all of us felt was worthy of copying.

The local minister was another role model, as were our teachers who were certainly key players in our daily lives. In fact, the camaraderie that existed between teachers and children and their families is in today's educational settings mostly a thing of the past. Some of these teachers lived in our immediate communities, others drove in from Augusta, some even from the adjoining state of South Carolina. All stayed in close touch with the parents and families of their students. In fact, we children knew that we could seldom hide anything we had done at school: "Mom will find out!" Teachers came to our homes and attended our churches on a regular basis to socialize, worship, and deal with issues concerning children and community. Our teachers wanted to know such things as, Do we work in the fields? Do we have time for homework? Are there any medical concerns? Is there sufficient light at home for homework?…

Perhaps one of the strangest things in our community was a strong and active grapevine. We had no telephones, yet news circulated at lightning speed. I remember one April Fool's Day, my brother Joe and I were walking to school. About a mile down the road we met an old man who did a lot of walking, and we decided to play a trick on him. We dropped a nickel on the ground and asked him if he had dropped a dollar. He responded, "You boys ought to be ashamed trying to fool an old man like me!" When we got home from school, our parents knew and gave us a stern "talkin' to."

Word passed from one person to another. It was expected. Our teachers or any adult would let drop a word about any child, either in passing or more explicitly. If they caught us beating the mules, for example, Mom and Dad heard about it. Cora was an old beast of burden. Queen was younger. Cora was slow, so we sometimes whipped her with the plow lines to get her moving. Any adult catching us gave us a warning and Mom and Dad heard about it. Nothing children did went unnoticed and the grapevine pulsed with gossip, news of our misdeeds as well as our triumphs.

Our walks to and from school were a time to romp and play, to enjoy nature and unwind. We sometimes wrangled with each other, but our mischief was innocent for the most part. There came a day, however, when the system changed and elementary and high school students were bussed to school. We still walked from our house up the two-rut road for a mile or so to where it joined the wider, red clay road, but we had been robbed of the freedom we enjoyed when walking to and from school. One of the memories that stands out is of how we built small fires on the side of the road in winter while we waited for the school bus. The bus rides themselves are a blur, except for the adults driving and in charge. They clipped our fun-loving wings!

9

What Mom and Dad Expected of Their Children

When we were not in school, we helped our mother at home and worked alongside our father in the fields, usually from sun to sun, planting, weeding, harvesting. We plowed, chopped cotton, pulled fodder off the corn and set it out to dry for animal feed before storing it. We did everything that needed to be done and that the season required. It was back-breaking work, and hot in summer when we wore wide-brimmed straw hats to protect ourselves from the sun. My father said to leave the sweat on our faces and necks to cool us off. Generally, we rose at dawn and did morning chores before coming in for a breakfast of eggs, grits, biscuits, and some sort of homegrown meat. As children we did not like fat meat. I still don't. However, our father reminded us: "If you're hungry enough you'll eat anything and the hog has more fat than lean." Saturdays and Sundays we had pancakes made with the flour ground from our yearly crop of wheat, and more rarely from store-bought flour. Having taken wheat to the mill in Wrens or corn to the one on the river banks, the grinder (driven by water-turned turbines) was fed by an attendant. We took home wheat flour and cornmeal that had to be sifted before cooking breads or cakes.

Morning chores, like evening chores, were by and large tending to the animals, collecting the eggs from the chicken house, milking our cows and bringing in the milk, boiling it, and after it had cooled, skimming off the cream that had risen to the top. This cream we kept in the icebox until we had enough to make butter in the hand churn—a porcelain container covered by a wooden top with a hole in the middle and a stick that you worked in an up-and-down motion until the milk turned to butter. The hardened butter would be removed, leaving buttermilk, which my parents drank. They also crumbled and dunked their cornbread into it, something my city-raised wife also favors. I tease her, saying she doesn't know any better!

We ofttimes had more butter than the family could use. Mother sold this extra butter or gave it to neighbors who ran short. What milk we didn't drink, we left on the end of the kitchen counter to clabber, or sour, using this clabber milk to make biscuits and cornbread. Our family had two methods of keeping milk and fresh meats cool. We would sometimes lower them in containers into the open-faced well. Other times, ice was delivered to the house by truck from Waynesboro. It was unloaded with calipers by the iceman and purchased in 25- and 50-pound blocks, which lasted two or three days.

Though we associated with any and all children in the fields and in school, our parents were careful about whom we interacted with on a regular basis. By and large they encouraged friendships with children who went to church. Those who did not were ones Mom and Dad were reluctant to let us play with. They were even wary of us waiting at the same bus stop. They made a conscientious effort to weed out the good children from the not so good. Children were often rated by what was known about their parents. If these were rabble rousers, drunkards, or people who hung around juke joints or were known to fight a lot, their children were to be avoided. Our parents had no problem with us associating with children from any one of the local churches, the good children. In Gough was the First Baptist Church, while a mile and a half from Cooper's Town was the Bryant Grove Church, the church nearest our home. Every New Year's Eve, we walked to Bryant Grove with Aunt Hattie Cooper and her family to attend Watchnight worship services, our way of observing and worshiping as the old year went out and the new year came in. It is, by the way, on Aunt Hattie's land that the Cooper's Town family graveyard is located.

Roberson Grove Church, where we were members, was approximately 10 miles southeast of us. These were the main churches in our immediate communities, the ones we attended. Pastors for our churches were essentially Sunday preachers. During the week they almost always had other jobs; they were farmers, truck drivers, railroad workers. Each was pastor for four, sometimes five different congregations. Some were schoolteachers or principals. One such person was my principal at Gough Elementary School: Mr. Benefield during the week, Reverend Benefield on the weekends.

In many ways, the business of teaching and preaching went together, and still do. In fact, these two professions along with that of undertaker represented the upward economic levels within the African American communities of my childhood and youth. Because they had regular incomes, these folks drove good automobiles, the men wore suits and ties, and the ladies had better clothes; some even wore silk, not cotton like us. By and large, they were highly regarded. I remember seeing young children stop whatever illicit activities they might be doing (shooting marbles, smoking, drinking, playing cards) if they heard the preacher or the teacher was coming down the road. They did not want to be caught, rebuked publicly, or worse, sometimes physically taken home where they would again be disciplined. People respected the teacher and the preacher. Even the white community had a way of respecting the teacher and the preacher. Perhaps, in their minds, they represented the best that our community had to offer—morally, educationally, politically, spiritually, you name it. The moral guidelines, for the preacher in particular, included being married to one spouse (and not divorced), not hanging around the night spots, and staying clear of alcoholic beverages, gambling, and, to a lesser degree, smoking. The preachers and teachers were more often than not people who had genuine concern for others, offered words of encouragement to children, and were willing to share what they had in terms of knowledge and economic resources. For the most part these resources, if not extensive, tended to be more than farm people had. A preacher who had sullied his name, however, was referred to as a "Jack" preacher. Be it the preacher or the teacher, if their walk did not match their talk, they were disregarded and even shunned.

The ministers who preached on Sundays received whatever pay or goods the congregations had for them. They would then get into their automobiles and drive back home, sometimes as much as 200 miles. The chairman of the deacons and the president of the missionary society took care of the needs of the people during the week. More often than not, preachers who did not have other jobs preached revivals.

Recently, the Calvary Baptist Church has invited three of the pastors of Roberson Grove as special guests for my pastoral anniversaries. In return, I delivered the Roberson Grove anniversary sermon in 2002. During the week of August 8–12, 2005, I was the revivalist preaching five sermons from John 6: "Feeding the People," "Not Just Some, but Enough," "One Who Can Do Anything," "Looking for the Master," and "Heavenly

Bread." Each sermon was designed for evangelism and growth. On this occasion, five people came forth in response to the invitation. What a thrilling opportunity to help draw others to membership and strengthen those already there!

But, to get back to the weekends of childhood...

Going to town on Saturday afternoons was the high point of the week. Mom and Dad made sure, however, that we did not go into those neighborhoods where the rough people hung out. They were very strict on us, controlling our goings and comings, whom we associated with. Mom would say without hesitation: "Where you been? Who lives there? Whose child is that you were playin' with? Whose daughter's that you were talkin' to?"

When I was old enough to date, or *court* as we called it, I borrowed Dad's car and went to see a young lady in Jefferson County. When I returned my parents asked where I'd been and I told them. They then said, "As long as you live in this house, don't you ever go back there or visit any of those girls!" Those girls, I was to later discover, were related to Mother by blood and happenstance. Their mother was an outside child, that is, born out of wedlock to one of the men in Mom's family, a married man. My parents had not brought up the subject until they detected my interest.

There were many things adults did not share with children or young people. If asked, they would likely respond, "We'll explain when you are older." We followed their directives, no questions asked.

My parents required that I be home by nine-thirty in the evening when I went courting. If I wanted to use the car again, I was well served to heed that curfew. Courting meant going to a young lady's home. We were never left alone, however. Her siblings might sit on the porch with us or play around us. Her mother would be in the next room with the door or the window wide open. In winter we sat inside the house, with others present. When I was old enough to drive, Dad lent me his car. Before that time I walked. Ofttimes, someone would go with me. There was always a third person in attendance. Who said three's a crowd?!

We children clearly understood our roles and what our relationship to adults was expected to be. We gave respect where we were taught respect was due. It was expected and required. When we interacted with white folk, we knew what our place was and how far we could go in terms of dealing with them. We would not dare step across that line. The same was true about courting. We knew we could get away with a little kiss, but anything more was out of place and could result in problems. Those were good days, though, because the strictures imposed on us kept us from getting into lasting trouble, like pregnancy out of wedlock. Of course this sort of thing did happen, although not so frequently in our community because the rules that all of the adults applied to all of the children were clear and the consequences were also very clearly laid out. We tended to comply. The old African proverb did apply: "It takes a whole village to raise a child."

When I was a teenager, no matter how old you were, if you got a girl pregnant a shotgun wedding was the very next step, or the girl would disappear to return alone in nine or 10 months. Some family member up North would mysteriously have a new baby. Most often, however, somebody made sure that the two of you got married. Many times those marriages did not last, so it did not always turn out for the best. I speak only as an observer!

Marriage was always very important in my family. My parents were an example of what we believed was a good marital relationship. There were ups and downs, of course, but there was a commitment to stick it out, to do what needed to be done to make it work. When my father moved out of the family home, just shy of my parents' fiftieth wedding anniversary, we were shocked, hurt, and disappointed. We had not seen it coming. Growing up we had never heard them fight, accuse one another, or discuss in a loud voice. My parents and their generation had very clearly defined standards of privacy and did not talk about their relationships. When they told us they were separating, we couldn't help asking why. They simply said, "We just couldn't get along with each other." Thus ended the conversation and we went on to another subject.

I still think about my parents' divorce and I am still in pain. Until today, my siblings and I do not really know what caused the rift that finally led to it. I think in many ways my parents stayed together as long as they did out of love for each other and for the welfare of their children. One thing we do know about divorce is that it is not just a matter between two individuals. It affects the entire family unit and creates great pain.

If there had been something I could have done to change that situation, I would have done it. I wonder at times if we, their children, had stayed around, would things have turned out differently? We can never know. But, one thing is certain. For each one of their children, Mom and Dad's divorce felt like a death in the family.

10

DEATH

MY THIRD OLDEST SISTER, ANNIE MAE, was the first of the Davis children to die. Having had heart problems, she was taken from us at the young age of 34, in August 1967. I was in Thailand, serving in the United States Air Force. She and I had become very close during the summer of my sixteenth birthday, which I spent away from home with Annie Mae, in New Jersey. Her death brought back memories of that summer and, of course, the pain of loss.

In his book *With Head and Heart*, Dr. Howard Thurman wrote, "Death was no stranger to us. It was part of the rhythm of our days." And so it was. These words came poignantly to mind when I buried my oldest brother Hildery on Saturday, August 20, 2005. James Hildery Davis was like a father to me. The years we lived together seemed as yesterday and I remembered how even family thought the two of us looked so much alike. Having considered his life, experienced my sister Annie's and my niece Doreetha's deaths at a young age, and officiated at the funerals of my father in October of 1984, of my mother in July of 1989, of my brother Joe in January of 1990, Dr. Thurman's words made sense to me.

On Friday, August 12, 2005, we had just come from preaching the revival at Roberson Grove Baptist Church. It was getting late when the phone rang. My daughter Grace said, "We are on our way to the hospital. They just called and said Uncle Hildery was not doing well." It seemed like a lifetime as I waited for her to call again. When she finally did, she was crying. "Uncle Hildery didn't make it," she said, and dropped the phone. It was like a bad dream. I had just talked to my brother's wife, Carrie, and to the hospital nurse not more than an hour earlier. Both had said that Hildery was doing well, just waiting for a Monday test and then he would be going home. My father's words were as clear as day: "Your wellest day, you are sick enough to die." Could Hildery really be dead? I called my siblings, promising to call again when we knew for sure. Grace called again, and then I knew that Hildery was really gone.

It was early Sunday morning. I had to preach two sermons for the first time at Calvary since my eight-week sabbatical, the first extended time away from the church in some 30 years. I felt numb and speechless. I preached anyway and Willene and I left Salt Lake City on a red-eye flight at 11:30 that same night. The flight was long, first going to Newark, New Jersey, before continuing to Fort Lauderdale, Florida. It took 12 hours. Once there, the family and I made arrangements for the viewing to be held Friday, August 19, and the funeral the following day. Hildery's remains would stay in Florida, near his wife and children.

The week passed slowly. Friday afternoon people poured into Bethel Baptist Church for the viewing. What an amazing tribute to his life of hard work, loving service, and patient listening! Saturday was a time of celebration. We had rented a larger church to accommodate the crowd. There were 12 or 13 preachers, half the pews were filled with family, and the choir sang his favorite songs. I preached the eulogy. Hildery was going home.

My earliest remembrance of death was that it was something scary, a time of great sadness and sorrow, a time when one had been left behind by a loved one. Hearing stories about ghosts abiding in our family graveyard added to that early fear of death. Thus, my first reaction to death as a small child was to be afraid and to try to stay as far away from it as possible. That meant, of course, finding the fountain of youth, as death was something that happened mostly to older folk. There weren't many young people dying in my community in and around Gough, except for those who died tragically as a result of some accident or some violence, self-inflicted or inflicted by someone else. I remember thinking that while I very much wanted to turn 18 and become a man, I did not want to be an old man, as I knew that the next step would be death.

As I grew older and became a man, I came to understand that death was a stage of transition, a movement, what the Bible calls moving from this earthly tabernacle to our home eternal in the heavens. So I began to view death as a relief from pain, as an opportunity to get away from the trials and tribulations of living in the world among human beings. In fact, I gradually began to look upon it with delight and pleasure as something to expect, to dream about, to get ready for. By the time my father and mother neared death, I anticipated it with a sense of peace, a sense of calmness. Yet, when my father died I was not as fully prepared as I thought I would be. I knew he was dying as he had been ill with cancer, but did not conceive of his leaving. His death brought tears to my eyes and a deep sorrow to my heart. I think my feelings were partly due to wondering if I had done enough to extend his life. But then, when I saw his remains after death, a look of peace and serenity on his face, I knew he had made preparations for his own death. When his time came, my father was ready spiritually, physically, financially, socially, and in every other way. Realizing this, I was able to accept his death knowing that he was out of the pain of his disease, out of the difficulties of human relationships, and that now he would be spending the rest of his time with God who made him.

When my mother died, although she was no longer able to speak and I was not there the moment she left her earthly body, I am told that she departed with a look of utter acceptance, as if finally on her way to a longed-for destination.

Death, I try to remember and remind others, should not be a time of despair and hopelessness, but a time of fulfillment. An old song that we learned at Roberson Grove Baptist Church when I was a youngster said, "Sit down, servant. Sit down, servant. Sit down and rest a while." I think those are the words that apply to the deaths of my father, of my mother, and of one of my first friends at Calvary, Mrs. Ella Louise DeBies. Mother DeBies was the elderly lady who took me under her wing when I was a young man just starting out in Salt Lake City. She was a friend and supporter and was instrumental in my becoming pastor of the Calvary Baptist Church.

I have asked my family to not come to my death with a great deal of sadness and sorrow on my behalf, reminding them of what the Bible says: "Weep for yourselves and not for them." I have ofttimes said to them that I have been in the dressing room getting ready for the day when I will have to go out from this life, when death will take me by the hand and lead me home. I have been getting ready, not morbidly, but rather looking at death as another portion of what life is really about. Not to die is also not to live. And so to live is to eventually come to the end of life.

As a Christian, I think of death as a time of rejoicing, of meeting my savior. I believe that God will be pleased when I reach the stage of my own death, my life having been a continual commitment to faithfully carry out what I sensed was my role in this life, doing what God would have me to do. So my hope is that my family will be prepared and will rejoice on my behalf. While they may share tears of love and weep because they are left behind, my recommendation to them is to go on, to fulfill their own roles, and make their own preparation for death. I can still hear my father saying, "Death is one debt that we all must pay. To die is what you must do!"

I have watched many people die and have seen some die with excitement, with a true sense of "I am going home now!" In fact, my wife's mother is an example. In her last days at the hospital, when asked what she wanted to do, she simply said, "I just want to go home." We rushed to prepare her house, quickly realizing that she was not speaking of her earthly home when the call came from the hospital.

As I think of death, I think of many of the African traditions regarding respect for the dead. I have wondered if it comes from a sense of the well-being that eventually sets in when a person gets to the place of death. Perhaps that is what markers and gravestones identify—that little dash between the date of birth and the date of death is all that really matters. My father lived life to its fullest and the dash represented that accurately for him.

If you were to mark my mother's grave, I think it would be appropriate to say: "Here lies a spiritual woman who went about doing good. She did all she could to help others." I was told at a family reunion that Grandmama Scoatney Cooper used to sing, "I've done all I could do. I've done all I could do. Go tell Master Jesus that I've done all I could do." That kind of sentiment would summarize the life of my mother and my father, two who lived well and were ready, when the time came, to depart.

The Cooper family cemetery is a reminder of what we really think about death and the importance that we place on our loved ones. Aunt Hattie, as I mentioned earlier, offered her property. Each one of us makes an effort to keep their grave sites neat and clean, to keep the bushes and weeds down, to keep the place looking good. I remember when I was a boy, if we found a sunken place in the ground due to deterioration, we went about providing cement tops and slabs for that grave and others. We made a point of keeping the grave space level and in good repair, even though the ground underneath may have given way. Now, we use vaults. We bury the members of our family in a neat fashion so that their graves are side by side, children intermingled with adults. At a recent family reunion, we asked each family member if they could give some money to help pay for upkeep. Because of a high regard and respect for those who have died, most gave. Though we still need to identify some of the earliest ones, we have erected markers for almost all of our graves.

As to the funeral, it is one of the loud announcements of what we think of the dead. The sermon is designed to be honest and truthful, to say that this is the person that we are burying. We strive to provide some comfort to the family and also to share memories that help us deal with the fact that we now are going to be out of the presence of the person who has died. If the person is one who had a strong faith in Jesus Christ and in God, then we approach the funeral as a celebration rather than as a time of sadness. We lift up the good deeds that have been done by the dearly departed and we are able, together, to celebrate this particular home-going. If the person lived life as a rascal, then we find a comforting way, if there be such a thing, to say so.

I heard a man ask not so long ago, "How many of you are ready to die?" No one raised a hand. He then asked, "How many of you are ready to go to heaven?" Everyone raised their hands. He said, "It is strange that everybody is ready to go to heaven but not one of you is ready to die!"

When my father was nearing death, he came to live with us in Utah. He had been diagnosed with cancer in Swainsboro, Georgia, and was being treated by a fine African American doctor who had joined the medical team in that town. He was capable and caring and took care of the needs of many of the African Americans who lived in the region. People drove from Burke County, 60 or 70 miles, to see him, as he had developed a reputation as one who cared. They trusted him. This doctor performed surgery on my father and sent him home with the suggestion that the time had come to take care of business. My father returned, not to his own house, but to one of his sisters' homes. This sister was heavily involved in root treatment, root working, and was what some folks in our rural community called "Doctor." Soon after he moved in with his sister, my siblings and I decided that it would be best for me to visit and try to persuade him to come home with me instead. To that end, I spent a couple weeks at my aunt's house, during which time I observed her placing pennies in the windowsills, sprinkling salt around the sick room, and preparing a variety of herbal remedies. Finally, Dad agreed to come live with me and my family. My brother drove us to Augusta, and my father took his first ever airplane ride. He was feeble and sickly, could not walk long distances, but was glad to be landed. Soon after we arrived in Salt Lake City, I took him to see a doctor who treated him with chemotherapy. Although sick, my father was still the John H. Davis I knew. He was alert. His mind was sharp and he was tuned to everything that was going on around him, even discreetly offering suggestions to me about family interactions, especially insofar as the children were concerned.

Dad stayed in the front bedroom of our home, a room which was spare, with a bed, a dresser, and a clothes closet. A window overlooked the front yard and the street. As Dad was not much for watching television, he gazed out of that window for hours on end. At first, he went to church with us and would sing those old country songs I had heard him sing as I was growing up: "How I got over, how I got over, my soul looks back in wonder how I got over." He was a good singer and would also read the Scriptures during devotions, and lead the congregation in prayer when invited to do so by the deacons of Calvary. His prayers were sing-song in style with lots of well-turned phrases, sometimes cliches. He would always include in his prayers a request that God teach him how to pray and what to pray for, and teach him to love to pray. He was indeed a man who believed in prayer and prayed regularly with his children as we were growing up. In Salt Lake City, he continued to participate with us. He would tell us that prayer is a way of moving the hand that is in charge of the world. One of our hymn writers says it this way: "Prayer is the soul's sincere desire, uttered or unexpressed. Prayer is the motion of the breast." I see prayer as a way of generating the positive energy that is within. It is also a means of summoning up help, a way of accessing the warranty or the guarantee that is there for us by calling upon the Creator, the one who knows best our needs. Of course, prayer is a way of sharing with those around us, a way of getting their participation, assurances, encouragement, a way of getting them underneath the burden or load, if you will. It certainly contributes significantly to healing, as research has shown. I can personally attest to it and my healing from burns confirms it. Prayer ofttimes repeats or restates a request being made. I believe that this repetition contributes to the process and progress of healing body and spirit. I can report here that God did answer my repeated prayers to leave my face unscarred.

As the illness took over my father's body, he spent more and more time looking out the window, watching my children, his gaze intently fixed upon us all, and in the last days of his earthly life he would point to things only he saw: "There's something crawling up the wall over there, why'nt you get it?" Could these have been extra-earthly beings which we could not see? Over time, his voice grew weak. He talked less and less and was no longer able to attend church. When he could no longer go out, the Lord blessed him and us with the Brown family. Sisters Louella, Viola, and Pauline provided food, while their brother Leon, who was a nurse and did not attend church, volunteered to take care of Dad on Sunday at no cost to us. I shall always appreciate their kindness. Eventually, hospice care was added, but it was my wife who was with my father when he died. When I left for work on October 4, 1984, Dad's parting words to me were, "It's going to be alright." I now think it was his clear announcement. He was ready to go and all was well with him.

Because we knew death was not far off, we had arranged with a local mortuary in Salt Lake City who committed to preparing my father's remains for the trip back to Georgia where funeral services and burial in the family graveyard would take place.

When my father died, funerals in Georgia (and in much of the rest of the South) were still managed by funeral directors based on race. Thus Carter's Mortuary took care of our needs, waited for us and the casket at the airport, and treated us like family as we had known them for as long as I can remember. And, because my father was so well known in the area, his funeral had to be held at the largest church facility in Burke County, the Rock Creek Baptist Church. Beechwood Baptist, my father's home church, was too small to hold the family, let alone all of his acquaintances, friends, fellow deacons, and pastors. Dad had not only been active in the Ministers and Deacons' Association, but also in the Walker Grove Baptist Association of Churches. He was also a leader among the Masonic bodies and when word got out that Deacon John Davis had died, people came from all over. Some drove hundreds of miles to attend and pay their respects. After funeral services, we all traveled some distance from Rock Creek Baptist to the family burial place in Cooper's Town to say a prayer and lower the casket into the ground.

I learned a great deal about respect for the dead at my father's funeral. People (black and white) would see us coming in procession, our lights on, and all would pull over to the side of the road to let us pass. The men, in fact, would get out, take their hats off and lay them across their chests. They would remain standing from the time they stopped until the last automobile in the processional had passed. I was fascinated by their high, high regard and respect for those who had died, even if they did not know whose funeral procession was passing.

At the funeral the family was all dressed in black and the ladies had veils on their faces. It was for many of my father's sisters, many of his family members, a very, very sad time. I have ofttimes wondered why they were so sad, why they cried so, why they made such wailing noises. As I looked back, I remembered that my father was the "point man" in the family, the leader. When his sisters needed advice and direction, even though some had husbands and other family members, they would seek out my father. They felt close to him. They trusted him. They relied on his good judgment, on his word. When there were legal issues that needed to be settled, when there were problems among family members, it was my father's voice that was the voice of calm and settlement. And so at the funeral there was a great sense of loss. Some, I think, felt loss because they had not treated my father fairly, family members who had borrowed farm equipment or money and had never returned either.

At the funeral were ministers, deacons, and churchmen who knew Deacon Davis stood for what was right and would stand up and speak if he felt wrong was being done that ought to be corrected. In fact, my father had left Roberson Grove Baptist Church for many years when two church members had committed crimes for which they had been arrested, and the congregation had been unwilling to discipline them. My father left in protest and joined Beechwood Baptist Church, again about eight and a half miles from Cooper's Town, on the Gough road. Even those people who had disagreed with him came to the funeral, knowing that his walk matched his talk. They remembered him as a living example of what it meant to be a Christian. All felt they had lost a friend and a good man.

For us children, although left empty by our father's death, we experienced his funeral as the home-going that we indeed believed it to be. Thus, it was also a time of rejoicing and celebration. It was what he would have wanted. We had watched my father work his fingers to the bone and make sacrifices for his wife, for his children, for others down through the years. We had watched him suffer in his latter years through a time of separation and divorce from my mother, and then watched him live alone. We had watched him deteriorate physically, but for us who watched through the difficulties and the pain, there was always a certainty about him as to where he was going after death. He used to say that we come here to practice our Christianity so we might be ready when it is time to meet our Maker. He confirmed what is said in the Book of Revelation, that there would be no more sadness, no more sorrow, no more tears. Dad knew that he was moving from this earthly tabernacle to a home not made with hands, but eternal in the heavens.

In the eulogy that I delivered at my father's funeral, I described Deacon Davis as a person who took care of his family, nourished and nurtured his faith, and set an example in our community. I encouraged the people to lift their voices in song and to sing with joy instead of moaning because now a servant of God was gone from his labor to his reward. After the service, when we left the Rock Creek Baptist Church, we made sure to drive by our family home en route to the cemetery, which was a tradition in our family.

Dad had always called home a place to hang your hat. Driving by was a ritual way of communicating that this was the final farewell to his home, his hat-hanging, stopping-off place that had sheltered him and his family for so many years. At the graveyard we would say our goodbyes, send up our prayers, and lower the casket into the arms of Mother Earth. When we placed the vault top and covered it with dirt, we had done one last thing on behalf of our father. We participated with joy and with tears, remaining by his grave until everything was complete, the dirt well packed, the grass replaced, and the identifying marker erected. We then drove our automobiles down the road to the home that my father had supervised the building of, the painted block house next door to the unpainted clapboard home where I was born, for a time of fellowship, a shared meal with family and friends. The paint on the new house was a symbol of the progress that my parents had made.

My mother, as she got older and more feeble, stayed in the homes of siblings and children, traveling between us from Washington, D.C., to Maryland, to Nashville, Tennessee, to be with my older sister, to Florida and James Hildery, to California and Utah. Her taste for travel never waned.

While with us, Mom took great delight in sleeping in the bed where my father had died and in just being in the room where he spent his last days. She plied us with questions about his behavior, where he sat, what he did. She stood at the window just as he had done and gazed out. I think she wanted to dwell in those places where he had dwelt as much as she possibly could. They had been husband and wife for 49 years. In many ways he had been her role model. People who had seen them together commented that they had come to look like sister and brother, behaving as if they were cut out of the same cloth. I think they were really still in love!

On Mother's last journey, she traveled with Willie Mae to St. Petersburg, Florida, for a June/July family reunion. Family members we had not met before ran the Cooper's Produce Market there. We had a chance to get acquainted for the first time, and had a grand time Saturday, eating barbecued goat and pork, and every possible pie and cake that you could think of. My mother enjoyed her two favorites, a coconut pie and a sweet potato pudding, and when Sunday came we went to church with our oldest cousin, Alberta Leonard. Her pastor invited me to preach and I did, using a passage I had ofttimes heard my mother refer to as one her father and brother favored. The sermon came from Psalms 37: "Mark the perfect man." I spoke of our family's heritage, our family history, about the elders and what they had passed down to us, emphasizing our spiritual heritage. We enjoyed the service, went to a cousin's house for dinner, and to another's after dinner, leaving Mom to visit with some of her classmates and relatives. We were having a great time at cousin Johnnie Bell's house when a car came down the street rather hurriedly and pulled into the yard. A cousin hopped out and informed us that something was wrong, that Mom had abruptly stopped talking. You needed to be acquainted with Mrs. Julia Davis to appreciate the significance of this statement! Mom was known as the life of the party, one who told stories, some based on true events, others just to keep a fire under the conversation. People gravitated to her. On the occasion of this last reunion, being the oldest member of the family present, she drew lots of attention.

We rushed to her side. She was silent. We took her to the hospital and learned she had suffered a stroke, yet her eyes were sparkly and bright as ever and she appeared calm. She was serene. We called her name, but she did not respond. My wife, the children, and I decided to leave her in the care of family and drive back to Salt Lake City to prepare to have her come and live with us. Two days into the trip I called back to check on her and was given the news that she had died. We continued on to Salt Lake City nonetheless and prepared for her funeral in Cooper's Town instead. The Calvary Baptist Church purchased airline tickets for me and my family and kept us in their constant prayers as we traveled to Georgia. Our Calvary family, as I said earlier, has offered me and my family their faithful support through the years, in good times and bad.

My mother's funeral was different from my father's. It was held at the Roberson Grove Baptist Church where a black-and-white group photograph had hung above the pulpit, behind the choir stand, for as long as I can remember. Pictured are a number of men, two of whom we have identified as Grandpa July and his brother Tommy. Interestingly, Grandmama Scoatney Cooper is the only woman in that picture. Grandpa July stands off to one side. It would seem that he always set himself apart. I have wondered about Grandmama being the only woman in the picture, but she was a founder and mother of the church. I asked to make a copy of that photograph and was sent the original. Today, it is all that has survived the fire that burned the old Roberson Grove Baptist Church down to the ground a few years ago.

On the day of Mother's funeral, so many came that there was standing room only with people spilling outside the church. The pastor of Roberson Grove was present, but the whole family and I conducted the services. As I had for my father's home-going, I delivered Mother's eulogy, setting the tone, wanting the service to be the home-going of a servant whose work was now to be rewarded. We started with songs, sung in jubilation. After the service the procession drove past the family house once again and we buried my mother beside my father in the Cooper family graveyard, already so filled with history and memories: Grandfather July, Grandmother Scoatney, my mother's brothers and sisters, my sister Annie Mae, my brother Joseph, my niece Carolyn...I have suggested that my wife bury me there, too, although I will not be alive to remind her!

After the final farewells at the cemetery, the family returned to my parents' house. On the way to the graveyard there had been sad, bluesy music, but on the way back the tone and the tenor of voices picked up, becoming more lively. This was a time of remembrance, the home-going of Mrs. Julia Cooper Davis. Some laughter was in the air.

Death is something to get ready for and yet despite our faith and our efforts, some part of us is never quite prepared. When I buried my parents, those were two days I shall never forget!

My mother and father are both gone and life is fleeting. We will be here only for a time and we had best do all that we can when we can. Dad used to say that opportunity knocks but once. How true!

11

Educational Opportunities

My parents made sure that their children had as much schooling as possible. My mother with her eighth-grade education had in fact taught school at one time. Going up to the eighth grade in her day, you were considered well enough qualified to teach the youngest children. Dad had to quit school after the third grade and go to work in order to help his mother on the farm and look after his younger siblings. Mom and Dad understood and made it clear to us that the level of schooling they had received would not be sufficient to get us very far. They were willing to make extraordinary sacrifices to insure that all nine of their offspring had the opportunity for better education. They insisted, "You've got to do better than we did. And you've got to be twice as good as your white counterparts." They also said, "There's one room that's never filled and that's the room for self-improvement. There's always some more that can be added to it." They emphasized that if you get to a place where you "know it all" and there is nothing more to learn, then it's probably time for you to die! Dad sometimes added, "I've forgotten more than you'll ever know."

At the time when my older sisters were ready to go to high school, there were limited opportunities available to African American children in the community. Mom and Dad had a standing invitation for the children to join Uncle Noah Cooper and his second wife, Nancy, in Washington, D.C., where they had moved in 1932. Uncle Noah and Aunt Nancy owned and ran some boarding houses in that city. Mom and Dad sent them their two oldest daughters. Lulu and Eunice lived with Uncle Noah's family and graduated from high school in D.C. A meaningful, yet informal arrangement had been made whereby my parents gave full authority to my uncle and aunt to oversee their daughters' education, safety, and medical treatments, and as required to correct their behavior.

My oldest sister Lulu is someone who has moved around a lot. After Washington, D.C., she lived in New Jersey, then returned to D.C., then home to Georgia. Today she lives in Nashville, Tennessee. I remember being amazed when Lulu gave birth to a baby long after she was mother to an adult daughter, Doreetha, who suffered from sickle cell anemia and died young. Though she is old enough to be my mother, Lulu teasingly calls me "the old man," saying I act like one. It was Lulu who sent us children still on the farm our first bicycle and small black-and-white television when she moved up North. In fact, my recollections of driving into Gough with Mom and Dad one Saturday afternoon and finding a large package waiting at the post office are vivid. The bicycle caused quite a stir and excitement as Cousin Solomon helped us assemble it. It was fire-engine red with silver fenders and a bar across the middle, a boys' bike. The Davis children rode it, crashing into the barn, the car shed, the back porch, falling repeatedly before learning to steady ourselves. Mom said, "Once you learn, you'll always know how." We enjoyed Lulu's gift for years until time took the glint off the fenders, silver turned to rust, and the red paint peeled. The memory remains, however.

As to Eunice, my second sister, I think of her as the one who we never saw upset. Her warm smile and laughter complement her soft voice and she enjoys the even temper known in our father. On one occasion, she and her husband, a chef for the president of a railroad, brought home a can of fried ants. I never got up the nerve to taste them!

In any case, Mom visited my sisters quite regularly when they were in school in D.C. She always took with her some kind of food products from Georgia, gifts to her family. She then brought back treats for those of us who remained at home. We looked forward to her return from these trips as our uncle and aunt never failed to send us candy, fruit, an item of clothing, or something in a bag that we were not accustomed to having on a regular basis.

While sisters Lulu and Eunice finished high school in D.C., the Boggs Academy became the place to go for the next four Davis children. My sisters Willie Mae, Annie Mae, and Daisy Mae, and brother James Hildery all attended Boggs, a Presbyterian-sponsored boarding school. Boggs was, in fact, the only institution in our area where African American children could continue their education beyond the ninth grade. Though by 1954, when the Brown vs. Topeka (Kansas) Board of Education decision said that schools ought to be integrated, many in our area still were not. Thus, the Boggs Academy was a Mecca for youngsters from our communities and a place where dedicated teachers could prove themselves, offer their best, be role models to their students and the larger community.

Willie Mae lived on campus and tells me she is still in touch with her roommate, Lula Kates Francis. Annie Mae and Hildery lived at home and were bussed to school, leaving before dawn each day. Daisy, on the other hand, boarded with Mrs. Carrie Cox, an older lady who lived across the street from Boggs Academy.

Sending their children away to school was costly. Mom and Dad had to make sacrifices in terms of money and labor lost on the farm. When it became possible to do so, they enrolled the youngest three of their off-spring in public schools in Waynesboro. Joe, however, left after his junior year and went to live with Cousin Lula Hatcher, in Augusta. He graduated from Lucy Laney, a high school named after a distinguished local African American. Immediately after, he joined the army and was stationed in California where he remained after being discharged, until his death on June 21, 1990.

Clarence, the youngest of the family, attended the first integrated public school, Waynesboro High School, graduating two years after I did. He then went on to earn a Bachelor of Arts and a Master's degree from Fort Valley State College in Fort Valley, Georgia, and returned to Boggs Academy to teach and serve as student counselor. Clarence lived in Georgia until joining me in Utah in 2006.

As for me, I attended Waynesboro High and Industrial School, still a segregated school in my day. My school mates and I were bussed to and from school and thus I had time to continue helping at home. My obligations precluded me from participating in after-school sports, though not from other opportunities like the New Farmers of America, an organization designed to develop young men into better farmers. With them, I traveled all over the state of Georgia, judging timber, animals, and farm techniques. We were taught up-to-date, modern approaches to farming. The use of tractors was a departure from the way my father farmed, using mules. We were also taught how to rotate crops to make the land more productive. In my last year of high school I became a member of the Honor Society (for persons not yet 18 years of age) and was voted class poet, for which I received special recognition at senior commencement. At that time, to join the Honor Society, one was required to meet certain criteria and pass a group initiation process. In my case, this process included crawling around in a dark room while blindfolded, hot wax from the candles held by others dripping on the backs of my hands, and responding successfully to orders shouted by members initiated the year before. Hazing would be the term for it today.

At our high school, graduation exercises were always held at night, in the gymnasium. The night of my graduation my parents, family members, and friends sat on the bleachers while we sat on chairs set up on the floor. The speaker was a preacher who delivered what seemed more like a sermon than a graduation speech. My father did not say much that night, yet I noticed a glint in his eye, a little light on his face, a little glitter indicating that a burden had just been lifted from his shoulders and that he was proud of his son. It was understood that after graduation we would get a job and move out. I remembered the many times he and Mother had said, "You got to do better than we did, you got to go further." Dad didn't give his children much for graduation. He didn't have much. But we knew he was excited and pleased. I remember that Mom, who always had a little money, gave me a $10 bill.

Immediately after graduation I got a job measuring crop land, determining the acreage over which certain crops were cultivated. I made enough money to buy a little black 1952 Chevrolet truck and subcontracted my brother, Clarence, to work with me pulling the chains or tape used to measure. Together, we made more money in three months than our father had in a year farming. That was the last full summer I would spend at home.

12

Church Homes

At home, the foundation for my life had been laid. Many years later, after leaving Georgia and ending up in Utah, I heard Dr. Gardner C. Taylor, one of my mentors, say in a sermon entitled "A Wide View from a Narrow Window," that underneath everything that has some worth and value is some "encourager," someone or some ones who were willing to make the necessary sacrifices so others could move to higher ground. In my case, my first "encouragers" were my father and mother. They were also the ones who made sure that I understood, upon leaving home, the importance of looking for two institutions in the place where I was going, no matter where that was. One was the barber shop where local gossip and conversation would be carried on. The other was the church.

For African Americans, historically, the success of moving from one community to another depended upon finding these. In fact, when I left home, my father's instructions were specific: "When you leave this place, when you get to the other place that you are going to, find a church home." The local church offered (as did the barber shop) a sense of connectedness. The church particularly was not just a place about religion and faith, it was also a place out of which everything else grew. When in Tuskegee, for example, I went to the campus chapel, Shiloh Baptist Church, Mt. Zion Baptist Church, as well as the local Presbyterian church. While serving in the United States Air Force, I attended the military base chapel in San Antonio, Texas. When transferred to Amarillo, Texas, it was the base chapel, Mt. Zion Baptist Church, and the Hopewell Baptist Church. In Thailand, I attended the base chapel as well as the leprosy colony's missionary site. I was never without a church!

The Calvary Baptist Church here is similar to those National Baptist churches all across the country, serving at least six major purposes. It is an agency for social control, determining what behavior is acceptable and not acceptable, defining such institutions as family and marriage, for example.

The church also plays a major role as an institution for economic development; if you want to get a job, if you want to start a business enterprise, find customers, have the necessary contacts in order to be economically viable, then, as an African American, you need to be grounded in the African American church. The church is also an educational institution. It is still true today that the earliest formal education beyond that which parents provide for young children in our communities comes out of the churches, starting in those little speeches delivered on special occasions and holidays, like Easter time. For example, my very first public speech before an audience was: "What are you looking at me so for, I didn't come to stay. I just come to tell you today is Easter day." A little jingle speech of that sort becomes the tune used to provide young people with the ability to stand before an audience with minimal stage fright, to develop speaking abilities, to find ways of communicating to the larger community. Later on, because they take education so seriously, it is the churches that help sponsor tutorial, pre-school, as well as higher education programs. We provide direction and training for very young children in how to read and write, and help with math and the sciences. Calvary also has a college scholarship fund.

Another role the church plays is one of political involvement—not partisan politics, but politics to the degree that they affect people's lives: taxation, justice, distribution of resources such as fire and police department services. Coming together in numbers in their churches, African Americans can make a difference. Here in Utah, it was through the churches that we were able to get a Dr. Martin Luther King Jr. Holiday Bill passed and name 600 South in memory of Dr. King. In the same way, we were able to get the county tax commission to stop taxing small, independent congregations and to root out unfair taxation of certain properties in the state of Utah. So the church plays a political role and is a gathering place for those wanting to be involved. Might I point out that when Martin Luther King Jr. was organizing the civil rights movement, he organized it through the church. It was a natural place. People were already accustomed to strong leadership and being a part of a following group that joined together in order to get tasks achieved. It is thus natural to turn to the church as the place of community, a place you can feel at home and not fret or feel like a stranger, an outsider, alone. My own personal experiences have included meeting what I call little old ladies who wanted someone to talk to and they were willing, in exchange, for an opportunity to be in fellowship, to share their food and their resources and the comforts of their homes. Those people I met at the church, and because they knew me as part of the church, I was welcome in their homes. Recently, I was talking to a banker who said that he was willing to extend credit to people who were part of one of our churches. There is a sense that people who are part of the local church community are willing to be accountable.

The most important role the African American church plays, however, is that of refuge. Many young people who cannot find their own family units (the basic unit of human existence), and cannot find role models elsewhere, can go to their churches and be identified with certain role models, play a part, and feel significant. For people who go to work daily, working for somebody they don't know, working for somebody who is not part of their culture or heritage group, who is not familiar with their life experiences; for people who have no clout in the larger community, the church is a place where they can play a part, be appreciated and respected. African Americans go to their churches and there they find a place of validation, a place of safety. They can say this is how we own, run, and control this place. They come dressed up as if they have everything in the world while all along they may have little or nothing materially. The church is also where they can get away from the hustle and bustle of the larger world, though of course it is primarily a worship center, a place to meet and be in fellowship with people who believe as you do, a place to be in touch with one's feelings as well as one's thoughts about God. It is certainly a place to participate in a lively and vibrant worship service. Our style is call-responsive, participatory. There are no spectators here. That's exciting!

Thus when one moves to a new town, when one goes from one community to another, then one can gather in church and find community. When students move, I always recommend to them that in addition to making their way on college campuses, they find a way to make connections with community through a church. Sometimes it means changing from one denomination to another. That's alright. The key role the church plays, especially in the lives of African Americans, is that of a home away from home, a safe haven both physically and spiritually. And so it was for me.

13

I Am Off to Tuskegee

HIGH SCHOOL GRADUATION WAS A SIGNIFICANT RITE OF PASSAGE, a time for moving on. Everyone in my community looked forward to a day when they would no longer be on the farm, when they no longer would have to work so hard. When our folks from up North came to visit, they reported that life was good in the urban centers of the nation. We saw them driving nice cars. They always seemed to have extra money in their pockets. They had enough to share and were expected to share, and were often asked by the elders. We wanted the same, our slice of the pie. I shall never forget once I was home visiting, on leave during my days in the United States Air Force. Dad walked up to me, asked if I had a piece of money that I could give to my aunt. I did.

In the fall of 1964, I boarded the Southeast Stages and rode off to Tuskegee, Alabama. We had picked Tuskegee over another college because they offered a training program in agricultural engineering that interested me, but mostly because my parents had no money for college and at Tuskegee I could work and study. I would pay my own way. My parents were excited. They had given me $27. I used fifteen dollars and change to buy a bus ticket, keeping the rest tucked in my Bible to use along the way. I shall always remember as Dad drove me to Waynesboro to catch the bus how my mother's eyes were watery. Her usual farewell when anyone left was tears. She had packed clean clothes, made sure I had soap and toothpaste, and fixed a shoebox picnic. I could tell she was anxious to see me going off into the unknown, as it were, and also proud to know her third son was now headed for college. Mother, Dad, and my youngest brother, Clarence, stood at the door of the station waving until the bus pulled out.

I had all of my belongings in a footlocker, stowed in the cargo hatch of the bus. I carried a small bag in one hand and the shoebox in the other. African Americans traveling in those days would invariably carry such a box as we were never certain where we could eat or for that matter whether we would find a drinking fountain or a comfort station we could use. My box had in it a chicken sandwich on light bread, fruit, and two or three slices of cake and pie. Mom always made sure there was something sweet to eat.

The journey from Waynesboro to Tuskegee was 10 hours long. To me, it seemed to take a lifetime. When the bus pulled into Auburn, Alabama, we had been riding all day. My picnic box was now empty. I was hungry and thirsty. I got off the bus and headed for the station only to be stopped at the front door. A little old lady said, "Get your sandwich and drink through the window at the back." I knew this was wrong but chose to accept the rules as they were at that time, burning on the inside. I had been taught to build up courage for other confrontations. Dad said, "Pick your fights, son." Gradually, I began to understand that I must find a way through the dark places in life and that the first step had to come from within. Next, I would need to reach out to others, in my case turning to faith groups for validation and support. There were times, I confess, when I wished I could shed my black skin. At such times, however, I remembered the old folks saying, "There are only two things you have to do: Stay black and die!" Later, when I read Langston Hughes, "Life for me ain't been no crystal stair. / It's had tacks in it, / And splinters, / And boards torn up. / And places with no carpet on the floor—Bare," I remembered my fears. But I was pressing on and my father's lesson was vivid: "Keep your feelings under control and aim for higher ground."

Setting out for Tuskegee was going into the unknown. When I got to campus I felt alone, afraid in unfamiliar surroundings. I wanted to go home, forget about college. I went to freshman orientation anyway. The gym was mobbed with strangers. When asked what I wanted to major in, I said, "agricultural engineering," a highfalutin term for a trained farmer.

I had enrolled in Tuskegee's five-year plan, which meant working full time and going to college part time the first year, then planning to work part time and go to school full time the next four years. Destiny would have it otherwise, but that's a story for another time.

I shared a dormitory room with one of a pair of twins who had also come to Tuskegee as freshmen. The twins were tailors. They knew how to make and repair clothing and thus earned their way sewing. They were also the drum majors for our college marching band. I mentioned them in a speech to the opening session of the 2002 Utah Legislature to commemorate the birth and work of Dr. Martin Luther King Jr., referring to the sermon "The Drum Major Instinct," which Dr. King delivered at Atlanta's Ebenezer Baptist Church on February 4, 1968, two months before he was shot to death.

Like the twins, other students had skills with which they earned money. One fellow was a barber, another was good at writing and tutored. I had no saleable skills, it seemed. I was assigned work full time in the dietary department of a hospital to cover school bills and was paid in Tuskegee scrip, a currency that was good only on campus. I needed another job in order to have some spending money and began to look around. I stopped at a number of places off campus, finally hiring out to Mr. and Mrs. Allen who owned Allen's Variety Store. They agreed they needed someone to clean up after store hours. It was the first time I had been away from my daddy's house since graduation, the first time I had the opportunity of earning money while away from home.

Mr. Allen was a short, quiet man. He was very light skinned and had relatively straight hair. He was the easy member of the team to get along with and to work with. He was behind the scenes, as it were, the bookkeeper. Mrs. Allen, on the other hand, was a large, stately looking, dark-skinned lady. She towered over everyone, including Mr. Allen. She was the demanding member of the team, attentive to details, to clients, and she was clearly in charge. They ran their business effectively and as the store was not far from campus, students and faculty shopped there, also stopping to eat and socialize in the little restaurant set up on one side of the store. Allen's sold clothing, school supplies, greeting cards, cosmetics, drugs, and souvenirs on one side of the store. On the other side was a small dining area with a few tables and chairs and a soda fountain where they prepared sandwiches and served ice cream and refreshments. When the store closed, I reported for work to tidy it up and clean. As soon as I established a routine, I was able to carry out my duties in half the time and still get paid in full. In what little spare time I had, I studied, hung out with other students, and talked to the girls. I took my job at Allen's seriously, however, working most nights from 10 p.m. until midnight. I swept the sidewalk in front of the store, mopped floors, washed windows, swabbed sinks, and stacked chairs before turning out the lights and locking up for the day. It was hard work, but I had learned from my father that hard work never hurt anybody and I soon made enough money to buy myself a record player with two speakers and some albums: Jackie "Moms" Mabley, who adapted the hardships of her life into a comic routine; Pig Meat Markham; the Swaney Quintet; and Mahalia Jackson, among others.

I had learned the skill of saving in high school, having dropped a dime at a time in a little metal cash register that opened only when this piggy bank had ten dollars in it. I had bought my first watch, a Timex costing nine dollars and ninety-nine cents, with what I had saved. At Tuskegee, in my freshman year, I was able to put aside enough to purchase new clothes and a radio on which I listened to the ball games and to a disk jockey named Randy, hailing from Nashville, Tennessee. I also bought an alarm clock, an instrument I no longer need today, but needed then. At that time I could not wake up alone as I was exhausted from my rigorous schedule, working full time and studying. Since I had to be up at four o'clock in the morning to get to work at the hospital, I set the clock the night before, placing it beside the bed. Ofttimes, however, when it rang, I reached over and turned it off. After being late for work a number of times, I learned to put the clock across the room.

Since I knew nothing about banks, I saved what money I did not spend in the back of my Bible, as I said earlier. Other students complained about things being taken from them. I put my dollar bills in two fly leaves at the end of the "Good Book" and taped the sides and the bottom. I left it in plain sight on my desk and nothing was ever taken from me. When I did discover that there was such a place as a bank, I opened my first account at First National Bank of Tuskegee. I learned how to write checks and seemed to have enough to take care of my needs with something left over. When I went home at Thanksgiving and Christmas, I could pay my own way.

On my first trip home from Tuskegee I rode the bus, taking a taxi to the station, which was located downtown. The next time, however, a lady who was employed by the food service department as a dietitian of the hospital, and who went home to South Carolina for the holidays, agreed to drop me off in Waynesboro on her way. I was company for her, and thanks to her the trip home for me was easier and certainly more direct.

By the end of November of my first year at Tuskegee, the push for integration of schools and other public facilities was well under way. Also, when I heard talk of a movement to register voters in Selma, Alabama, I was curious and was willing to do what I could. Shortly after Christmas break, I joined the civil rights movement. I was excited (we all were) and was convinced that now was the time we had sung about in one of the old Negro spirituals: "My Lord's a writin', my Lord's a writin', my Lord's a writin', he's a writin' all the time. He sees all you do. He hears all you say. My Lord's a writin', he's a writin' all the time." We understood this song to be a song about how God was keeping a record of the injustices of "separate but equal" and that there would come a day when the oppressors would be put in their places and the oppressed elevated.

I returned to school after Christmas that year, but instead of going to class, I began to participate more and more in the movement. I said nothing of my activities to my parents, and I don't know what they would have done if I had. Tuskegee was an exciting place in the '60s. Many of the shining lights of the era visited the college and students had the opportunity of interacting with them. It was there that I met Dr. Martin Luther King Jr. and joined him in the march from Selma to Montgomery. I met Malcolm X there as well, coming under the spell of this riveting speaker. You could listen to him for hours, even seated on the hard bleachers of the gym, which is just what I did, later writing about him for the school newspaper. Certainly, these were memorable experiences. Not the least of them was meeting Mahalia Jackson, Harry Belafonte, James Baldwin, James Farmer, Stokeley Carmichael, and Peter, Paul and Mary, among others.

Ultimately, my involvement in the civil rights movement led to my neglecting my studies. I failed in math and at the end of that first year I received a letter from the college informing me that I was no longer welcome to return. I knew Ralph Ellison had been kicked out of Tuskegee for leading a protest march on campus in his day. I may have been in good company in that sense, but I felt sad, disappointed, and embarrassed. It took me some time to admit to my parents that I would not be returning to Tuskegee for a second year. When school was out, I packed up my belongings and went home, where I immediately got a job at a pre-school in Gough. By the last week in August, I had saved enough money to accept an invitation from my brother James Hildery to join him and his family in Fort Lauderdale, Florida, where they had made their home.

My father had ofttimes reminded us that God opens doors that no man can shut and shuts doors that no man can open. In September of 1965, holding fast to Psalms 91, "I will say of the Lord, He is my refuge and my fortress," I saw the open door and set out on my new journey.

14

FLORIDA AND THE CALL TO PREACH

I WAS ON MY WAY TO FLORIDA. I would live with my older brother James
Hildery and his family. The Vietnam conflict was picking up. I knew that
as a young man who had dropped out of school it was just a question of
time until I was called to join the military. In the meantime, I decided to
look for work and explore my newfound freedom.

I had never been anywhere like Fort Lauderdale. At night, I could
hear the traffic go by the windows of my brother's apartment, lights flashing on and off through the frosted glass, tires screeching. Someone was
always walking by, talking, laughing. It seemed as if people never went to
bed. Florida was hot and humid. Lizards dotted the ceiling of my brother's
living room and darted above me as I slept, frightening me at first as I was
sure they would bite. When I discovered that they were friendly and
helped to control the traffic of mosquitoes through the house, I looked for
them with the eye of welcome.

It was 1965. I began to look for work and my brother helped me. I
applied and was hired as a dishwasher in the cafeteria of Burdine's, an
upscale department store downtown. I was told that with my limited experience, however, I could not be trusted to wash dishes. Instead, I would
scrub pots and pans, some almost as big as I was, big enough to climb into.
It was heavy work. I earned $50 a week and got two meals on the job. One
day, however, my cousin, the late Thomas Braswell, said to me, "Why don't
you come apply for a job where I work? The pay's by the hour and you can
make better money." This is how I went to work at the aluminum window
factory where my cousin was employed, fabricating and assembling window frames. It was dirty work, but I made more money than I did at Burdine's. I worked during the day and did not have to worry about studying
or going to classes. I had the evenings to myself. I explored, went to movies, night clubs, and church. What a mixture of experiences!

As my brother did not take rent money from me, but suggested I give his wife $20 or $30 toward food, I found that I had enough to buy a car. I quit riding the bus and now purchased a 1955 Chrysler automobile for $60. This automobile was green, two-toned, and missing a front bumper. In those days, in the African American community, a car without a front bumper distinguished its driver as a "hot rodder." The police seemed to get a thrill out of stopping me, finding reasons to issue tickets on a regular basis.

My Chrysler had a powerful little engine. It was apt to be driven. It was ready to go. I drove it, and being a young man with an automobile opened doors. It made me popular in the area. Others wanted to be my friends, hang out with me, have me pick them up, take them where they wanted to go though most never had money to buy gas, or were not willing to part with it if they did.

One of my friends and I were dating two sisters who sang in the choir at the Bethel Baptist Church on 22nd Road where I had become a member soon after my arrival in Fort Lauderdale. The pastor, the Reverend George Houston, had actually grown up with my mother in Georgia. I began to sing in the choir, to usher, to assist with receiving the offering, also helping to lead devotional services. Whatever was going on at church, the Davis brothers were part of it. I remember preparing diligently for a concert at church one evening, feeling excited about my first solo in a choir musicale. That Sunday morning I attended worship service and came home to a huge meal my sister-in-law, Carrie, had fixed. I ate and ate and ate all that she had served me, having been taught at home to eat all that was put on my plate. Plus, it was good! When I got to church that night I sang three or four lines, my stomach started churning, and I got sick. My brother had to step out of the choir and take me home. We joked that Carrie's eyes were too big for my stomach!

I continued all the while to get letters indicating that I should make sure I was properly registered for the draft. I decided I would not wait to be drafted, probably into the army or the marines. Going down to the recruitment office of the United States Air Force, I was able to strike a deal. They agreed that once I got my draft notice, I could report to them and promptly enlist in the Air Force. This is exactly what I did and was shipped out the same day I received my notice, arriving at Lackland Air Force Base just before midnight.

In Fort Lauderdale, however, trying to make sense of things, to weave strands of my life into a viable tapestry, a pattern emerged. I began to understand that while I could to some degree steer a course for myself, it was really God who was ordering my steps, directing me to a higher calling. I prayed, talked with family and friends, shared by letter with my parents in Georgia, finally sensing that the higher calling I sought was indeed to be of service in the preaching ministry.

We have always believed in our churches that the ministry, the preaching ministry, was a specific calling from God. We were taught that we would recognize the call when it came. Others could confirm it, but only the individual called could fully acknowledge having received it. The call came with a distinct realization that there is a word of worth and of value that is worth sharing, worth passing on from one generation to another, something beyond us and yet something that required a commitment in the here and now. The traditional spiritual came to mind: "This little light of mine I'm going let it shine…All in my heart…All in my house… Ev'rywhere I go…Out in the dark…, I'm going to let it shine, let it shine, let it shine." I remembered Mrs. Fannie Lou Hamer, the great Mississippi civil rights leader, as she lifted her voice singing it. This "testifying" song, based on Matthew, chapter 5, verses 16 and 17 in the Bible, reminds us of what Jesus said to his disciples: they are the light of the world, a city on a hill that glows for all to see. He urged them not to hide their light.

Another version says, "Let your little light shine, let your little light shine, there's someone down in the valley trying to get home." As I felt God calling me, thought of "Mary's little baby," I pondered John, chapter 8, verse 12 in the Bible, which so clearly describes Jesus as the essence of divine light: "I am the light of the world." I wanted to take strength from that light and to let my own light shine forth. And so, during the course of that year in Florida, it became clear to me that each of us as an individual has a responsibility to let our part of the light shine. We are to be (each in his or her way) lighthouses so that others can see and find their way off the seas of trouble, the maze of life's storms and circumstances to a landing place of harmony, peace, and rest. It seemed to me then (even more so now) that if we hide our light we may be responsible for the shipwreck that another may face. Also, it is not enough to talk and do, one has to literally *be* what one is talking about. In my case, it was to become a minister.

When I sensed my calling and decided to make it known, I promptly went to see Reverend George Houston. "Well, I always knew it," he declared and suggested that I study the two Books of Timothy and the Book of Titus to familiarize myself with what the Bible said were qualifications and responsibilities incumbent upon a man of God. He also talked to me about a trial sermon and began coaching me on how to go about preparing one, reminding me all the while that it was the congregation who would vote to license me as a preacher or to deny licensing.

"The trial sermon ought to be three parts," Reverend Houston instructed me. "The first part should address your acceptance of Christ, conversion experience, and baptism while in the second part you should say something about how you sensed your calling." The third part, he explained, would require me to take a passage from the Scriptures and build my message around it. He emphasized how the Scriptures were to the sermon what leavening is to bread. I left Reverend Houston feeling exhilarated and excited. After that, every chance I got, I read the Bible, prayed, and worked on sermon preparation.

On April third of 1966 an evening worship service was scheduled at Bethel during which I was to preach my initial sermon. The Reverend Houston introduced me and as I stood before the congregation I felt relatively calm. I believed that God had called me to do His work and I trusted Him to empower me to do the best that I could. I delivered my trial sermon not from the pulpit, but from the floor, an old custom. It is one to which I still hold and am perhaps one of the few who does.

As I delivered my trial sermon that day, I felt the congregation's enthusiasm and gratefully received their "Amens" and "Say its." When I was done, they offered me their vote of confidence, licensing me, meaning that I could preach the Gospel anywhere a congregation and its pastor, out of the kindness of their hearts, extended an invitation to me. Reverend Houston and the church's clerk, Mrs. Carrie Sheffield, signed the official papers.

Since that long ago day in Fort Lauderdale, my goal in life has been to be the best that I can be and to help others, regardless of who they are, be the best that they can be. "Do what you can while you can. Then when you can't, you don't have to worry about it. You will then be confident in having done your best and be at peace," I remind the people at Calvary.

Isn't that what the Gospel and preaching are all about?

15

COMMON SENSE AND HONORING PERSONAL NEEDS

DAD USED TO SAY, "DON'T QUIT, DON'T QUIT."

From my father, I learned about perseverance as well as common sense. My mother's mother and my father's mother persevered until they owned something. Their own parents owned nothing. They were, in fact, themselves owned!

My wife and I likewise make sacrifices so that our children can go forward, do better, become more than the two of us. Imagination, faith, and perseverance can unlock doors, and if doors open, don't ask if you can go in. Go in even if you're told you have to go out. This has been one of my steadfast rules.

Life was not ideal for our parents and their parents, but they tended to keep their eyes focused on some distant point, some high road, and they taught us to do the same. They constantly reminded us that the downward road is a crowded road! "Keep your eye on a higher calling," Dad said, "and match your walk to your talk."

One of my role models in this respect was my old Georgia mentor, the Reverend John R. Tarver. He was one about whom you could always say, "There's a real minister! There's one who lives up to the calling that we believe God has given him in his life, one who matches his walk with his talk." He had integrity, and integrity is the kingpin for any person's well-being, but even more visibly so for one who is in ministry. Integrity is being what one truly is, what one says one is, and what one would teach others to be; to be genuine, to be real, to be sincere and honest. My father put it in simpler terms: "Be what you is and not what you ain't because if you ain't what you is then you is what you ain't." Talking to the Pharisees, Jesus placed prostitutes and thieves above hypocrites who by their nature exclude themselves from the better life, one guided by conviction. The Bible reminds us: "I know thy works, that thou art neither cold nor hot:

I would thou wert cold or hot. So then because thou art lukewarm, and neither cold nor hot, I will spew thee out of my mouth" (Revelation, chapter 3, verses 15–16).

The Apostle Paul put it in more passionate terms when he wrote: "When I was a child, I spake as a child, I understood as a child, I thought as a child: but when I became a man, I put away childish things. For now we see through a glass darkly; but then face to face: Now I know in part; but then shall I know even as also I am known" (First Corinthians, chapter 13, verses 11–12). So to have passion, to be passionate about where one is and about one's convictions, is a part of integrity. Without it we cannot demand nor command respect. In fact, where we get in trouble (particularly in ministry) is when people discover we are teaching them to do one thing and we ourselves are doing something other than that. Like my father, like the Reverend Tarver and other mentors who have been role models for me over the years, I strive to match my walk to my talk. Also, I keep in mind a lesson we learned as children, namely that the negative places are those that you aim above. When we went hunting, Dad pointed out to us that the birds in their natural habitat always go upward when danger comes.

My parents and their parents made sense out of life, made it exciting, by looking forward and by looking up. They believed that while you may now be in the fields, mud getting in between your toes, dirt crusting your shoes, you are going somewhere else.

As I go forth, committed to a life of service, I make sure not to overlook my personal needs. To that end, I introduce variety into my days and make time to be alone. I am rejuvenated when I move from one situation to another, from one kind of experience to another; going from home to the university, from the university to the church, then to some project that is being done in the community. My father, who planted cotton, corn, peanuts, sugar cane, wheat, and oats, always rotated his crops: "The land will be replenished by the residue from rotating crops. One crop may have drained the soil of certain nutrients when a second crop would be planted to replenish it," he explained. Both Mom and Dad repeated hundreds of times, "Variety's the spice of life!"

Solitude is another way of rejuvenating myself. I have learned that I can be alone even in the middle of a crowd by tuning in on my own wave length, thinking my own thoughts. In fact, I can be happy sitting in a chair doing nothing, just going about the necessities of life. An hour of sitting down doing nothing is for me as valuable as a week of vacation for some others. Quiet reflection pays high dividends. Sleep is restorative. I have trained myself to release the content of the day the minute I step into the bedroom. When I go to bed, I'm generally off to sleep rather quickly and sleep for five or six hours. However, if I wake before the five hours are up, then there's something to do. I get up and take care and do whatever that is. Likewise, it is relaxing for me to get on an airplane and go from a very demanding church situation to a meeting where I am just a part of the group, sitting in the meeting. I am comfortable with a book or a bicycle. In fact, I read off and on all the time, sometimes as many as four or five different books simultaneously: a biography, a volume of poetry, a collection of short stories, a thriller, a theological treatise....I always have something to read at home, in the car, in the office, something with me at the doctor's office, on an airplane. I go to bed at night with a book in my hand and in the morning the first thing I do is spend some time reading. Every now and then there are opportunities to read aloud or in conjunction with another person who is reading the same resource or who may be interested in the same book. That, too, is refreshing. I don't have to have all of the noise and activity that my children require. In fact, I don't understand how they can concentrate while doing homework with all of the bompety-bomp music playing at ear-shattering levels.

It seems that I have more time to do because I take less time than many people I know to rejuvenate. And I suppose if you want to talk further about the way I balance my time, it's more on the basis of quality than quantity. If I make a commitment, I try to keep that commitment regardless of where. My father called it going to get your name. I write into my scheduling not only what I have to do for work, but also what I would do for pleasure and family, thus making it possible to balance the time available to me. I also take advantage of opportunities that come as a result of being a pastor to sit with significant leaders in the community, to attend events, to go to banquets and dinners. Yet, I enjoy just as much a simple chicken dinner at home or at church. My wife says that I've learned to live wherever I am and to make the most of that living while I'm there.

In a nutshell, my life is based on doing what I have set out to do at the time I am doing it. When it is done, I move on to the next thing. I do not go back over it. What's done is done!

16

A Full-Time Obligation with My Family's Arms Around Me

THE PREACHING MINISTRY IS A FULL-TIME OBLIGATION and responsibility. I am glad that I received the call before I got married so that my wife understood that there would be great demands on our family associated with this calling of ministry. Sometimes there are frustrations that come with it. For example, when I walk in the door and the phone rings with an emergency or a call to go someplace and take care of a particular need. At times, this stretches our relationship. I am finding more and more the need to say "no" to some situations. By and large, however, it has worked well because both of us understood the obligations and responsibilities incumbent upon a minister from the start.

When I was called to ministry, my parents responded with a great deal of joy and thrill. My mother's father, her brother, and a number of her nephews were ministers. But to have a minister in their own home, one of their own children, was a high-water mark. They acted as if they expected it, that it was not a surprise, and made it their business to show up at various events, to puff their chests and lift their shoulders. Their eyes had a little more glitter in them and their faces were brightened each time I, their son, would do the work of ministry in their presence.

I have never had any doubt about my decision in terms of my call to ministry. The one area that has given me some second thoughts is whether it would be better to be a minister with a family, or to be a minister without a family. I read in one of Paul's letters that a minister without a family can dedicate one hundred percent of the time to the work of ministry. One with a family has to juggle. I've thought about that a good deal and I've had mixed feelings. Pastors have developed a reputation of not being there for their families. So, one of the challenges for me is to be at the church for the people and at the same time to be a husband and father. I have to make sure what time I have is spent wisely. In our home, we made it a habit to take our children with us to many of the places we went so that they might be involved and able to see for themselves what we were doing in terms of ministry. However, when this was not appropriate or possible, my wife stepped in and took over. She drove all over the West, taking our children to their various athletic and musical events. Sometimes I was there, other times not. We sacrificed so that Willene was home with our children as they grew up. As a result, we count our blessings that all of them have been in good health and none of them have been involved in abrasive lifestyles or criminal activity. All have completed or continue to work toward their higher education goals. We have tried to let each be themselves but have expected them to be the best at whatever they are. We taught them to love God, to respect others, to love one another, and to appreciate the blessings that come their way. Early in their driving careers, all four wrecked automobiles with major property damage but no bodily injury.

Carolyn Marie is the oldest of our children and was born in California. She has a strong sense of humor. She is very independent, a leader in our congregation, and has her own family and home. She attended Tuskegee University and later graduated from the University of Utah with a degree in health education. In 1991, Carolyn was diagnosed with leukemia and given a few weeks to live. After various treatments, doctors recommended a bone marrow transplant, but no match could be found. An experimental bone marrow re-infusion was the next step. Doctors drew and froze her stem cells until enough were gathered to replenish her system. They killed her blood and her body peeled. She received the frozen stem cells, recovered, and has been doing well ever since. She works for the State of Utah as a social services fraud investigator. Carolyn is the mother of Cedric, who attended Rowland Hall School and graduated from Lutheran High School in 2005. He loves basketball more than anything else and even appeared in a TV movie, released in July 2005, as a basketball player. He plans to attend university, perhaps to study electronics or engineering. Our second child, Grace Elaine, was born in Salt Lake City. She and Carolyn are quite different. Grace is small in stature but more willing to venture out. She attended Utah State University and graduated with a degree in elementary education from Grambling State University. After teaching school in Texas, she branched into security and was a policewoman for Baylor University Medical Center. In 2002, Grace moved to Florida, ran a boys' home for a year, taught school for two, and is receiving her Master's Degree in Criminal Justice. She is the director of her

Hollywood Church music department. She has clearly fallen in love with larger African American communities and makes only occasional visits to Utah.

Our only son, France II, was also born and raised in Salt Lake City. He was a member of the track team at Skyline High School and later at Georgetown University, taking part in long, triple, and high jumping. He held many of the national, state, and regional records for track while at Skyline and when he was subsequently courted by Georgetown University, one of the coaches came to Salt Lake City to visit us. He did a good job of assuring us that they would do everything in their power to insure that France would graduate if he chose to come, that he was not just "a piece of meat" to be used and once used to be discarded as in the case of some school athletic programs. At Georgetown, France qualified at the Olympic trials but was unable to compete due to injury. He graduated from Georgetown with a degree in theology and sociology, attended Interdenominational Theological Center in Atlanta for a semester, and has worked and lived in New Orleans, Vallejo, and Salt Lake City, conducting West Nile Virus research. He is developing plans to be a business owner and is currently attending Marywood University Medical School, in Scranton, Pennsylvania, in a special program for physicians' assistants and medical administration. He seems to enjoy the urban areas and has learned to live anywhere.

When Willene joined me in Utah, I had been living there a year. Having lived briefly in married student housing with Carolyn, we soon moved to the house that the church provided and where my wife and I still live on Meadow Drive. When Carolyn was five, we enrolled her in the Jordan school district. Those early days were difficult because she was the only African American in her school. There was some name-calling, announcements made over the loudspeaker about attending the "Primary" of the dominant religious group after school. Carolyn was left in the dark. My wife and I subsequently developed a practice of going to her school on a regular basis. We talked to the principals, to the teachers, I did presentations about African American culture and heritage, and Willene assisted in the classroom. We were able to soften what seemed initially to be a hostile atmosphere. Carolyn did indeed finish Mountain View Elementary School and when she went on to middle school she had become a popular student. In fact she was elected as a student body officer one year and in her final year was president of her senior class.

Certain experiences leave their mark, however. Going to public places was sometimes stressful for us and our children as people stared either at us or through us. Some commented on our skin color; some wanted to touch our hair. In restaurants and stores some servers and clerks simply ignored us, while others would follow us around as if we might take something. A few years ago, walking out of the stacks at the university's library, a staff member rushed up and said, "Can I help you?" I let such incidents slide. I am determined to do what I can to reach out, educate, and hopefully bring about change. I'll speak about this a little later.

Now, to return to our children and to Willene...

Grace attended the same school as Carolyn with minimal conflict. By that time, we had established precedents for how we expected our children to be treated, also indicating to neighbors what we would not tolerate. I even talked about mistreatment to the press. When Grace got ready to go to middle school she was fortunate in that the Granite school district had space available. Diane Hesleph had become one of the earliest African American school principals in the state of Utah, at the Wasatch Middle School. We chose to have Grace attend Wasatch where she would have at least one person like herself—the principal. Grace became popular and was later elected vice president of her student body at Skyline High School.

As to Mrs. Davis, I call her a master mother. When other people don't seem to be able to handle some children's situations, she is able to handle them with style and class. Having helped raise her own sisters and brothers, she has skills for how to quiet a baby as well as the gentleness for how to encourage and support a teenager. I watch her sometimes when a new mother has a babe that's crying. She simply takes the babe and with pats on the back and rocking she is able to calm that baby. She is no nonsense, however, applying discipline as well as tenderness. Children sense that she truly cares about them. I discovered these qualities in her after we were married, though I knew before that she had helped rear her sisters and brothers as both her parents worked outside the home. I did not realize then how this experience would impact the rearing of our own children, however. It has proved an invaluable attribute. In fact, in addition to her duties as a mother, Willene is able to share in the lives of so, so many people in times when they are becoming frustrated and wondering, "Where do I go from here?" I encourage her to work with new mothers, to help them learn the art of mothering. My wife is also active in the reading group at church, an extension of her love for children. This is a group that starts with 18-month-olds. She has the opportunity to direct the lives, the social interactions, and behavior of young people and at the same time to help them learn to read. In fact, our goal is to have young people entering the first grade already reading at the second-grade level. Thus, we see two-year-olds excited about what they are learning, so much so that they are becoming their parents' teachers in some cases. The Bible says, "And a little child shall lead them" (Isaiah, chapter 11, verse 6). How true!

To see my children and grandson, to have a loving and caring wife has meant so much and has made the work of ministry easier in many ways. I've had mixed emotions when thinking at times that I could have done more in terms of ministry if I did not have family responsibilities. On the other hand, having a family has made possible much of what I have done. Certainly, I have been protected from a lot of temptations and challenges. I am also well aware that one needs some kind of release from all of the demands and obligations of being a full-time pastor. Thus, to go home and have somebody say "I love you," and have children want to play, to have a family who throws their arms around you and accepts you as you are, not for the duties you perform, makes all the difference for me as a minister. I deeply appreciate my wife and children. I know for sure that if nobody else cares, if nobody else appreciates, these are the ones who truly do care and appreciate. Not only do they say so, but they act in a way that lets me know without a doubt that they love me and that they care about me.

A loving family also becomes a good example, reflecting teachings of the Bible. Having a loving family and being able to model that family for others is perhaps a more powerful teaching tool than any words that I could ever utter. The visible church combines family and teaching.

17

A Good Name

ALL THE MINISTER OR PASTOR OF A CONGREGATION HAS IS A NAME. When that name is maligned, the pastor and the congregation are likely to suffer. There have been several unexpected challenges that have made a lasting impact upon my life. I learned to live with them and God has given me the victory over them all. Here are a few examples that come to mind readily.

I have a hate mail file that has grown far thicker than my friendly mail file. One letter came to both my home and my office the day after Dr. Martin Luther King Jr.'s holiday. It offered to burn me with gasoline, wished that I might catch AIDS and drop dead, thrown into the dump along with the garbage, and sent back to Africa. Such letters are numerous and unsigned with the exception of those ending: "The KKK is active, alive, and well. 5,000 strong in Utah!"

Perhaps the most bizarre challenges came by mail to both my office and my home. The one to the house was addressed to my wife. This letter was from another preacher. It was written some 14 months after I attended his banquet and greeted his wife with a kiss on the cheek. He complained, threatened me, and later six sticks of explosives arrived in the mailbox near my office. They were old and the city's bomb squad took them away.

We planned a day of reconciliation at the graveyard in Price, Utah, to acknowledge the lynching of Robert Marshall in 1925. Soon, a police officer attached himself to me, and everywhere I went, he went. He told me that someone had called in a threat, saying they wanted to "get" me. It was a young man who was ultimately identified. He intended no real harm.

Another time, a vicious rumor was traced to a non-church member of a local benevolence club, the former son-in-law of a Calvary deacon. He alleged that I had been caught compromising within the church facility. My pain was for the reputation of the other person accused and for the name of the congregation. I confronted the issue head on. It was denied and soon died out.

While some of the threats over the years have been directed at me personally, most have been attempts to halt good community-building work, I believe. The challenges cause me to push even more for the causes I feel are right.

I am not afraid!

18

Mrs. E. Louise Debies

When I joined the Calvary Baptist Church soon after arriving in Salt Lake City, I very quickly found a dear friend in one of the older members of the congregation, Mrs. E. Louise Debies. She was in her 80s at the time and very actively involved in the church. In fact, one could probably say that every time the doors of the church were open, as long as she was able, Mother Debies was there. She walked the block and a half from her home to the church when she had to, and after we became friends I frequently picked her up to get her to the church. On Sundays, she refused to ride in the front seat, indicating that this was the "wife's seat." She was a deaconess, member of the Missionary Society, a teacher in the Sunday school. She also sang in the choir.

I remember it as if it were yesterday, my first Sunday in Utah, the first time I walked into the Calvary Baptist Church! I sat on the aisle, on a bench about four rows from the front, on the right side. The adult choir (under the direction of Mrs. Phyllis Grayson) sat in front of me and on the opposite side was the children's choir. Mrs. Gladys Hesleph was in charge of the children and played the organ. Her young son, Brian Hesleph, played the piano. The time came during the worship service when a young lady from the congregation stood up and said, "We want to extend a welcome to all of our visitors. We ask you to please stand and identify yourself. Tell us who you are, where you're from..." So, I stood up, introduced myself, and indicated that I was an ordained minister. I was promptly invited by the pastor, the Reverend Henry Hudson, to join him in the pulpit. Soon after that, I became an associate minister.

In the days when I first went to Calvary, there was still a real trust that a person was what they represented themselves to be. There was a belief that to be a minister was not something that you played with. So, because of trust, perhaps because of the way I was dressed and handled myself during the worship service, Pastor Hudson was very open. I had been taught to come to church dressed in my very best. In fact, I remember as early as age three my father saying, "You must dress up for God. God's been good to us and we must present ourselves at His house looking our best." The way I was dressed separated me in some ways from the local young men who came neatly clad in shirts, some in ties, but many without a jacket. I had just arrived from Berkeley and I wore my hair in an Afro, one bigger than the young men at Calvary wore at that time. That, too, distinguished me, perhaps pegging me as something of a radical. The congregation at Calvary had the reputation of being an activist congregation and thus with my neat, yet less-than-conservative look, I must have attracted their attention. Soon, however, I discovered that the people who were the most friendly toward me at church were the more senior. Mother Debies was one. After the service on my first Sunday at Calvary, she made a beeline for me, coming from the choir stand to introduce herself and to welcome me.

I have always had good relations with older people in every community I have lived, calling certain elders "Mom" and "Dad." There is a reason for that. It gave me a sense of grounding, a sense of connectedness, and allowed me to be tied to the more established members of a community or congregation. It also provided me with a place I could go where I could find a listening ear, where I could gain from the insights seniors were willing to share. Ofttimes the elders were people I could bounce ideas off of. Being a long way from home (at least 500 miles from my nearest family member) I needed somebody I could feel at ease with. Many readily invited me to their homes, to sit about their tables, to share a meal. As a struggling young student and teaching fellow at the university, I could always be assured of something to eat at a senior's home, and certainly of some conversation. So, I became familiar with older people and participated in a number of their groups: the Missionary Society, Sunday school, the Mass choir, which had people of all ages. In fact, I sang with the choir, did narrations, and soon became an active participant with them in whatever events and programs they were going to do. I gained a reputation for what Mahalia Jackson called "talking a song up." My voice was fairly well trained and certainly distinct. As a matter of fact, the Reverend Lafayette Moseley called it "the only voice of its kind." So, I gradually became a spokesman for the choir in many respects and that provided me with a natural group of people to interact with. In fact, my best friends at Calvary came out of that group.

Gradually, I began to take on more ministerial duties at Calvary, becoming, in 1973, the interim pastor. How that took place, I'll talk about a little later.

Mother Debies was particularly interested in visitation and going places. She wanted to be wherever I and the Calvary congregation were participating. So, she was always there. For me this was fortuitous. As a young minister who had been labeled by many as "too young to be a pastor," I encountered obstacles. Problems could arise. For example, traveling with a lady was considered inappropriate. After I married and started a family, my wife was busy at home rearing our children and making sure the home front was in good stead, in good repair. She could not always accompany me. Mother Debies, because of her age, was a good companion, in fact a godsend.

Mother Debies lived alone and was excited about the possibility of getting out. So, if I was going to the hospital, I'd stop by and pick her up without having to give her much notice. She seemed to be ready to go anywhere and to go every day. I still remember how, if I walked into a sick room, patients came to understand that Mother E. Louise Debies was going to walk in, too. When we went to people's homes she always had a kind word for those who were downcast, reminding one and all that God was still good and cared about them, that God would take care of them at the right time. She was an inspiration.

I remember on the third Sunday in June of the year I was burned my brother Joseph and I, Brother Edward Miller, and a pastor from another Baptist church in Salt Lake City drove to the National Baptist Convention, held in St. Louis, Missouri. Mother Debies had a relative in that city and wanted to go along. I reminded her that it was a long trip, but she said she wanted to go anyway. That afternoon we loaded the car and started driving. Along the way I would ask her if she was sleepy and she answered with no hesitation, "No, son, I don't sleep when I'm ridin' in an automobile." So as we kept riding, she would nod off. I would say something to her and she'd say again, "No, son, I don't sleep when I'm ridin' in an automobile." When we reached Denver, she was sound asleep. We pulled into a fast food place, bought boxes of chicken, and took off again. After a while, Mother Debies woke up and said, "Boys, don't you think it's about time we stopped to get somethin' to eat?" We reminded her that we had and that her box was on the seat beside her. We never said anything more to her, but chuckled to ourselves.

Mrs. E. Louise Debies was a lovely lady who had strong concern for me, my family, and my welfare. One of the things I learned from her was that you can do anything you want to do and that whatever resources you have, they can more than cover your needs. She would say, "I don't make much, but when it comes time to do my part, I'm gonna do my part." I constantly reminded the officers of my church to look at Mother Debies. What a grand example of one who did not have transportation, who was old and in some ways feeble, who didn't have many resources, but yet was a model for everybody else of what was possible, what could be done!

I spent a lot of time in her home, talking. We went on more visitations together than I can count, stopping by the hospitals, the jails, homes, and churches. After a while, if she was not there with me, people asked, "Where's Mother Debies? Where's Mother Debies?" They wanted to know.

I can say without a doubt that Mrs. Debies' friendship contributed to my name and reputation as a pastor who was about doing what's right. Her proximity also gave my wife a sense of comfort.

Mother Debies, the strong, spiritual woman living alone knew how to manage her resources well. I remember she called me one time and said, "Come by my house. I want to talk to you about my house." One of her grandchildren had been arrested and had called her to put her house up for bail. She said to me, "Reverend, my husband always told me, don't ever sign anything that would obligate your house. I don't want to do it!" I agreed with her.

I remember another occasion when she called me and asked if I'd come by and throw some trash away that she had at her house. I went and as I looked at the trash I noticed a couple of pieces of jewelry and a watch. She told me that these things didn't work anymore and that she wanted me to just throw them away. I asked her if I could look at the watch. It was an old watch with a glass top that would open, like a watch for a blind person. You could open it and feel the hands and see what time it was. I asked if I could get it fixed for her and she responded, "You just take it and do whatever you want with it. If you can get it to work, you can have it." All it needed was a good cleaning. It is to this day a prize piece that I intend to hand down to my son when I pass on my heritage.

When Mother Debies took sick, in her 90s, she was taken to the hospital, then confined briefly to a nursing home. Though she never returned to her house, her "home-going" was the funeral of a lifetime and a grand celebration. The songs that we sang at her request were all upbeat. The program participants were not uttering grunts and groans and moans of sadness. Even the family recognized that here was a soldier who on the battlefield of life fought well and now was entitled to go home, to be at rest, to take her rest. Some of the songs were old and familiar church hymns: "Amazing Grace," "I'm on the Battlefield for My Lord," and of course, "Precious Lord Take My Hand." Brother Nelson Styles led the congregation in singing "When my work down here is done, I must now go to the setting sun…" I delivered not a eulogy but a sermon that by her request was to speak to the needs as I saw them, not hers, but those of her family. It was a reminder of the words that Jesus said in the Bible as he was preparing to be crucified: "Weep not for me, but weep for yourselves…" So, it was a service, not of sadness for her, but one that was directed toward helping her family to grow. Her son, who had been a student at the University of Utah in the 1920s and who at the time of her death lived in Alaska, came and stayed in our home. She also had two adopted children who were here in Salt Lake City.

Everyone who knew Mother Debies seemed to have a high regard and trust that she would do her utmost to insure that those around her would do the right thing. When she spoke to children or to young people, she always had good advice and was very firm with whatever it was that she had to say to them. She carried a big stick, if you will, and she was instrumental in my becoming pastor of the Calvary Baptist Church. Mrs. E. Louise Debies got me started on the right track and helped me in establishing the best of reputations. She took the time, she stretched herself in old age and overcame many frailties, becoming my champion and friend from the day I set foot in the Calvary Baptist Church to the time I became pastor. She was determined to do all that she could for Calvary and this included doing her utmost for the one she called her "boy pastor," me.

19

DESTINY

My work at Calvary took a turn in the early 1970s. In the winter of 1972, Reverend Henry Hudson had asked me if I had ever thought about pastoring a church. I said, "No." I thought he might be alluding to a vacancy in town; another Salt Lake City church had just put their pastor out. I wanted no part of that and was planning to leave Salt Lake at the end of the school year with the intention of going to graduate school at Morehouse College.

Reverend Hudson had been at Calvary for over a year about that time, having come from Oakland, California. He was familiar with where I had come from and was very open to having a person teaching at the university as part of his ministerial team. In fact, it seems to me that during that year, I preached as much as he did and performed a number of marriages. He was traveling quite often. I remember these as being exciting times and remember Reverend Hudson as a good person to learn from. He had a strong business mind and was precise with numbers. He had an accounting approach to how to manage church resources, something I had not learned anywhere else. He taught me how to put together a budget, how to manage the resources that would be given to the church, and how to manage time. He was highly disciplined and whatever he was going to do, he gave it his all in a timely fashion. I learned a lot from him.

Winter turned to spring and summer. School came to an end. It was June of 1973 and my thoughts were on my coming move. I went to Calvary for the morning service and listened to Pastor Henry Hudson deliver a sermon from Matthew entitled "Shake the Dust Off." After the sermon he excused the guests, pointing out that church members in full standing had some business that they needed to take care of. When they were gone he said, "I want to read a letter to you." It was his letter of resignation. He let us know that he had in fact already moved his family out of town. (He is as of 2005 at the Williams Chapel Baptist Church in Oakland and is the only living former pastor of Calvary.) On the day he resigned, Reverend Hudson also suggested that I be asked to fill in until a pastor could be found. I accepted by way of being helpful, but told Calvary's congregation that I must first go back to Oakland to get married. They agreed.

My ministry had taken an unexpected turn. I would fill in as interim pastor, earning $50 a week. Some of the younger ladies in the congregation were not so pleased to see me with a bride on my arm, but the elder people gave Mrs. Davis a warm welcome. In fact, they threw their arms around us and sponsored a second wedding reception at the church. Mother E. Louise Debies was our primary mentor.

In September of that year, I was appointed as a full instructor at the university and continued to carry on at the Calvary Baptist Church, to conduct their ministerial affairs until March of 1974. Meanwhile, the congregation was interviewing prospective pastors, ministers coming from various states. They listened to them deliver sermons, considered their credentials, and asked about their desire and willingness to come to Salt Lake City. Finally, they called a business meeting, ready to take a vote on two of the candidates. It was February of 1974.

A week or so before the vote Mother Debies called and asked me if I would come by her house. I went. She said to me, "Reverend, I just want to hear it from the horse's mouth. Did you tell our deacons that you wouldn't take our church?" I was startled by her question and let her know that no one had asked me. She then said, "Thank you. That's all I need to know."

The night Calvary was voting on a new pastor, my wife and I went to a banquet sponsored by the Trinity AME Church. The banquet was being held at the First Baptist Church's multi-purpose building. I was participating with my friend the Reverend Alvin Larkin, pastor of Trinity. Near the end of the banquet, I saw Deacon Harding Jones of Calvary coming into the hall with smiles on his face. His wife was already at the banquet as she was a member of Trinity. Brother Jones informed me that I had been chosen as pastor of the Calvary Baptist Church and that the vote had been nearly unanimous. The news he brought surprised me. In fact, I was shocked.

The meeting was presided over by the Reverend D. A. Washington, a retired pastor. The first nominee was a man from Texas, one with the sorts of credentials that the congregation was looking for, at least in the eyes of the leadership of the congregation. He was presented by the Committee for the Selection of a Pastor and endorsed by the deacons as their candidate of choice. Brother Jones related to me how Mother Debies stood up and made a nomination from the floor. Reverend Washington, a master parliamentarian, announced to the congregation (to the committee's disappointment, it seems) that they would take the vote on the last nominee first. He called for those who were in favor to stand. All but a very few of the leadership and members rose to their feet. Now keep in mind that I had hosted all prospective candidates, taken them to dinner, given them rides here and there, and I was certain that Calvary was looking for an older, more experienced minister than myself. Destiny would have it otherwise.

On the fourth Sunday in April of 1974 I was installed as pastor of the Calvary Baptist Church in Salt Lake City, Utah, and I have been serving there ever since. Although I had not been looking for a church, not interested in being a pastor at the time, I was truly honored. I knew that Calvary had a long history as the oldest of the predominantly African American Baptist churches in the state of Utah. I knew the congregation to be an activist group of people, as I said earlier. Also, I had some notion of the significant role to be played in the larger community. It was a congregation with a rich heritage, in a capital city, boasting members with long tenure and good memories. In fact, Calvary was a place where people met to experience what the Reverend Jesse Jackson has called "somebodyness," a sense of belonging, a sense of connectedness, a sense of place and being. The Calvary Baptist Church in Salt Lake City is the center of that kind of experience. Thus, to be called as its pastor was a real honor. To be given the opportunity to help shape and mold the lives of a whole group of people (at first African Americans, later people from the community at large) was a real tribute. I accepted it with humility and also with high hopes for what I could accomplish with God's help and the support of the people. If God guided and directed my steps, then the people would be able to catch the vision and follow.

It has come to pass.

20
—

The Visible Church

An important role the pastor plays is that of insuring that the resources needed for the effective running of the church and its programs will be available in a timely fashion. That is to say that the money required to pay bills will be on hand. I take that very seriously. I believe that if the funds are not raised through the efforts that are put forth by me and the Calvary family, then we are doing something we ought not to be doing, trying to pay a bill we ought not to be paying. And by the way, I never ask people to give unless I first show them that I am giving. So, at a given time during the worship service, I will say, "Here's mine, now you bring yours." And this kind of example has insured positive results. Because I am paid by the church, people know what resources I have to work with. So when they see me giving liberally, then they can say, "Oh, if the pastor can do it at that level, I can do it, too." We suggest that members of the church start by giving ten percent of their income, that being what the Bible calls Tithe. Some folks cannot see their way to tithing at that level and so we encourage them to give regularly at whatever level they feel comfortable. We encourage members to give every Sunday, having discovered that when people do that, even if the amount given is small, it tends to take care of needs and to move the church ahead. We have also discovered that people will give when you ask them. There is a beautiful little teaching in the Bible that says, "You have not because you ask not." So we take the position as a congregation and as the leadership of the Calvary Baptist Church here in Salt Lake City to ask for what it is we want. By asking we have been able to meet most of the needs that were there. Our building fund, for example, was near what it needed to be as we broke ground for our new church on State Street. The members of the church stepped up and gave. Then, people from the larger community were willing to participate with us. We used a poster board thermometer to keep track of the funds coming in. Watching the red line rise with every gift heightened the interest and sparked fresh participation. Although we raised enough money to pay more than three-quarters of the cost, the thermometer reading did not reach the top. Church members continue to contribute regularly and friends make special gifts. Our goal is to reach the summit within the next five years of the start date. To grease the legal and political wheels, we got letters of support from everybody we could think of. For example, with endorsements from both the mayor and the city council, getting through the city processes with their building regulations went more smoothly.

The building process was church ministry at its best. We met with the design and construction team weekly to discuss progress and any changes. Then, on a cold winter day I will always remember, members of the Calvary family, both young and old, gathered with the construction crews, tramping through the snow-covered mud. Wearing hard hats, armed with our Bibles and thick permanent markers, we climbed on platforms and rode lifts to inscribe Biblical passages and song lyrics on steel framing. Where prayer would be offered, we wrote about prayer. I chose to write in the preaching place, "Go and preach the kingdom of God" (Luke, chapter 9, verse 6). And, over the door of the sanctuary, "Go ye therefore, and teach all nations, baptizing them in the name of the Father and of the Son, and of the Holy Spirit" (Matthew, chapter 28, verse 19). Where there would be singing, we wrote words of songs or about psalms. Where there would be food and recreation, we chose appropriate passages from the Bible like Jesus' feeding of the five thousand, or the wedding dinner. And in the office spaces, we inscribed passages about business and administration. In the classrooms one of our long-term Sunday school teachers wrote, "So they read in the book in the law of God distinctly, and gave the sense, and caused them to understand the reading" (Nehemiah, chapter 8, verse 8). In the children's "crying room" areas we wrote, "Suffer the little children to come unto me and forbid them not, for of such is the kingdom of heaven" (Matthew, chapter 19, verse 14). Each and every one chose a favorite verse or song and left their mark on the girders, to be covered over when construction continued. We had found the precious gem and were burying it in our building's foundation to radiate for years to come. This was a moment of unbridled imagination and a dream fulfilled before our very eyes. We were witnesses to all who would see!

Perhaps one of the most meaningful and memorable facets of the building ministry was feeding the workers. Every other Friday, the ladies of the church would cook and the men would provide soft drinks, which they delivered for lunch. Members of the congregation and building crews sat down side by side, sharing a meal and conversation. I was always there and always started with table grace. The conversation, although light-hearted, always included something about Calvary, her history, her missions, and her beliefs. Sometimes the choir would host the meal. Their inspirational gospel singing filled the air between State and Main. The workers enjoyed the soul food and the congregation minimized her costly change orders. For example, dead space beneath the stairwells was converted into storage closets as an afterthought; the dividing wall in the convocation room used for large Bible studies and community meetings was eliminated at no additional cost.

With scripture on the walls and the congregation's ministry, the construction workers acted as if God might be present and walking among us. From the time we broke ground at 1090 South State Street in January of 2001, to the October completion and move-in, I never heard one curse word, one foul utterance on the site. It is a stereotype that construction workers commonly swear and use colorful language. What could be the reason for their restraint on this job?

Finally, one balmy fall day, escorted by the police, carrying bottles of water, wearing comfortable shoes, pushing baby strollers, children carrying our nation's and church's flags, we marched from the old church at 532 East 700 South to our new home, adding people along the way. Camera shutters clicked, lenses flashed, groups broke into song, and all walked jubilantly. We had met our commitment to remain in the inner city. We had made inroads toward being a positive influence in the area. We had honored the mission of those who had been on the battlefield before us, in 1892 when the Baptist Prayer Band met at individual homes under the direction of "Mom Jack," Mrs. Emma Jackson. They no doubt raised their voices as we were doing on the day of our first worship service at the new Calvary Baptist Church: "Let the Church be the Church, let the people rejoice. Oh we've settled the question we've made our choice. Let the anthems ring out, songs of victory swell for the Church Triumphant is alive and well."

We were walking the talk and growing a congregation with loving compassion. A new day had dawned. We held our first worship service and the church came alive with song and sermon.

21

SERMONS

WHEN I VISITED FORT LAUDERDALE A FEW YEARS AGO, a family friend and the barber who used to cut our hair, Mr. Willie Morris, came up to me and said, "I remember your trial sermon, Reverend Davis. It was about what a man will do in exchange for his soul." He was right. The sermon in fact bore the title: "What Manner of Man is This?" and was based on Matthew, chapter 16, verse 26.

Since then, I have delivered more sermons than I can count, but growing up, I would ofttimes hear people report, "Reverend sure preached today!" They would say it with great excitement, communicating that they had a great time in the worship service. But then, ofttimes too, when these same people were asked "Well, what did the preacher have to say?" they didn't know or could not remember. Perhaps the most popular minister during my lifetime was a singsong, whooping, highly emotional preacher. He was in such demand that he was scheduled years out and when he came to town you would have to get there an hour before just to get in the door. After his death, the minister who followed him said to me, "The church never heard him, Reverend. They watched!" When I asked, "How did you know that, Reverend?" he said that he had been reading some of the sermons by this very famous and popular preacher. The words, the messages were sound. If people had heard them and acted accordingly, they would have been true Christians. This was not the case, he indicated. The congregation was high on emotion, on shouting, but low on substance and thought. They had been distracted from the message and thus didn't have much to carry them throughout the week. A sermon that is all substance and no emotion, on the other hand, would have the effect that the apostle Paul writes about when he says that the "letter" by itself kills.

From some ministers you learn what to do, from others what not to do. I have aimed, since I have been a minister, for a balance between the educational and the emotional, the inspirational and the informational. I try to provide something that your mind can grasp, but that can be grasped equally effectively by your hands, your feet, your emotions, if you will. What you understood, what you learned, would then give you a reason to get up and go do something about it. This is my hope and my goal as a preacher and pastor. It is a delicate balance to maintain, as every audience is a mixed multitude. There are those who are believers and those who are non-believers. There are those who are mature and those who are not. Some are committed and some are not. It is a challenge to provide something for everyone who is present. Sometimes, you have to leave certain things unsaid. There the imagination takes over, allowing application within each hearer's experience.

Sermons grow out of three major wellsprings. They grow out of a time of prayer, from reading and studying, and from language aimed at the head and the heart. I learned from an old preacher that one must pray oneself hot and preach oneself empty. So, sermons grow out of communication, communion with God, spending time alone, in reflection, in meditation. Then great study of everything you can get your hands on is next. Reading, but also experience, are key. A preacher must be a people watcher, an observer, and one who interacts with people regularly, studies them. The old preachers called it "studying oneself full."

How do you get people to listen to you? What language do you use, what examples make sense and apply, so that people can identify with the message? This comes with having regular interactions. One pastor friend of mine says that he spends all morning in the word and all afternoon in the world. That is he studies and prays and does physical preparation in the morning, then in the afternoon he interacts with people. I find that works for me.

Ideas for sermons come through the imagination, from inspiration, much as poetry does, or music. After one has studied and prayed long, plumbing the depths of one's own being, then comes next sharing it with others, followed by the message. David would say in Psalm 23 that when one's head has been anointed with oil then what runs over from the full cup is the sermon. The sermon is the overflow of one's own life. As a preacher, as an individual, having learned a lesson myself, I can then develop it in the sermon and pass it on. The preacher must preach first to himself, then and only then preach to others.

In my own sermon preparation, I always begin with the Bible. A passage from the Bible is the centering nugget of the thoughts that eventually come together. If it is Fathers' Day, for example, I might talk about the love of a father for his children and base my sermon in Luke, chapter 15, the story of the prodigal son. This story talks about the father who waited for his son to return and who was just as available to his son who was at home. This seems to be a passage that demonstrates the kind of love that a father would have. And, as I think of my own father, or fathers that I see, they become examples, modern-day examples of what Luke talks about. Inspiration comes out of that. I sit down and read the passage over and over and over again. I familiarize myself with the language, with the words, with the parts of speech. I try to decipher the meanings of words, both for the time that they were written and for today. So, I start with the passage and spend a lot of time with the passage.

Sermons grow. They do not just pop out. They are not full grown when one starts. They grow out of the passage, out of life experiences, out of what one reads, out of one's prayer time, and out of one's imagination. It takes a good imagination to be a preacher, especially in an African American Baptist church context. You must bring to life what was written many thousands of years ago by painting pictures so that people can visualize what they hear. Thus, words must take shape in their minds, helped along by the fertile (not exaggerated) imagination of the preacher. The sermon must sing with insight, foresight, and sight. The message, the words and pictures must literally get up and walk in order to convey a dream about what is rich and powerful in the lives of people. So I start with the word. I immerse myself in the word. I listen and look for examples everywhere, ones that relate to a chosen passage. I then sit with pen and paper and say: "Speak, Lord, for thy servant hears." It just seems that it all comes together at the right time, having grown, having become…

There once was a passage that I read and got excited about. Very quickly, however, I concluded that I was not mature enough to deal with it. It was many years before I was able to preach about backsliding, for example, what it really means: sliding away from that which is the better, going backward instead of forward. It was many years that I studied, prayed about, read about the subject, but even more years until I felt I could deliver an effective sermon about it. I had a good, clear idea about where I was going, but then I would put it aside, gather fresh insight (or ooze out) before going further in the direction I initially set out to follow. In some cases, I go in a new direction altogether.

Insofar as the delivery of a sermon is concerned, I mostly preach from memory or from short notes. The secret is to have three or four main ideas and three or four clear examples to put forth. Start with one idea: "God loves you," for example. Next, read a verse: "For God so loved the world that he gave his only begotten son that whosoever believeth in him shall not perish, but have everlasting life" (John, chapter 3, verse 16).

I might begin by saying, "My subject today, sisters and brothers, is God's love for you." Then, from the verse of Scripture, I see if there are two or three main ideas that are right in the passage itself that I can lift out, illustrate. "God so loved..." He loves us. I would illustrate that by what he did. He gave us life, food, shelter, provisions... Secondly, I would say that he so loved the whole world that no one is excluded, that it's not about being black or white, young or old, male or female, native or not... I would say that and illustrate that.

Lastly, I would remind the congregation "that he gave his only son so that we might have life..." I would talk about that gift of his only begotten son. All of these ideas would have grown out of, jumped out of the passage itself as main points to be delivered and then illustrated. Then, of course, the last part is to bring it home, to conclude, to say this is how you can apply these truths to your daily life.

When delivering a sermon, eye contact is key. Also key is addressing people in the congregation directly, calling on one person here and there in some cases. I may say, "And Brother so and so, or Sister so and so, I want you to know..." then make a statement having called somebody by name. They then are reminded that the message is for them. To read it would make that much more difficult. In fact, I find reading a sermon too dry, and personally only refer to notes, making sure I take some of my cues from the response of the congregation. I seldom read because I am convinced that to be caught up in a piece of paper is to lose the audience.

Preaching in the dark just does not work!

The sermon delivery is a two-way street in the African American tradition. It is call and response. It is one person leading and others following. It is the congregational response to what the preacher suggests. Ideally, there are no spectators. The best of all worlds is to involve the congregation to such a degree that they feel, that they sense, that they know what it is that the sermon is about. They can say, "Amen!" or "Yes, Amen, right on!" to what the preacher is saying. I am always listening for the response and the overtone, if you will. If there are no "Amens," if there is no echoing of

passages, if there is no verbal reinforcement of the message, then the sermon is not likely to be much. It's not likely to make contact or reach a con-
clusion that ignites a spark in the hearers. It's not likely to be very long,
either. Thus, if the heart and mind are in the delivery, the preacher, to be
effective, must listen for the people's interactions and responses. If the
preacher gets the sense at any time during sermon delivery that the people
don't understand, don't hear, can't make sense out of what is being said, it
behooves the preacher to then change course or to find a graceful exit.
When it comes to audience participation, the preacher must preach as you
would drive on the freeway, always looking for the best exit.

Many times, when dealing with an audience that is perhaps unfamiliar with the Bible, I have had to change the examples. I have at such times
changed the thoughts and presented them in a different way because I saw
that the people were not engaged, that they were not involved, that they
did not truly hear what I was saying. Let me see if I can illustrate the point
I am trying to make with the example of a particular sermon. I preached a
sermon from the Second Book of Timothy, chapter one, verses 6 and 7:
"Wherefore I put you in remembrance that thou stir up the gift of God,
which is in thee by the putting on of my hands. For God hath not given us
the spirit of fear; but of power, and of love, and of a sound mind."

My subject was "Stir Up the Gift." I picked three main points based
on the verses and soon sensed that the audience was not connecting. So, I
decided to change direction and said to them, "Well, let me give you an
example…" I used the image of stirring up yogurt in order to get the fruit
that is at the bottom mixed in with the stuff that does not taste so good.
Lots of people could identify with that. What I was indeed alluding to was
the desire to get to the fruit of your faith experience. But then, there were
some older folks in the congregation who did not grow up with yogurt, but
who, like me, had experienced rural homes, heated with fireplaces. I asked
them what they did to get the most warmth, the greatest heat, the bright-
est flame from the fires in those old fireplaces. There was laughter and the
following response: "Stirrrrrrrrr up the logs!" Take the poker and stir up
the logs! To drive the point home to yet another group, I reminded the
cooks about stirring beans as they simmer on the stove. "To keep them
from sticking," some chimed in. I wanted to convey the message: don't be
like stagnant water, don't just stay where you are. For my final thrust, I used
the example of my preferred dinner drink: Kool Aid. I described how I
make Kool Aid and how my wife makes it, pouring the water on the pow-

der and sugar mix. "If you want to get the sweetness, the color, the substance of that Kool Aid, you have to stirrrrrrrr it up!" It was exciting to watch the response of different groups of people in the congregation. Hence, to the degree that the pastor can engage the audience and get them actively involved, then the sermon will have meaning and will be exciting both to the ear and in application to everyday life.

Perhaps one demand on the preacher seldom talked about is physical. Lots of energy is exerted in standing and preaching. Maybe that is why some preachers in the Bible sat down to preach. I remember one Sunday, our First Aid Team was checking blood pressures. When the nurse checked mine immediately after the benediction, she said, "You need to go straight to the hospital, Reverend!" Of course I knew and did not go until the next day. The doctor said, "You have an athlete's blood pressure," which was good.

Sermon preparation and presentation is no small matter. It takes many hours, sometimes days, weeks, and in a few cases perhaps even years to make sense out of a passage of scripture in light of life experiences. I try to stay ahead, to always have something on the back burner, as my mother would say, where the fire is not so hot yet. I try not to be surprised when called upon to preach unexpectedly. And, I advise young ministers (especially those with whom I work) never to set foot in a place where ministry ought to be done unless they are prepared to do what that ministry is. Even if someone else is scheduled to do it, even if they have not been told that they are expected to perform ministry, they must be prepared to do what is needed and to represent themselves as wanting to do it. They must always have a sermon ready and be prepared to deliver it. I remind them that we must practice what we preach and see ourselves above all as servants.

The people will forgive the preacher for almost everything except the failure to preach!

22

THE PASTOR AND HIS FAMILY

BEING A PASTOR IS A CALLING FOR THE PASTOR. It is not a calling for the family members. It is a sense of responsibility and duty for the pastor. It is not one for the wife and the children. However, the expectation in an African American community, particularly in a predominantly African American church, endows the pastor with respect, but also responsibilities that extend to his family. The pastor is expected to be a preacher on Sunday, a counselor on Monday, a lawyer on Tuesday, a businessman on Wednesday, a social worker on Thursday, and a problem solver on Friday. On Saturday he is expected to be the financier. People turn to the pastor for all sorts of needs. I will never forget the time a lady called me to ask how to spell a certain word. I asked her if she had a dictionary under her and suggested she open it.

In our tradition, the people around ministers have come to expect that ministers will be well dressed, that they will drive nice automobiles and live in decent housing. Congregations will make it their business to make those provisions available as best they can. They will sometimes buy a new suit, a set of luggage, more significantly a car or a house. Recently, Calvary's congregation deeded the house at 1912 Meadow Drive to me, their gift on the occasion of my 30 years as pastor. It was actually done year by year with equity as a 30-year mortgage. As to clothes, Calvary's members have learned from experience that to buy me a flashy outfit or ask me to buy one or wear one, to expect me to drive a new model luxury car or live in a big, fancy house, is unrealistic. It's not me! My dress Monday through Sunday is a conservative suit and tie. Now there was a time, when I was younger, that I did wear clothing that was very colorful, with different patterns and so on. But, the older I become, the more conservative I tend to dress. In fact, my wife and others comment sometimes that I ought to wear something other than the dark colors I now favor. However, I am comfortable wearing dark colors, or a discreet pin stripe, wearing a necktie almost every day, everywhere, except when I am home and getting ready to go to bed. I sometimes even cut the grass with my suit and tie on. My wife shakes her head! But that is just my way of being me. I don't recommend it to others, but it's me. You will notice in some of our family photographs that I am at the beach playing near the water with my children, out in the fields hunkered down, picking peanuts, or walking about doing some other task—dressed in a suit and tie. That's just me! The clothing that I wear as a minister simply serves as a way of helping to identify or define me, while the suit and tie is my personal choice of daily wear as well as my uniform some Sundays.

One of the things about being a minister here in the United States of America is that there are some specific outfits that clearly identify one as a minister. To wear what is called a clergy shirt, mostly black (though now it also comes in colors) with a white collar is a way of indicating instantly who I am and what I represent. If I am meeting with law enforcement officers, for example, or a judge, or if I am going to court or to a hospital, I don't want anybody to hassle me as I walk in or out. To that end I choose to don the clergy shirt. I also wear it on the first Sunday of the month, the time we perform the two ordinances of baptism and the Lord's Supper. The Lord's Supper is for us an evening worship service when the congregation can take communion. The garb we wear is again a way of being in uniform, all of the ministers on that Sunday therefore being dressed as much alike as possible. And, by the way, the deacons on that Sunday always wear dark suits while the deaconesses wear white dresses and hats. On other Sundays I wear robes or a suit. Often, there is a lot of sweating when delivering a sermon and a robe is one way of not ruining the fabric of a suit. Having taken the suit jacket off, I replace it with a robe. Wearing a robe is also a way of not drawing attention to oneself. Ofttimes a suit may be too distinctive because of its color, style, or cut. A robe, similar to that worn by other ministers anytime, anywhere says, "Don't pay attention to me, to the way I am dressed, but to what I am saying." The different robes that I wear (sometimes black, sometimes white, sometimes with crosses, a Kente cloth or a plain satin lapel down the front) do not have any major or ritual significance, but are just a way of changing up. As I said earlier, when younger I enjoyed wearing a red shirt or one of a high yellow color. Now, I generally stick to whites, blues, and shades of brown. The clergy shirt I wear out in public lets everybody know there's a minister here. There is also no mistake when wearing the robes as to who I am. I believe (and give such instruction) in avoiding flashy garb and in not drawing attention to oneself when sharing the Gospel.

The clothes for me then literally speak for themselves. They serve to communicate a certain message without, hopefully, drawing attention in terms of style. I like to remind young ministers that the preacher's garb does not make the preacher. If a minister's behavior, preparation, and prayer life are not on solid ground, then what he wears doesn't mean a thing. To step out with a clergy collar around your neck and then to spout foul language, use mind-altering substances, or behave unbecomingly, is a terrible mark on the reputation of a preacher. I remind them of the sanctions in the Book of Proverbs, some of the writings of the Apostle Paul, as well as the Books of Timothy and Titus in the New Testament. Some restrictions are particularly emphasized in Baptist churches. We try to encourage people to not do anything that is going to cause them to be out of control, to harm them physically and mentally: imbibing alcoholic beverages, couples dancing, sex before marriage, smoking, and the consuming of pork are a few. Some of these prohibitions grew out of the sense that people need to be protected from temptations that alter the senses or over-stimulate them. Exercise is recommended. As to the dietary sanction, it is one that is problematic, as pork is favored in traditional African American cuisine. We believe that to follow such guidelines helps to make us more of what God would want us to be, to experience an abundant life, to live to the fullest of our potential. These are some of the guidelines that have become a part of the Baptist tradition, truly a way of saying that we wish for you the very best that life has to offer. If people must indulge, we recommend moderation, reminding them that the Bible instructs us to "shun the very appearance of evil." We also sing, "Yield not to temptation, for yielding is sin. Each victory will help you another to win."

When one finds oneself in a position of leadership, such as a pastor, temptations tend to be more readily present. In counseling settings, for example, the person being counseled is hurting. There is the temptation to comfort and comfort can sometimes lead to more. Recently, a number of clergy have found themselves admitting to going beyond discretion and getting into moral trouble. Those kinds of temptations require a strong person to avoid them. One has to be able to manage one's own behavior to such a degree that you know how to say no. The temptations are bound to come, but you have to be able to say "No. No, thank you, not me, not today" and be able to walk away from a given situation. I exercise the rule of three to guard against any difficulties or insinuations of misbehavior. Implementing this rule is simply having a third person present, nearby, or at least the suggestion that a third person is nearby. Sometimes that third person is simply God. Other times, it is someone just outside the door, just down the hall, or someone who may even be a participant in the process. Also, where there are witnesses, where there are other people who can say, "You shouldn't do that," that helps to manage the kinds of temptations that come, that we as ministers might yield to. For most who have yielded to temptations, I suggest that opportunity played the role of chief culprit. Having the opportunity without some kind of buffer, without a third person present, without someone who would object, makes it easy for many to follow through.

Whenever Jesus sent his disciples out, he never sent them out one by one, but at least two or three at a time. Matthew, chapter 18, verse 20 reminds us: "For where two or three are gathered together in my name, then am I in the midst of them."

In my daily life in ministry, I try to not participate in or expose myself to certain situations unless there is another person present. One practical suggestion is to avoid places, times, and circumstances that are a set-up, where you could set yourself up to yield to temptation. If you are in an office, for example, keep the door partially open, or have a glass door as a preventative measure. We had a minister who was invited at a late hour to come for a visit. He was wise enough to take another minister along. In this particular case, sure enough, when he got there he discovered sure signs that there had been ulterior motives to the call. Had he gone by himself, he would have been in serious trouble. So, we have to find a way and hope that we will learn to deal better with temptations as time goes by. We also must be willing to come forward and admit to having messed up and get back on the right track if we have yielded. It is important to remember that when you give in to what you believe is wrong, you destroy your own sense of well-being and confidence. You cannot be the person that you were, or the person that you can be. In the same way it is the person who forgives rather than he who is forgiven who nets the greatest benefit; he who does harm suffers greater damage than he who is harmed. If you are a minister, then you hinder your own presentation by not being true to yourself. If you have a heart full of guilt, you cannot preach with gusto and vigor. The feeling that you have done wrong tears away at you and keeps coming up, destroying your effectiveness as a minister.

As a teaching-pastor, I make it my business to urge young ministers to consider that without a good name the rest of what we do is mockery and has no lasting worth. The preacher has to be careful of all behavior whether at church, driving down the street, at home, or in the community at large. There has to be a sense that there is always somebody watching. A man of the cloth is not made virtuous or effective by the cloth. What the preacher wears is not where the real substance is. It is in the person, in the individual. Furthermore, to conform to what is outside is one thing. But to be transformed from within is the greater. That ought to be what every preacher strives to do. "Walk worthy whatever it is that you wear!"

If the congregation wants their pastor to look a certain way and provides him with the wardrobe to meet their expectations, this can sometimes create conflict. I made the conscious decision and let it be known from the start that I have to be myself. What I am on Sunday, I try to be on Monday and Wednesday, Tuesday and Thursday, Friday and Saturday as well. To put on airs, to pretend, to act like something that one is not is to confuse those with whom you are communicating. They will not understand the message you are trying to convey. The outward appearance needs to match what is the inner minister and in this way he will be more successful at delivering the lessons and, if you will, setting an example.

Another issue that arises for a minister such as myself is that people ofttimes will invite the minister and his family to join them for meals, to come to their homes to eat. The food at those meals is usually very plentiful. Sometimes those who invite will say, "You didn't eat much, Reverend. Go ahead and have some more. Don't you want seconds?" The fact that I eat more fruit than meats, for example, that I refuse to do as I am expected, can create feelings of hurt when food has been prepared with great care and effort. If I refuse to respond to an invitation or when I respond but do not do as I am expected, that can cause a conflict. My wife will tell you that I eat the way I eat whether at home or out. Again, it's just me.

Another area that sometimes raises conflict is that often there are sensitive topics that preachers are not expected to dwell on, not expected to talk much about. In these current times AIDS is one. AIDS as a disease is not a topic that a lot of people want to hear anything about. And so, when you approach one of these subjects, people will often say that they don't want to hear about such things in a sermon and that if you insist on bringing them into the sermon then they will do something about it, meaning they will try and dismiss you as pastor. This creates a conflict. I do believe that my responsibility as pastor, however, is to share the whole of the Gospel, all of the Bible, and not just the pleasant and the pleasing portions, not just that which makes people feel good and at ease. I feel I must also share that which causes one to want to change because of the pain that it brings. And that, as I said, can cause conflict. However, my determination is to be faithful to my calling and to follow the leads that I believe I am getting from God, and also what I perceive as the needs of the people, not only their desires. When the desires and the needs come together, then that makes it all the better. Where there is conflict between the two, I will do what I believe God would have me to do.

Perhaps the scariest thing that I as a pastor must face is the notion that there are hundreds of people who are dependent on me for leadership, for guidance, for direction in terms of their lives. Trust must be earned. Members of the congregation have come to trust me with their affairs, with their stories. I just make it a regular habit of not talking to anybody at all about what I know. For example, if a husband comes and shares with me details about himself and his wife, I exercise discretion. If the wife were to come, I would do the same. When it is over, I try to put it all in a can and seal it. Law enforcement officers will tell you that the worst situation you can ever get into is to be caught in conflict between spouses. I take that seriously and thus as a counselor will ofttimes tell an individual, "If you would like your spouse to know what you just said to me, you tell them. I will not." In this way I avoid coming between spouses, having to be accountable, and possibly getting labeled with having said certain things. Hence, as a minister I know that most of what I talk to other people about is not repeatable. I have to live with that. In fact, I often suggest that individuals share with God first and come to me if they must with practical considerations, the sort of matters I can help with. There are some things ministers cannot help with. And sometimes it is not to an individual's or a couple's benefit for me to know everything about them. As much as I would try not to judge, there are still some resulting opinions and feelings that come once you know everything. The counseling setting is one of confidentiality. The minister's sense of discretion must be watertight. More than 50 percent of my time is spent going to court, visiting the sick, helping with budget and financial problems, and just working with individuals trying to get through the day.

After getting others through the day, it's time to head home for some tender loving care. Willene is there.

23

Willene, Pastor's Wife

My wife is the second oldest of her parents' children. The oldest is named after her father. Her father, Willie, had wanted another boy whom he planned to name William. When a girl was born, he used part of the name anyway and named her Willene. I was, by the way, blessed to have great in-laws. They never shared with us what they thought about our married life, saying, "What God has joined together let nothing come between. It's your family. It's your home. We'll come visit, but we won't interfere." And that is how it was with them.

I met my wife, Willene, in a rather strange way. It was 1967. I was in the military on my way to Thailand from Nellis Air Force Base in Nevada. In order to make the trip to Thailand I had to fly to California to take a military transport from Travis Air Force Base, some 50 miles from Sacramento. I decided to route myself through Oakland to see my brother Joe and his family before shipping out. Joe's wife invited me to attend worship service at the Center Street Missionary Baptist Church where she was a member. I went and when guests were invited to introduce themselves, as is the custom, I got up and did so. The Vietnam conflict was in full force and I pointed out that I was on my way to Thailand with the United States Air Force and would appreciate receiving letters from any persons who would like to write. I left my address at the church and with my sister-in-law. For soldiers, mail call can be the high point of the day, or a low point if there are no letters from home. In any case, Willene's mother, who was present, told her (or so the story goes) about this nice, young military man who also happened to be a preacher. Although we had never met, Willene wrote to me and I wrote back. We communicated regularly for several months. But, one day, the letters stopped because she was dating someone. It was not until my tour of duty ended that I saw Willene.

In 1970 I had been honorably discharged from the United States Air Force and resolved to go to back to California to live with my brother Joe and go to school. I also became a member of the Center Street Baptist Church in Oakland. Willene and I waved and spoke casually until one day, at an ushers' board meeting, the ushers (all young people) talked about going bowling. Everyone paired up, leaving only Willene and myself. When one young man (who later, along with my brother Joseph, stood with me at my wedding) asked me if I was going, I replied, "Only if Willene will go with me." After that, we began to date and participate in group activities until one day I asked if I could visit her at her mother's house and she responded that it would be fine. The rest is history. But, here it is in brief.

Willene and I got to know each other real well and fell in love. We decided to get married. My daughter Carolyn was a toddler, born in September of 1968, around the time when Willene's letters stopped. Our wedding took place in September of 1973 at the Center Street Missionary Baptist Church, Reverend R. L. James presiding. Willene and I then left on a whirlwind honeymoon, driving to Los Angeles where we attended the National Baptist Convention, then on to San Diego and Tijuana, Mexico. I had accepted to serve as interim pastor of the Calvary Baptist Church by then and now was ready to return to Utah, Willene and Carolyn at my side.

In April of 1972, however, I was about to graduate from the University of California at Berkeley. I was seated in my brother Joe and his wife Barbara's house at 1515 26th Avenue when the telephone rang. I answered, but did not recognize the voice or the name of the person on the other end of the line. The caller said, "My name is Rick Rieke from the University of Utah, in Salt Lake City. We would like to offer you a teaching fellowship and an opportunity to pursue graduate studies here at the U of U." I was stunned. Where did he get my name? Only in 2004 did I discover from him that he had read about me in a magazine. Speak of destiny! In any case, curiosity got the better of me and I decided to accept the offer and I am still in Utah more than 30 years later!

In the last days of August 1972, still a bachelor, I sold my Beetle, bought a Chevrolet LUV pickup, loaded all of my worldly possessions into it, and drove to Salt Lake City. Now, keep in mind that I knew little or nothing about the beehive state and wondered what it would be like to be a Baptist in Utah, not to mention an African American Baptist. When I arrived, I was warmly welcomed by Dr. Rieke, Dr. Robert Tiemens, and others who had also helped, while I was still in Oakland, to make housing arrangements. I had paid a deposit on an apartment and installed a phone, but when I showed up in person was refused. I pursued the matter. The landlady hedged, informing me that carpet was being installed. She said to come back the end of the week. When I did, the apartment was occupied and this is how I ended up living at International House, a building on campus, mostly for international graduate students. Dr. Boyer Jarvis, associate academic vice president at that time, secured a room there for me and became my advocate. He and I remain friends and he attends every award ceremony on my behalf.

At International House, each student had a private room, but the kitchen and bathroom spaces were shared. I could walk to campus and lived frugally. I figure I spent about a dollar fifty cents for food a day, eating Corn Flakes with a little carton of milk for breakfast. I kept a bowl and a spoon in my room. Mid-afternoon I went to Chuck-a-Rama for their dollar-nineteen-cent buffet, eating my fill. That was my routine the first year in Salt Lake City. I studied, taught in the Department of Communications, and remember with pleasure working with experienced teachers like Neff Smart. Eventually, I was promoted to Instructor and taught a full-time load with committee assignments, participating in the re-publication of *Broadax*, an African American newspaper, developing a course called Minorities in the Media, and serving on various community boards. I was studying for a master's degree in journalism and news writing and thinking about going on for a Ph.D. When I mentioned it to one of my advisors, he said: "Davis, it took me eight years to get my Ph.D. It's going to take you eight years." But, I was on the fast track. I was already working as a minister and could not envision this outlay of time. Besides, I did not really need the degree to serve effectively as pastor of the Calvary Baptist Church. So I said thank you and no thank you. Interestingly, some years later, I received an honorary doctorate from the University of Utah as well as from Salt Lake Community College, the third African American to be thus honored. The other two were Dr. Alberta Henry and Dr. John Hope Franklin. What a tribute! I considered these degrees earned through the experiences of work and toil and participation in the larger community and remembered my father saying, "Experience may not be the only teacher, but it is certainly the best teacher."

But, to get back to starting life as a family man in Salt Lake City. When I returned to Salt Lake City with my little family in 1973, we moved into one of the married student housing courts, living at 802 University

Village. The year before Willene and Carolyn joined me, however, I spent the summer harvesting fruits and vegetables wherever I was invited to do so. I canned, and made jellies, marmalades, and puddings in anticipation. When my wife and daughter arrived, Mason jars filled the kitchen cupboards and we received more canning equipment as wedding gifts!

At the university, we had some great interactions with others, among them a young man who became and still is a best friend, Dr. Ronald Coleman. Like us, he and his wife lived in the married students courts. Another lasting friend to me is Dr. Wilfred Samuels, now Director of African American Studies and Coordinator of Ethnic Studies at the University of Utah where we are colleagues. Yearly, for Black History Month in February, he organizes programs shared by the university, Calvary, and the community. He sings in the Calvary Male Chorus and is an exemplary mentor for our youth.

But, pardon me, I got ahead of myself...

Before Oakland, before moving to Utah to teach and study at the university, before even dreaming of becoming pastor of a church, much less one in Utah, I spent over a year of lonely times in Mountain Home and Boise, Idaho. I was completing my tour of duty in the United States Air Force, working at the YMCA, and doing ministry at the Saint Paul Baptist Church, a historic church in Boise. It was a year of honing my skills in ministry, certainly one of personal growth.

24

THE MILITARY AND ELSEWHERE

AFTER MY TOUR OF DUTY IN SOUTHEAST ASIA, I was posted to Mountain Home AFB, Idaho, a military base in the middle of nowhere. Winters were said to be bitterly cold and the wind was reputed to blow without respite, sometimes sandblasting the paint right off an automobile. Before the completion of my tour of duty in Thailand, I was warned that Mountain Home was a place you went only under duress. I decided to extend my tour of duty in Thailand by six months in exchange for a better choice upon transfer, but I was sent to Mountain Home anyway. I was amazed to see sand dunes not too far from the military installation and to observe how the wind literally picked them up and moved them, practically reconfiguring mountains. I had never seen anything like it!

Despite the harsh climate, Idaho turned out to be a good experience for me. For starters, my boss from Thailand had been posted to Mountain Home and was already there when I arrived. He and I got along well. He gave me a choice of where to work and I indicated my preference for anything indoors. "Sergeant Davis," he then said, "today's your day. I've got two jobs inside." I picked the one that involved training and evaluating aircraft mechanics. I was one and had been recognized as "Mechanic of the Month," "Mechanic of the Quarter," and "Mechanic of the Year" while still in Thailand.

The job on the base was principally an office job. I had a regular eight-hour shift, a good deal of freedom, and I was sheltered from the elements. I went on the flight line when I needed to and did not have to respond to emergencies as I had in Southeast Asia. I could call my own shots, something I truly appreciated. Once I had my routine set, however, I made a conscious decision to spend my time off duty in Boise, partly because worship services at the military base chapels I had attended were a far cry from the African American tradition I cherished and African American chaplains were few and far between, although every now and then one would appear in an assistant capacity. I was eager to find a church home, to take part in ministry in a Baptist church, and to serve in the local community.

One Saturday morning early, I drove into Boise and located two churches that were by and large African American in makeup: the Saint Paul Baptist Church and the Church of God in Christ. The Saint Paul Baptist Church was then at 124 Broadway, right across from a school, a dirt parking lot on one side of it, beside it the parsonage where the pastor lived. It was then (and still is) the sole predominantly black Baptist church in town, and dated back to the 1900s. It was housed in a wooden building with a little pitched roof and had half a dozen steps leading up to the sanctuary and a dozen or so to a meeting hall in the basement.

The Saint Paul Baptist Church has now grown and moved with new leadership to another facility. The historic building where I attended worship services back then was relocated to the Julia Davis Park (same name as my mother) and is now the Idaho African American Museum. On July 16, 2005, my wife and I visited the museum. When we introduced ourselves to the docent, he said, "We have a book written by somebody from Utah. Here it is." He handed us a copy of *Light in the Midst of Zion*. He did not recognize me as the author pictured on the cover.

My very first Saturday in Idaho, I drove into Boise and walked up to Saint Paul's Baptist Church. I checked the time of the worship service and the Sunday school. Sunday morning I returned, and to my surprise no one was there. I waited. Eventually people wandered in, started the service, and finally the pastor arrived and delivered the sermon followed by the invitation. I responded and became a member.

The pastor of Saint Paul at the time was a very good preacher, always had a warm smile and a big laugh. His wife was a great musician and they both opened their home to those of us in the military who needed a place to stay overnight on Saturdays so as to attend morning services on Sunday. Many of us did. I had been a member of the choir in Fort Lauderdale, Florida, before shipping out to Southeast Asia. I now joined the Saint Paul choir. Interestingly, all the men in the choir but one were in the military while the women were from downtown. We were all single, except for the pianist, who was the pastor's wife. We traveled and sang all over the region: Montana, Oregon, Washington State. There would often be an opportunity to speak as part of the concert and I was soon identified as one who would be able to do that with great emotional push. I became a kind of spokesperson for our choir.

Singing is, of course, a very important part of the style of worship in African American churches. In fact, an old preacher once said every preacher ought to have three books: a Bible, a hymn book, and a pocketbook. Until that time, I had not paid much attention to the second book, the hymn book. I began to pay more attention to it and learned to sing. I sang solo parts as well as other parts in the choir and at the same time I preached every opportunity I had, which was pretty much on a regular basis, always in black churches, however. In Boise, at that time, African Americans rarely attended churches that were predominantly white unless we were invited to sing.

The Church of God in Christ was another predominantly black church, which had come out of the Baptist tradition in the late 1800s, early 1900s. It was one that I could easily identify with and as the worship services there were held after the Baptists had finished theirs, I could go from one to the other. The congregation was very open and the pastor gave me the opportunity to preach from time to time. I felt welcome and at home, but decided I would join the Saint Paul Baptist Church and was soon invited to become an associate minister. I gladly accepted, asking him what he wanted me to do. His answer surprised me. He said, "Davis, I want you to help me out with whatever you see around here that needs to be done." I asked him to repeat what he had said: "Yes, anything that you see that needs to be done, I'd like you to help me out with that."

With the pastor's clear, public instructions to help him out, I decided to begin with the issue of timeliness. Whatever time was advertised for the service should be the time to start, as this was part of being what you say you are. The next Sunday, when the pastor walked into the church, the church service was in full swing. I was doing what needed to be done because he had encouraged me to do just that. However, from that day on until the day that I left (and the day that he left that church, too), he was never again late. We became good friends as a result of the shared experience at the Saint Paul Baptist Church in Boise, Idaho.

During that time in Boise, I also worked at the YMCA and had regular interactions with young people there. It was an opportunity for me to share with any who would listen my belief in Jesus Christ as my savior, explaining how he had made me whole and suggesting they try Jesus. I also invited them to come and be a part of what we were doing at Saint

Paul. It was a witnessing opportunity. Acts chapter 1, verse 8 says: "And ye shall receive power, after the Holy Ghost is come upon you, and you shall witness unto me." So, witnessing...

Those were exciting days in Boise with challenges as well as opportunities as my ministry continued to grow. While working at the YMCA, for example, I met the editor of *The Intermountain Observer*, a local weekly with an alternative viewpoint. He was a white man concerned about social justice and issues surrounding civil rights in the community, a man willing to do what he could to open doors for all people. He asked me if I would like to contribute some articles and I wrote about my experiences in Boise, about the Saint Paul Baptist Church, about the local job corpsmen, many of whom were African American. I wrote about what it meant to be part of that endeavor in those days, far from home, from family and friends. I had a great experience developing my writing skills and considered it part of my ministry. In fact, everything that I did was ministry in the short term and preparing for ministry over the long haul.

After some time in Mountain Home, I decided that since I spent the weekends in Boise, I would move there. Finding an apartment near the church, I began to commute to Mountain Home AFB during the week, driving directly after to my job at the "Y" where I manned the front desk, enrolling people in various programs, issuing and checking memberships. Meanwhile, I continued my ministry at Saint Paul's and in the community. It was a time of rich experience as well as a time of challenge.

I remember late one night, returning from work to my apartment complex, I was met with flashing red lights from a police vehicle. I was surprised, as Boise was normally a quiet place. A police officer stopped me and asked if I lived there. I said that I did. He informed me that neighbors had reported loud music coming from my apartment. I invited the officer to step inside where he saw for himself that I had no stereophonic equipment of any sort. I resolved to move, not ready for confrontation. Again, I remembered my father's counsel to "pick your fights."

Jeanne Troutner was serving as executive director of the YMCA and it was she who hired me. Eventually, she came to mean a great deal to me, not only as my boss, but as a friend. But, it took time. Being from the South where one of the problems that plagued young black males was the white woman, I was suspicious of her motives when she extended the hand of friendship. I found excuses not to accept her invitations to dinner with her and her family, hedged when she suggested I join them to go here or there. She persisted. When I was singing in the choir or preaching, she wanted to know about it and made a point of attending. She would then ask again, "Well, why don't you come over? Why won't you come?" I don't know if she ever understood how my own baggage and history would not allow me to accept her friendship. I had never experienced this kind of response from a white woman before and didn't know what to make of it. Could I trust her?

The day came when a couple of young African American airmen started attending programs at the "Y" and Jeanne invited them to her home. I think she must have realized how lonely we all were, far from home, far from family. When they went, I went, too, figuring there was safety in numbers. I couldn't help thinking of Mom's stories about her uncle, her father, the Klan, and the dangers posed by the white woman. Although my fears were not based on personal experience, Mom's warning voice echoed in my ears. Eventually, the ice was broken and Jeanne and I established a high level of trust that continued until her death in 2004. She left instructions in her will for me to conduct her funeral, and I did. I now suggest to others who feel as I did that there is some risk you can take and that it is less scary when others are around, when interactions start in a social setting. I also advise to take people at their word until they prove you wrong. Most people mean well.

In February of 1970, I was honorably discharged from the United States Air Force. I remained in Boise for a month or so, deciding what to do. While the military had been an education in itself, while being an Airman from April 1966 to February 1970 had offered experience and exposure, it was time to seek other opportunities. In the Air Force I had been in the field, firing a rifle, repairing an airplane, marching to orders, training others, learning better how to follow directions, and certainly how to work as part of a team. None of that experience was wasted on me. I felt the time had come for more formal education and training.

One morning early, I bought a train ticket and set out for Portland, Oregon. I visited relatives, continuing on to Oakland, California. I remember thinking back to my life as a boy in rural Georgia, watching trains go by. When I got to Oakland I went directly to my mother's brother, Uncle Willie. I had never met him as he was in the merchant marines, always on the high seas. My uncle invited me to stay with him awhile and offered me his car so I could visit my brother Joe and look around the town. I first drove him to a friend's house and when I returned to pick him up there was an ambulance and flashing lights. I flashed back to Boise, but Uncle Willie had died of a heart attack.

When we took him home to Georgia to conduct his funeral and bury him in the Cooper family graveyard, I took the opportunity to look at some colleges. When I discovered the cost to be $7,000 a year on the average, more than my G.I. Bill would cover, my brother Joe suggested the University of California. Berkeley's tuition at the time was $1,200 a year.

"You can live with us," Joe encouraged, "and go to school essentially free here on the G.I. Bill."

He did not have to insist!

25

A Student and His Ministry

By the time I finished the military, I had become completely convinced that the only way I would ever get ahead in life, the only way I would ever make a meaningful impact as an African American, was to get as high a level of formal education as was possible.

There were all sorts of schools around Oakland. I decided to try more than one and enrolled in four colleges at the same time: Merritt College, Laney College, and the University of California at Berkeley, while also attending Bay Cities Bible Institute as a non-matriculating student. In fact, I graduated in one year from the first three colleges, having carried a full load (15 hours). The courses at Merritt College emphasized African American studies and helped me to take a good look at who I was, to come to grips with my history and heritage, and to make some sense out of the experience. At Laney College I studied language and speech making, receiving a degree in Arts and Letters. I never lost sight of the fact that (as an African American minister, especially) I needed to be as good a speaker as I could possibly be and to develop skills in analyzing others' speeches and writings. I added rhetoric to my list of courses and studied rhetoric at Berkeley, where one of my first exercises was to look at Dr. Martin Luther King Jr.'s "I Have a Dream" speech in terms of the kinds of appeals he made and who his audience was. I won first place on that paper and was awarded (along with some others) a ten-day trip to an international youth conference in Quebec, Canada. It was a fascinating experience for me. As French was the language of the conference, we were assigned interpreters, many of whom were priests or nuns. I learned a great deal from them and was particularly interested in the insights one of them shared about celibacy and priesthood. I had not given it much thought at that time in relation to ministry.

At Bay Cities Bible Institute, I took courses in theology, church history, Bible interpretation, and hermeneutics. I learned a great deal from ministers who were actually practicing the trade and teaching in the evenings. There, one of my role models was the Reverend Earle Stuckey, who taught preaching and other courses and was an associate minister at Progressive Baptist Church in Berkeley. When this very popular preacher took me under his wing, I remembered my parents' saying that nobody gets anywhere in this world by themselves. He invited me along when he had a preaching engagement and if he could not accept one was kind enough to recommend me as a speaker. I studied the way he delivered a sermon, the way he carried himself, how he dressed. I took note of his demeanor, his facial expressions, his attitude. I looked at his family and observed him in his role not only as a minister, but as a husband, father, friend. I noticed how his personality, his style and values mirrored those I saw in my own father, Cousin Horace Cooper, and my earlier mentor, Reverend J. R. Tarver. Perhaps this was one of the reasons I found it easy to relate to him. We had a great time. Every new experience, every opportunity I was able to take in the course of my journey, everything was for me a way of making myself more of what God could eventually use in his service. Of course, I knew that good preparation was crucial to my success as a preacher and minister.

I remember the first wedding I performed at Calvary: Mr. Jesse Crenshaw to Ms. Pattie Piggee. Reverend Henry Hudson, who was still pastor at that time, had called upon me to do whatever it was that needed to be done when he was away. On this particular occasion, I felt a thrill when signing my first marriage certificate and bringing a family together. Shortly after this Reverend Hudson asked, "Davis, have you thought about pastoring in Utah?" I said, "I am not looking for a church."

While taking school seriously, I continued to be involved in ministry in the local community. I took to heart the commission of the Bible to visit the widows, the orphans, the sick, and the shut-in. I began to participate on a regular basis with Reverend James Hunter of the Center Street Baptist Church. He was one who had both the resources and the willingness to take his ministry to the hospitals, nursing homes, and jails. He included me. I went along with him and we became good friends.

In the Bible it is written: "For I was an hungered, and ye gave me meat; I was thirsty, and ye gave me drink; I was a stranger, and ye took me in; Naked, and ye clothed me; I was sick, and ye visited me; I was in prison and ye came unto me" (Matthew chapter 25, verses 35–36). In this spirit, Reverend Hunter and I visited San Quentin and other prisons in northern

California. I did not know any of the inmates at these facilities, but he did. Going with him gave me an opportunity to see what was happening inside while providing some outside contact for the inmates, some of whom were lifers. It was there that I became aware of the concept of "conjugal visitation," a privilege inmates had to earn. Those who had spouses and families could spend personal time with them in little houses right on the edge of the prison. At the time I also became aware of the "hard coreness" of some of the inmates who—while they looked harmless and powerless—had, I knew, carried out vicious crimes, some unspeakable. However, interacting with them was an opportunity to further develop my ministry and was indeed a useful stepping stone to the decade or so of work I would be charged with in the corrections system when I came to Utah.

One of the things I learned by working in prisons was that there are essentially three sides to every story: the official side, the inmate's side, and then (strange as it may seem) the guard's side. The guards often had a different slant on the story: "I know what the record says, but..." "I know what the inmate says, but..." This observation served me well in family counseling. I learned early in my role as a pastor to try to sit down with all of the parties that are involved at the same time to get each one's side of a story. "Always get your information from the horse's mouth," Dad used to say when we were youngsters. I do my best to keep in mind this advice.

Another thing I learned while visiting prisons was that inmates ofttimes find themselves confessing religion and beginning to practice a religion. We always take that with a grain of salt yet with some hope. An example of one who was "saved" while in prison was one of two sisters involved in a murder and serving long terms. Our prison ministry at Calvary visited them regularly and one sister sought us out when she was released. She became one of the most active members of our congregation and when it was "shoutin' time" she had something to shout about and did not mind saying, "Look where I've come from!" She was a marvelous lady who always sat in the first pews, near the choir at the old Calvary. Many remember that she had to be held and fanned by the ushers as she would frequently be "moved by the spirit." I have found over the years that some who are physically confined can find redemption, be spiritually free if given a chance.

A choice blessing came my way in 1971. In September the National Baptist Conventions of America held their annual meeting in San Francisco. I became an active participant in the youth department, going daily for a week, participating Monday through Thursday in the study and discussion groups. Thursday afternoon came around and with it an opportunity for youth department members to stand before the entire body and present a summary of what we had learned. I was chosen as one of the two presenters to speak before an audience of some ten to twelve thousand people. Present were some of the best trained, most experienced, most popular preachers in the country. I was scared, my knees shook, and I felt nervous. I encouraged myself with prayer and with the assurances from those who were seated behind me, the people in charge, the president of the body, the audience. They helped me along with their shouts of "Amen, say it, say it, right on…" With such remarks echoing in my ears, I finally settled down and the message flowed. I subsequently received preaching invitations from all over the country. One that sticks in my mind was from a Reverend Johnson, a minister from South Carolina who had preached earlier that day and had really stirred the audience with his delivery and with his message. However, as he dropped out of that convention and joined another soon after, we lost contact and I never did go to South Carolina.

When I was growing up, I knew we belonged to a large pool, but I had no sense of just how large. It was not until I became a full-grown adult that I came to understand that this body (our National Baptist Convention) spreads across this country and into the international arena. It is by choice, however, that a local congregation decides whether or not to pay dues and participate. There are some advantages in participation: help with missions, education (sponsoring a college, for example), and to a limited extent help for a retiring minister or full-time Christian worker or help with construction or remodeling of a facility. Belonging to a convention certainly gives a congregation the opportunity to interact with others of like faith, to share in spiritual and practical matters, to see how other ministries go forth.

There are four major Baptist conventions, about 16.5 million members strong. The National Baptist Convention U.S.A., Inc. (of which I became a member and still am a member today) is the largest. The National Baptists of America, Inc. (the one I spoke to in San Francisco) is the second largest of the conventions. Progressive National Baptists (made up of people who are the most academically well-trained ministers) is third in size. The Missionary National Baptist Convention is the newcomer. The National Baptists U.S.A., Incorporated and the National Baptists of

America both claim to be the same age. Someone has dubbed these Baptist conventions "the sleeping giant."

But to return to that thrilling day in San Francisco. After I spoke, the response I received from the audience was like sparks of a fire. People rose to their feet as I concluded my message. Some responded verbally, many flocked toward the stage to express congratulations and thanks. That day I vividly experienced the payoff from the various forms of training I had received in Florida, Texas, Thailand, and Idaho. I also realized the benefits of my schooling and formal work in the Oakland area, especially the courses I had taken in public speaking.

Was I now ready for full-time ministry?

Three months after speaking to the convention, I was officially ordained by the Association of Baptist Churches in Oakland, at the Center Street Missionary Baptist Church, 940 Center Street. The Reverend R. L. James was the chairman of the catechizing committee of some eight or 10 ministers. After checking me out to see how much I knew and how well I was prepared, they agreed to issue me papers of ordination, thus confirming that: "Yes, we trust this young man to go now and do the work of ministry without our having to be there to oversee, to make sure that he does it right."

I was now declared fully qualified, fully available, fully authorized. From the day of my ordination on December 5, 1971 (also my birthday), until August of 1972, Reverend James encouraged me to do every facet of ministry at the Center Street Missionary Baptist Church. I learned how to perform marriages, baptisms, and funerals. I learned by watching and by doing. This experience paid high dividends because when I arrived in Salt Lake City and united with the Calvary Baptist Church in September of 1972, and the Reverend Henry Hudson called on me to help him bring some order to some of the organizations in the church, I was prepared. I could do whatever needed to be done, meeting with the Missionary Society, working with the choir, teaching. I remember one particular lady who came to classes regularly and made it her business to challenge everything I said, perhaps because I was not the pastor, perhaps because I looked so young—"boyish," some people said. She tested my patience, was a thorn in my side, but I learned an important lesson: Always speak from a firm foundation and always present evidence. In fact, the Bible speaks for itself. I remember exciting challenges and thrilling moments in those early years at Calvary.

Calvary Baptist Church's congregation had built a new facility on 700 South in the 1960s. They moved into it in 1966, but by 1972, when I joined, the congregation itself had dwindled and people were not populating their new space. I wondered: "How does one build a congregation of people?" I was moved to start with fellowship, spending as much time with people as I did in study, teaching, sermon preparation, and prayer. I determined to get to know who people were, to inform myself as to their desires and their needs, and to respond whenever they were hurting. If people were grieving, I let them know that there was help, that there was solace. If people were sick, I could utter a prayer, give a word of advice, read a passage from the Bible. What this said to them was, "Here's somebody who cares about you." Of course, I made a point of inviting people to participate with us as visitors, to join, or to return to the church.

I remember many a time when I would bump into someone and ask, "What church do you attend?" "None," many said. "Why is that?" I would pursue. More often than not the answer was, "Nobody ever asked me." The Bible says, "Ask and ye shall receive." So I took the approach that if I was going to "grow" a congregation, I had to ask people to come, to be a part, assuring them that they had a place and opportunities within the community. I knocked on many doors in Salt Lake City those first years as an associate minister at Calvary! Many responded, becoming energetic and active participants. Brothers Robert Handy and Jim Dooley come to mind.

Robert Handy had been an active member of Calvary, helping to do some fund-raising for the building of the new church at 700 South. At some point he drifted away or perhaps found a reason why he should not return. I visited with him and rather quickly he committed to come and be of help to me. As I said earlier, in those days, some talked about me as the young "upstart." I was 28 years old and, in the eyes of many, too young to be a pastor. Robert Handy was willing to help this youngster to get on the right track. Jim Dooley, on the other hand, was very active in the community, doing civil rights work. He had moved to Utah from Arkansas, where he had been a member of a church. He was one who had not bothered to seek one out in Salt Lake because no one had reached out to him. When I did, he came, became an active member of Calvary, and in fact helped to write one of the early histories of our church. He remained a member until his death, as did Robert Handy. That's building congregation! That's connecting with people! That's letting people know that they have something of worth and value! And in the words of the Reverend Jesse Jackson, that's encouraging them to remember that "everybody is somebody"!

One particular hurdle I knew I had to cross was attracting men to join the congregation. Women naturally tended to come more regularly and voluntarily than did the men. Historically, men have not been the core group and finding ways of speaking specifically to their needs was a challenge. I knew I must strive to make them feel they had real value, a significant place in the life and leadership of the congregation. In fact, they needed to be persuaded that they would not be "trampled" upon, that they had something to contribute, that their role in the family would be enhanced by their role in the church.

Another challenge was how to reach out into the community, make all people feel welcome, be inclusive. Over the years, and by design on my part, the Calvary Baptist Church has become a melting pot. When I first came to Calvary there was only one member who was not African American. At various times she made comments that she was treated differently because she was of Swedish descent. I made it my business to make sure that she was included in whatever we were doing, inviting her to become part of the leadership of the church, celebrating with her at the times that she was celebrating, offering comfort in her times of distress. Eventually, she began to bring members of her family. She became an example of how the power of love can gather people into the circle. A similar example was that of a teenager who came with a friend from high school. She enjoyed the music at Calvary and wanted to take part in what we were doing. We invited her to travel with us as we went to national meetings, to participate in various projects. She soon became one of the youth leaders. Trust and respect was developed between those who were different, people spread the word, and those who had come in tentatively (some out of curiosity) became some of the stronger, more active members of the congregation over the years.

Goodwill, I have found, is more frequently than not reciprocated. Thus, as the congregation grew and the old church filled to overflowing, we began to envision a new facility and to reach out for help. This was no easy task: Calvary is a historic congregation and people become attached to a space they believe is part of their history. To get some to agree to the value of change requires vision casting, discussion, one-on-one contact. I was prepared to cast a vision and did so through sermons, written documents, conversations with people in their homes, and meetings. With

God's help my efforts motivated the Calvary congregation to cooperate with their pastor. We began to raise funds.

In January of 1995, we invited everybody to bring as much as they could for the "kickoff." At least one Sunday a month I put special emphasis on the building fund. Adults set aside a specific amount based on their ability and their level of commitment. Children added their pennies, nickels, and dimes to a big bottle that they could watch fill up. Pastor's friends and friends of members of the congregation said, "We'll help you." Many ultimately made regular contributions. We sponsored a number of community-wide events, such as a golf tournament once a year. Our choir went about the community singing. We determined we were not going to sell any kind of merchandise in order to reach our goal, however. At some point in their fund-raisers, the congregation had sold dinners, candy, pies, cakes, all of which required great effort with meager results. We made a point to recall Jesus' efforts to cleanse the temple of merchandising. I reminded the congregation that the Bible instructed us to give as we could and commit from within our own hearts. People were moved and the dollars began to grow until one day it was possible to see that the vision that had been cast could be realized. Having secured one-third of the funds needed among ourselves, we then approached larger community foundations. We asked them if they would participate with us. Fortunately, the George S. and Dolores Eccles Foundation agreed to match the dollars we already had. We began to look for land. Another faith group came forward and offered us the property on which our new church now stands at their cost.

One of our goals had been to remain in the inner city in order to meet the needs (as Calvary had historically) of an inner-city community; another was to build our new facility and march into it debt free. By and large our prayers were answered. The help we received was no doubt the result of God moving hearts; there was clear manifestation of goodwill toward the African American community of Utah. Although Calvary has traditionally been an African American church and is thought of as one still today, it has in fact become an integrated congregation, demonstrating where the power of love and goodwill can lead. Of course, wherever there is more than one human being there will always be friction. Friction, though, is the principle on which mechanical instruments operate. Cars run because the piston rubs against the head, the head creates friction causing the engine to fire up and run, and so on. I consider love as the same thing as oil in an automobile engine. It is what keeps the friction from becoming an explosion, what keeps the engine running smoothly. At Calvary, our goal continues to be to do all we can to make sure that people have more and more love, instead of less and less.

Another of my efforts at reaching beyond the church and into the community was getting the choir to do its first televised concert, on KUED. I remember this concert vividly. Mrs. Gladys Hesleph played the organ and her son, Brian, played the piano. Brian was such a marvelous performer that the camera spent more time on his hands than on the choir. I was the narrator for that particular concert and thereafter developed a name around the community for doing just that.

Music has, of course, been a central part of the worship experience at Calvary Baptist Church. We appreciate strong voices and the message of song. When I came to Calvary, Sister Phyllis Grayson was the choir director and Sister Gladys Hesleph was the musician. As time went on, a number of instrument players joined us and became a part of our team. Christy Anderson joined as organist and director for the Women's Chorus, which sings on fifth Sundays. Later, Shelly Smith and James Anderson played on the bongos. Vernisha Sterling and Mychael Johnson came on board also to play the drums, while James Jackson Jr., Tony Mason, and Cal Isom play guitar and bass. Merilyn Hesleph plays the piano as does Courtney Smith, who has been in music ministry since a young age. He started at old Calvary and developed primarily on the piano and organ. Laura Eady came to town as an experienced pianist and singer. We have a broad range of musical talent with an angel choir, a youth choir, a male chorus, a women's chorus, and an inspirational choir. We needed all the help we could get! We tried several approaches and our search for a minister of music took more effort and time than we had hoped. Our choirs continue to draw people to Calvary by providing music for all the worship services at Calvary, as well as at other churches and in the larger community. We appreciate our musicians and of course our directors who include Brian Hesleph, Minister Anthony Bennett, Merilyn Hesleph, Laura Eady, Jackie Jenson, Peggie Wright, James Jackson III, and B. Murphy, who conducts yearly a Gospel-inspired "Messiah" at Salt Lake Community College. God blesses us with harmony and spiritual music for each worship experience, preparing the people for the coming sermon. One of our long-term members, Loralee, took a signing class and volunteered to sign in our main worship service. It has been a special treat for those with hearing difficulties.

So, my early days at Calvary were times of invigorating spirit, connecting with community, and fulfilling my life vision and goals.

But, allow me to return briefly to the years that led up to that time. The two years I spent in California after leaving the military were completely filled with the work of ministry and with formal schooling. Interestingly, the courses that posed the greatest challenge for me, the ones I found hardest, were the theology courses. I found, however, that by applying all of what I was learning at one school to the course work at the other schools, I could keep my ship afloat and benefit from all of the courses I was taking. So, what I was learning about the African American experience at Merritt, I used when I went to deliver speeches at Laney College, and the speech that I delivered at Laney had content that was helpful when I went to Bay Cities. When I went to the University of California, the papers I wrote for Laney were the starting places for papers I wrote at Berkeley. At times, doubts crept in. I wondered if I would ever make it. However, the Lord showed me ways, guiding my hand as I wove different strands into my calling. For example, I used Margaret Walker's *Jubilee* as the basis for a paper in rhetoric. I then converted this paper into a sermon. This interweaving made it possible to complete my course work and to go forward with my work of ministry. All the while, ringing in my ears were my father and mother's words: "You have to be better than I … You have to go further than we did … We got by with minimal education, you have to have more." Also, I never lost sight of the fact that I had to do better than my white colleagues if I was to distinguish myself. I remembered the people in my community who were doing well, recognizing that they were people who not only had on-the-job training, but also had a good deal of formal training. I visualized each and every one of them, and their example firmed up my resolve to stay the course. I felt family at my back, bolstering me. My brother Joe was steadfast in his support, giving me free rein of his house, access to his resources, validating and encouraging my efforts. Of course, the G.I. bill was a godsend. Though I sometimes had a mind struggle, especially about taking on so many different courses, I was steadied by my faith and by the conviction that I was doing this for myself, for my family, and for my people. I was never tempted to quit.

Having freshly returned from my tour of duty in Southeast Asia, I had a mixed accent of Southern drawl and Thai. People would ask what country I was from and be surprised when I responded, "The U.S. of A." My education and boldness, along with my availability, opened many doors. I was a youth minister with the then elderly Reverend R. L. James, pastor of the Center Street Missionary Baptist Church, at 10th and Center Streets in Oakland; I went where the Reverend Stuckey gave me an opportunity to go and I preached. When Reverend James gave me every third Sunday as "Youth Day," I also preached, gaining meaningful experience and exposure.

While still in California, an exciting opportunity came to attend a meeting of the Baptist Associations. There, I met the Reverend A. Paul Jones, pastor of the New Hope Baptist Church in Sacramento. He was known as the "Dean of Preachers," a doctor among his peers. He invited me to preach for him at New Hope. I did. He liked me and I liked him. A few years before his death, Reverend A. Paul Jones came to Salt Lake City to install me as pastor of the Calvary Baptist Church. He reminded me of what the apostle Paul had said to Timothy: "Let no man despise thy youth." I was 27 years old.

26

INSTALLATION

As I MENTIONED EARLIER, I was called as pastor of Calvary in February of 1974 and the installation service was scheduled for the fourth Sunday of April. The worship service consisted of lots of music from the Calvary choir, strong prayers, readings from the Bible, all of which culminated in an exchange of vows. The pastor made commitments to the congregation and the congregation made commitments to the pastor, much like wedding vows. The leader of the association of churches gave the charge to the pastor. A local minister gave the charge to the congregation. When the ceremony was complete, we went downstairs to the social hall of the church for a full-course meal of soul food prepared by some of the best cooks in the area: Sisters Viola Goff, Lula Flake, Pauline Brown, and also Robert Handy and his daughter, Mary. A special cake was provided by Milford and Olivia Simpson, Olivia being a member of Calvary. It was a small cake in tribute with my name on it, which Mrs. Davis and I took home. We ate instead a larger sheet cake. Calvary's congregation and guests all took part in this installation, the official acknowledgment that I was to be the pastor of the Calvary Baptist Church for an indefinite time. Churches of various denominations came to take part in this installation service as did people from around the region and the nation. Politicians and preachers, choirs and members from other churches, community leaders and college professors, students, young people, old people all came to be a part of the service and to hear guest preachers preach. It was a high spiritual time. I felt overwhelmed and could not imagine what the future would hold.

Before my installation, however, I had already presented to the congregation a ministry plan communicated at the church's business meeting; a written copy was voted on and accepted. The plan had spiritual goals first and foremost, encouraging members and guests to spend as much time in prayer and Bible reading as possible, to fellowship with others, to visit the sick, the shut in, and those in prison. It also included a financial packet that defined the pay the pastor would receive, for example. In fact, it was during this presentation that I indicated there would be no selling of goods to raise funds, that the congregation would instead be expected to give liberally, freely, and to set aside a portion of their income for the support of the church. I asked the officers of the church to remain in place and give me an opportunity to take a look at what they were doing, to see first-hand whether we could work together. These were the deacons, deaconesses, trustees, chairmen of each of the auxiliaries, presidents of the various boards and groups such as the choir, the ushers…They were to be example-setters for the entire congregation and were expected to "match their walk with their talk," as was I.

This was an exciting time because it meant lots of study groups, lots of teaching and training that first year. I didn't go anywhere for the most part and spent long hours at the church conducting classes. I suppose you could say that I was passing on my own style, my own beliefs, making sure that others had the opportunity to catch the vision directly from me. I remember that one deacon did not attend the classes and did not show up for the confirmation meeting, the time for renewing commitment. I took with me a group of the deacons present that day and went to his house. We talked to him. He finally informed us that he was going to step aside and said, "Put one of those young fellows in my place." I did just that and we promoted him to what is called a "senior deacon," which for all intents and purpose meant that he was retired. He continued to come and go, but not on a regular basis. So, we trained the deacons and spent time training other officers and heads of departments so that they might become familiar with how we would conduct business: requests for finances, upkeep of facilities, missions, operational routines…One of the little-discussed facets of a church operation is how it is a business corporation operating with all of the essential requirements of any other kind of corporation in addition to being, of course, a spiritual center.

At Calvary we soon learned what was required to make sure that funds were there so that the congregation could move on. From the Book of Malachi and the Book of Corinthians we studied about the importance of bringing to the Lord's house a portion of what we have received, a dime from everyone, so to speak. We, as a congregation, also decided that we would sponsor and have available to the entire community, one week out of the year, a concentrated preaching revival, inviting a guest minister to preach for five days. This sort of revival is different from a prayer revival, which is more internal. The preaching revival has become a tradition and is held one week before the church's anniversary, on the second Sunday in the month of November.

Although I did not know it then, February 1970 to June of 1972 were years spent in preparation for Utah. During the week I was in school full time, though my brother Joe sometimes enlisted me in his painting business. I made a little extra money that way and also by babysitting. On most weekends, however, I traveled, preached, did the ministry work I wanted to do. I was applying what I was learning in school to my calling. The traveling that I had started in the military continued, especially after I was able to buy a new car—a baby-blue Beetle. On frequent weekends, I drove to Southern California, to Portland, Oregon, to Las Vegas, Nevada, where I had a "church family," and returned in time for school on Monday. I applied myself throughout the week, but on the weekends it was time for fun, for relaxation, for witnessing, and for preaching. I had a great time and became a well-known and respected youth minister. The hands-on experience I was gaining along with formal education was all invaluable in my long-range plans. A dream grew out of what Dad spoke of as a higher calling: I wanted to be the best-prepared minister available anywhere in the United States of America!

When I moved to Salt Lake City, the dream blossomed into a long-term commitment. And, when I accepted the Calvary Baptist Church's invitation to become its pastor, I knew that along with the exciting times and the satisfaction of doing the Lord's work, my family and I would have to learn to henceforth live in a "glass house."

27

Glass House

A pastor lives in a glass house. In fact, because everybody is looking in on him and his family, noticing the example he sets, the pastor's house sometimes becomes the only "Bible" some read. They will tell you what's appropriate and inappropriate by what they see the pastor do, and by what the pastor's family does. Living in a glass house means that people are always looking in for guidelines for their own behavior. One of my daughters is bitter because she was held up as the example for many of the children in our community. Their parents would call and ask to speak to her. They wanted to know if she was going to be attending a particular party or event, if she was going to a ball game, if she was ... If she was, then these adults felt it was okay for their children to go. To place that kind of responsibility on a preacher's kid (or PK, as they have come to be known) is going beyond what ought to be. Thus, many PKs don't measure up to what is expected of them. Many of the pastors' wives are expected to be docile, quiet, and easygoing, obedient to their husbands, and the example of what a "good" wife ought to be. Really, what does it matter if they are happy and it is okay with their spouses at home? In the larger community they are labeled because of the expectation of the congregation. In short, to live in a preacher's house is to have imposed upon you expectations beyond those that are imposed on other people. I remind some of the people at our church from time to time that the same thing it takes for a pastor and his family to get into heaven is what it will take for them to get in. However, the pastor's house is, in some places, a "twenty-four seven" proposition, which means being open 24 hours a day, seven days a week for whatever it is that the congregation needs. As a result, ofttimes, the pastor's own family is left without the presence of the pastor, without the attention of a husband and a father. I suppose some of the loneliest ladies that I know are pastors' wives!

In my opinion, a pastor who is truly successful is one who is able to balance doing for others and doing for their own families, their interactions in the larger community and their participation at home. When all is said and done, however, I can say from experience that a pastor does not have much time he can call his own. People don't mind calling anytime when a need arises. My wife believes I ought to put in more time at home, delegate more of my responsibilities. However, when a member of the congregation calls it is their pastor they want, the person they have elected as their leader. They are reluctant to turn to the assistants or to the deacons. Nonetheless, to the degree that one is able to spend adequate, quality time with family and congregation, one is therefore a good pastor.

In my estimation, a good pastor's wife is one who has a mind of her own, is able to provide support, but also is able to do things that she wants to do; not a slave to the pastor. Pastor's wives are neither to be walked on nor to be lorded over. They are helpmeets. My wife has truly been one. Often the congregation expects the pastor's wife to hold certain offices, including help with the children at church, attending missionary society meetings, opening the home to people who come by, being good at hospitality, and so on. Fortunately, at Calvary, my wife is allowed to be primarily my wife and the mother of our children. Mrs. Davis has in fact spent most of her years in our marriage taking care of the home front. She has helped me to be able to work evenings by being the one to attend most of our children's school events, for example. I have stayed involved, but home and family have been primarily her responsibility. The role she performed has sometimes meant that she has not had a lot of time for herself. But, now that our children are grown she is branching out in a number of different directions as she becomes weary of having an empty nest. We have both adjusted our schedules and timing so that we can take care of each other a bit more. In general, my wife is an indoor person. I am more of an outdoor person. Fishing would be fine with me. She would like to go to a movie or a musical program. When the children were at home, I suggested she take them and go where she wanted to go. Every now and then I would take her where she wanted to go. Now that the kids are gone, I try to take her where I am going and to go to some of those places she would like as well, doing some of the things she wants. So, give and take. There ought to be some sense of fullness, fulfillment on behalf of both parties in a marriage.

As to the pastor's children, they ought to be allowed to be children. I think one of the reasons a lot of people say that the preacher's kids are the worst kids in town is not because they are any different or any worse than others, but just that what is expected of them is different. I remind my congregation that "my family, my children are children just like yours. My wife is a wife just like yours. Don't expect any more. They were not called to be the pastor of this church, but I was. Leave them be." There are, in fact, a number of books that have come out recently where ministers' wives express their frustration at being placed in a glass house, of having others always minding their business. Expectations are sometimes not spoken, but other times they are: "And you call yourself a pastor's wife!" Or, "And you're a preacher's kid!" Calvary Baptist Church has been less demanding of the pastor's wife and children than other congregations I have had the opportunity to know about. Now and then, however, I do have to send forth the reminder: "It takes the same effort for a pastor and his family to get to heaven as it does ordinary folk!"

The responsibility for changing attitudes toward what constitutes a good pastor, a good pastor's family, a good pastor's house, perhaps ought to be in the training, the teaching provided by the given pastor to the congregation. To have people depend on you for everything may give some a sense of value and worth, but if one knows who one is oneself then one ought not have to depend upon what others expect as a way of defining oneself. Frederick Douglass talks about how the slaves valued themselves in relationship to the value and wealth of their masters. Unfortunately, that is often the case in the church's arena. And it ought not to be. Each individual, each person has to know who the pastor is and be convinced that he is no more or no less than anybody else. Whatever is required of one person is the same that is required of another. That has been one of my convictions. I believe that I do not have to depend upon anybody to define who I am. I am who I am and am going to be that. I am France Davis and not some other person. I do what I do, not what some other person tells me to do. That is one of the great things about being a Baptist, by the way. Baptist ministers have the individual freedom to do what we are convinced God would have us do. We do not have a hierarchy. We are independent, distinct, and self-governing, if you will. The role of the pastor, as I have emphasized, is to help people be all that they can be. In effect, a good pastor will endeavor to equip people to do just that. As pastor of Calvary, I see my job as being one to help my congregation know from within who they are spiritually, to be fully equipped with a sense of hope, faith, and love; those are the three things that will abide with each of us throughout life. Beyond that, whatever causes the members of the congregation or community to hurt, it is my task to help equip them to be able to face that as well. It is not my job to do for them, but to equip them to be able to handle what they need to handle in life. If housing is an issue, then we need to help people find decent, safe, and affordable housing. If education is an issue, then it's the role of the pastor to help equip people to be able to find that educational opportunity. If they need legal help, it is not my task to be their lawyer per se, but to be the one who can help them to find the lawyer they need. So the role of the pastor is that of "equipper," one who helps people realize the fullness of their own potential.

I think that the success of the Calvary Baptist Church in Salt Lake City over the last three decades can be traced to our ability to help more and more people to deal with life daily. In fact, when I came to Calvary in 1972, there were not more than two handfuls of people I knew who had finished college. Now, there are hundreds of people who have been able to graduate and earn degrees and go on to be self-supporting members who take care of their own needs. So the congregation is expanding, not just in numbers, but in personal growth and development. That is where real growth ought to be.

One of my colleagues, the Reverend James Gates, used to say: "We ought not be so concerned about numbers, but we ought to really be concerned about numbness." Indeed, if I as a minister can keep people from feeling numb about life, if I can help them to overcome feeling insignificant, unwanted, worthless, put away or put down, then I have done well what I believe would be the task that God expects of me.

28

Time and Tasks

As I have tried to explain, one of the greatest challenges for me as a pastor is the balancing of time and responsibilities. Over the years, I have had to find various ways of balancing my time at home and at the church. Sometimes I've had success, and sometimes I haven't been successful. My wife, I suppose, if she were here, would say that I have not done a good job of it and that I have been gone most of the time. And indeed I have been gone a lot. However, as I touched upon earlier, one of the ways I do that is by handling everything when I handle it. When I'm done, I leave it. If I get a letter in the mail that requires my attention, I pay attention to it, answer it if need be, and move on. If I must make a telephone call, I make it promptly and move on. When I go to the hospital to visit the sick, I visit the sick and give them my undivided attention while I am visiting them at the hospital. But, when I leave the hospital to go to a wedding or a blessing, I give these my full attention. When I leave the wedding to go officiate at a funeral, I am fully engaged in the funeral. When I leave the funeral to go to the courthouse, I focus on the matter at hand. When I go home, I leave whatever it is that I have at the church. I leave it there and go home and am engaged at home. So, by handling everything fully the first and only time that I handle it, I can avoid a second visit to the same old matter or situation. That is hard for a lot of people to understand and many ask how I can move from a wedding to a funeral. I believe that it is one of the gifts God gave to me.

All in all pastors operate with a great deal of freedom. I am free to make my own schedule, to set my own appointments, to go and come as I please, except for regularly scheduled church services and meetings. Because of my own nature, however, I tend not to take a day off on a regular basis. Rather I take an hour here and there. That is a kind of freedom.

Pastors of African American churches have also operated in the larger community with a certain amount of freedom nobody else seemed to have.

They could go in and talk to the powers that be and express themselves without worry of repercussions, without the fear that they would not be hired, or lose their jobs. They have had a higher sense of a calling. They do not have to worry, by and large, about someone looking over their shoulders all the time. I am grateful to be able to make my own decisions and work at my own pace. Except, as I said, for worship services that involve other people, my schedule is my own, though being pastor of a church is all encompassing. The task requires not just the excitement of the Sunday sermon and the worship time, but also a dedication to meeting the needs of the members of the congregation.

In the Gospel according to Saint John, Jesus asks Peter, "Do you love me?" When Peter responds in the affirmative, Jesus reminds him that he must watch over his people: "Well, if you do, feed my sheep, feed my lambs." This is indeed a commitment the pastor ought to make and keep. Feeding the sheep and the lambs is his single most significant role.

29

MINISTERS

MINISTERS ARE EITHER GOOD EXAMPLES OR THEY ARE BAD EXAMPLES. And as I say to young ministers nowadays, you can learn something from every minister. From some you learn what not to do. From others you learn what to do. That includes how to conduct yourself in visitations, how to interact with members of the congregation, and certainly how to deliver a sermon. Jesus reminded his disciples that the power to help and heal comes with much fasting and much prayer. Young associate ministers, "sons of the church" as we call them, may sometimes mess up, may not be able to get the job done, may not even know how to get it done, and certainly may not be able to do it to the satisfaction of or at the same level as the pastor. But part of their training requires that they have room, space, and the opportunities to try to do the best that they can. I make it a regular habit of suggesting to the sons of Calvary that when they are inexperienced at a particular task, they try it with me present in the room. Then, after they have tried performing a wedding or a baby blessing successfully, they can go out and do it on their own. In this way the pastor, in relationship to the sons of the church, is a teacher and mentor. Hopefully, the information that is passed on, the experiences that are shared can nurture and prepare for ministry.

At Calvary, the sons of the church have specific assignments, which change every month. One of the sons is responsible for preaching, another for teaching a particular class, still another for sharing brief devotionals, another for visiting outside of the congregation: the jails, the rescue missions, the prisons. Others will be responsible for visiting the sick and the shut-in. Those assignments are made by me and the group as we discuss what needs to be done. We then expect that all will do what they have been assigned to the best of their abilities. They are held accountable. Training is on-the-job training, which includes preaching. After a sermon is delivered, we meet as a team in the office and discuss the weaknesses and the strengths, making suggestions, saying how we would have approached the sermon, the message, the subject that is being shared.

At Calvary, we take very seriously the business of training young ministers and helping them to grow and to become the very best that they can be before we turn them loose to go and practice among the people, the sheep, the flock or any other congregations. I believe that we as "trainers" must be accountable to God, to other people, and to ourselves, as must sons of the ministries who are in training. All three are important if one is to successfully carry out the work of ministry, preaching and sharing the good news. Jesus told us that when he comes again he will separate the sheep from the goats. He will ask you what you did for the kingdom. Did you visit the sick? Did you visit the prisons? Did you feed the hungry and clothe the naked? Did you care about others? You will be accountable for your stewardship. Service is the key word and I remind some of my colleagues that we have to be careful who we "turn loose" on people, on congregations.

Sons of the ministries have a responsibility to be supportive, to help lighten the load that the pastor carries, to volunteer to be of help, not always waiting to be called upon. This, of course, is patterned after what Jethro says to Moses in the Book of Exodus. Thus, a son of the church "holds up the arms" of the pastor as Aaron held up the arms of Moses during battle. I say to those who have made the choice to become part of the Calvary team: "I expect that you will be here. I expect that if you're not you will let me know. I expect that you will be prepared to do necessary tasks, and that you will do these as if you were me. For example, if you are given to long sermons and I am given to short ones, you will follow my example. I expect you to be in support of what is going on (verbally and in terms of your participation) during the worship service, even if you disagree. If you don't like or do not agree with the pastor, I expect you to hold your peace in public and air your issues only in private. And, above all, I recommend that you be what you say you are, the same person you are in the street as you are in the church house, and to be prepared at all times to preach and to do everything that needs to be done." As a pastor and as a congregation, we are looking for education, for knowledge of the doctrines and beliefs that are taught in the Bible. We are looking for demonstrations and evidence of a regular life of prayer. We are looking for a spirit of humility, meaning that one knows one's place and is able, until promoted, to cheerfully accept things the way they are while they are that way and then when they change to move on to a new and different place. Paul says: "I have learned in whatsoever state I am therein to be content."

Associate ministers remain sons of the church until they are called to pastor a church. Once they are called, they become pastor-sons. *Associate* simply means that they are members of the church and that they are serving there. Being pastor of a church means that one has a charge of one's own. Some associate pastors may not yet have reached the level of qualification that allows us to be comfortable in sending them out. These are sons who are in the developmental stages, whereas sons who are pastors have completed that development and training. They go on. The men who sit behind the pulpit with me are sons and also happen to be associates. In the afternoons and for special programs we may have other sons who come from their own places of responsibility. Those who are there regularly during the two morning services, though, are ones who are associate ministers, sons of the church still in training, like Reverends Anthony Bennett and Clarence Giles. Some, like Reverends Wilson, Wright, Stewart, and Miller, have been pastors before but have sensed the need for additional training and have returned to the church for training and fellowship.

Now, all of these ministers (whether sons or pastors) express to the pastor first and then to the congregation that they believe they have been called into the ministry. It is a personal conviction. The Book of Timothy says that it is an urging within one's own being that God is calling one to the work of the preaching ministry. People thus called are then given an opportunity to stand before the congregation and tell them that they sense they have been called. After the congregation hears their expression about their belief in a call, they are then scheduled for a time to deliver a trial sermon, as I did in Florida back in 1966. They are given a time frame and will have spent time working with the pastor in preparation. Because we are a congregational church, the congregation decides whether they want to issue them a license or not. Once licensed, however, they then have (with permission from the pastor) the opportunity to be part of the ministerial team. In short, licensing means being able to practice what you believe to be your calling in ministry whenever opportunity allows. One is not fully qualified to render all of the services of a minister, however. Licensed ministers are not allowed to give communion or perform marriages. They are, however, authorized to bury the dead while being directly supervised by the pastor.

After being licensed, ministers who are prepared are then ordained. They are examined in terms of their knowledge, their life experiences, their lifestyle. If found to be worthy by a team of pastors and ministers, they are then declared qualified and can do any of the tasks the pastor does. Once ordained, however, if they do not do as they ought, it is very difficult to "sit them down." So, ordination is serious business. However, before ordination, a licensed minister can be "sat down." The pastor can say, "I don't think you're doing what you ought to be doing. I don't think you're making the effort…I don't think you're preparing yourself…I don't think you're living as you ought to live as a good example..." and deny the person any further opportunity. To sit an ordained minister down, however, requires that written charges against that minister be presented and defended. So, the responsibility of the pastor is paramount and most important in overseeing not just the congregation, but also the work of new ministers, associates, and sons of the church so that they learn as much as they can and behave in ways that are acceptable and appropriate. In fact, a list of the character traits required of those entering the ministry is found in two or three places in the Bible. In the Book of Acts they are defined as people who are filled with the Holy Spirit, and who have wisdom and good report both within and outside of the church community. Those three characteristics summarize what is a much longer list of expectations found in the Books of Timothy and Titus. These include being grave, holding the mystery of the faith, ruling well one's own household, being the husband of one wife, not given to wine, not proud, and not greedy.

Ministers are on "trial" when they are first licensed. Thus people are constantly looking at them, even expected to report anything that is contrary to what Timothy and Titus, or the Book of Acts, tell us are the qualifications for a minister. Furthermore, ministers who are not willing to learn, who are not humble, who are not obedient to other leaders, who are unwilling to invest themselves, "pay their dues," these ministers will encounter the reluctance of their leaders when it comes to ordination. They must put in the time and effort to become what they ought to become and to be willing to not be in the forefront, but be in the background for a time. They must support and encourage the leader—the pastor, that is. Sometimes this means doing menial tasks, ones that get your hands involved in the work, if you will. They must be willing to play the role that Aaron played, holding up the arms of Moses in the time of battle. Lifestyle, daily walk and talk, everything a minister does to demonstrate a call to ministry is noteworthy. While the call is indeed a gift from God, the practice requires personal effort to make of this gift the best gift it can be.

Some ministers behave themselves in an unseemly fashion, in ways that would not, I believe, be pleasing to God. Some who step up have not, we believe, truly received the call and in fact don't actually have the gift. This business of ministry can be learned, of course. Some can learn to go through the motions quite effectively. In fact, there is a place in the Bible that talks about false prophets creeping in unaware. Before you know it they have become so popular, so influential, they are making such an impact that it is hard to distinguish them from those who have received the gifts. I have seen those who will tell you: "I know just when to raise my voice during the course of a sermon and I know just when to lower it. I know exactly when to move a certain part of my anatomy and when to keep it still as a way of 'slaying' the listening congregation, having an emotional effect on them." It has been my experience that the good fruit and the bad fruit are eventually separated. The one who is genuine is able to withstand the trials and show accountability, whereas the one who has learned ministry is likely to fall by the wayside.

Every now and then there are those who emerge who will tell you that they can teach you how to do the work of ministry without your having the calling. And, yes, they know the technique. When it comes to passion and feeling, however, they frequently miss the mark. They lack the shepherd's heart, the love for the sheep!

30

LESSONS

ONE OF THE THINGS I FIND TO BE TRUE is that the more people have in common and the more they know the Bible, the easier it is for them to relate to one another. Sermons of the church are designed to talk, among other things, about what we have in common. We all have problems. We all run short of money. We all work. We all have opportunity to go to school. We all have worth and value, insight and vision. By emphasizing the things we have in common more than our differences, we become closer. And I believe we have more in common than we have to make us different.

EQUALITY

The evening sun left night and me
To find our way around, you see.
Invisible!
Free from the vulgar separate tide
Just alike and side by side.
Harmony!
Jet! Black as Black can get
And no two are blacker yet.
Ebony!

As we think about what we are trying to achieve, we are talking about being more human. We are talking about being more fully what is within us as individuals. That is the starting place. That is an aspect of what the sermon deals with. Each person has to start here, with self. Each of us must work on self, know who self is, get self under control, and then we can interact with others out there, beyond self. The philosophy with which I imbue my sermons goes back to my parents' teachings, my father's little jingles, my mother's "urgings" that you're are no better or worse than any-body else. Now, you may get treated better or worse by others, but that does not give you the right to mistreat others. Always treat people the way you would like them to treat you is what we learned from the earliest days of our lives. I made a personal choice based on my parents' teachings. I decided to take the "road less traveled." I chose to go the loving, caring way. I decided to consider a more tender approach to life. I don't think you can make a choice, an appropriate choice, unless you know what the options really are. Children who have never been exposed to spirituality, for example, cannot make a spiritual choice. Those who have not had an opportunity at education can't rightly make a choice about whether educa-tion is valuable or not. My choices have been informed choices. They direct how I perceive my life's mission, my role; to take those little gems of truth that I collected over the years and use them to better a whole community, to help others become what they can become. The good that I see in myself, I want to pass on to others. Preaching is one way to do that. In fact, one of the reasons that I made a commitment to stay in this community was that I believed that what I am doing and where I am is where more and more people ought to be. I have something of worth and of value that is worth being shared. I can make a difference. Sometimes I feel tired and weary. Sometimes I want to quit and give up. Sometimes I think it's not worth it, it's not paying off. But I wake up the next day and say, "Let's get at it again!"

I am convinced that there is something beyond us, that there is more than this physical person that we look at. I try to find my way there and take others with me. Many times, we convince ourselves or others con-vince us that our circumstances are so bad that it is useless to even dream, to visualize, to imagine. But isn't that what really makes us distinct as human beings? The duck goes about the water, in the water, and on dry land because that is what a duck does. But a duck never does anything that a duck wouldn't do. People do things, I believe, that people have never done before because they have visions, dreams, imagination. When one imagines, one can go beyond. When one visualizes, one can go beyond. When one dreams, one can go beyond. So, it is my job to remind those whose lives I touch that more is possible.

One of my mentors, Dr. Howard Thurman, told about the power of the imagination. One morning, he was sitting in the living room at a house where he was a guest. A child rode into his presence on a cardboard box.

He stopped in front of him and said, "Mr. Thurman, will you help me? My car has a flat tire." My mentor agreed to help, going through the motions of changing a tire. The child climbed back in the box and promptly declared, "Mr. Thurman, my car won't start." So they checked the batteries. The child walked around to one side and then another, opened the hood and the gas tank and said, "Oh, Mr. Thurman, the problem is we're out of gas." So saying, he ran to the kitchen, got a glass of water, got back in his car, drank the water, turned the key and the car started. "Thank you, Mr. Thurman. Thank you," he said as he drove off. That's dreaming! That's imagination! That's the power of seeing what is not and making it possible because one has a vision for something great. That's what we have to do-take flight! We can't just focus on where we are. Oh, yes, we live here and we have to understand that we live where we are, but we have to take the past and remember where we've come from, look at where we are, then rush quickly to where we are going. One of our hymns says: "I'm pressing on the upward way, new heights I'm gaining every day..." An old worldly song says: "Keep on pushing..." Adam Clayton Powell said, "Keep the faith!" And that is what keeps us going in spite of circumstances. So, I try to remind people with little stories, examples, that others have indeed made it. You can, as well. Gwendolyn Brooks said, "Live and have your blooming in the noise of the whirlwind." You may have to be around in the circle for a while, but eventually you wake up and discover that you are no longer where you started. My parents instilled this in their children. They insisted we go further than they did. I can almost hear my father's voice saying, "I have a third grade education, that's all I was able to get. You've got to get at least to high school." When we got to high school he said, "Well, why don't you think about going on to college." And of course, once I caught the bug, college was just the beginning. Before he died he was able to see some of us go on to graduate school and teach. To him that was the ultimate achievement. In fact, there were a number of ways Dad expressed his pride. One was when he needed advice (though 50 years older than I), he found a way to talk to me and ask for advice in terms of his own life. He was also willing to turn over to me part of what would have been his legacy to his family, which he entrusted into my hands—his land, his property. And perhaps the greatest expression of his pride was when he wanted to come and live in my home and share with me toward the end of his life. In fact, he died in my home, in a place of comfort, a place of ease, no worries or uneasiness about where life was going. He came as a teacher, as an experienced man of wisdom, but he also wanted to have this association and to be present with me, living miles and miles away from where I had started. I had gone beyond what he and we had imagined. One of the things that brings delight and pleasure to a parent is to be able to look back at where they have come from and to see how their children have done a little better, gone a little further than they did, and to be able to say, "That's my child, that's my son, that's my daughter," and feel proud as they say it, to hold their heads a little higher. Mahalia Jackson sang, "Move on up a little higher..." My father thought of it all as a job well done. With a sense of humility he could enjoy the last part of his life knowing all was well, that the overflowing of the cup was finally coming his way. He could see a brighter side and could truly say, "Yea, though I walk through the valley of the shadow of death, I shall fear no evil..." (Psalms 23). It is, after all, the journey, the going through, that makes it all worthwhile. I remind myself regularly that while there are others who are carrying on in my hometown in my absence, I have a responsibility to pass the teachings, beliefs, and principles I received from my elders at home to a new generation right here where I am. It is a "bloom where you are" philosophy, if you will. I think that when I feel I have done what I can do to make a difference here, it is incumbent upon me to find somewhere else to do something, or to retire, whichever is more reasonable in light of age and so forth. For the time being, I make an effort to pass on what I can to my blood family and also take seriously my responsibility as pastor of the Calvary family and my work in the community at large. Many of the responsibilities that I have taken on as a member of the Housing Authority's board, the Board of Corrections, the Conventions and the Salt Lake Career Service Council, and the Visitors Bureau, for example, take away time that I could dedicate to something else. But I do them because I believe it is incumbent upon me as a person with my charge and responsibilities to help others to realize as much out of life as is possible. I want people to have good housing. I want people who are in prison to know that they don't have to go back if they get out. I want everybody to understand that we all can be educated, even the least educated of us can learn and become better at whatever we are. Thus, if there is any one legacy that I want to be known for, it is that of being an "encourager."

Much of what guides my life strategies today came home to me as I yielded to the disciplines of military service.

31

Basic Training

Six days after I preached at Bethel Baptist Church in Fort Lauderdale, Florida, I got the notice from the draft board. I rushed down to the recruitment office of the United States Air Force and promptly enlisted. I had already taken the tests and thus was ready to sign the papers. The air force, like every other branch of the military, was actively looking for people. Almost anyone who showed up at the door was welcome, even more certainly those of us who had passed their test and had some college behind us. That same night, I was given a ticket to board a plane going to Houston, Texas, then transported by bus from the airport. By midnight I was at Lackland Air Force Base in San Antonio, reporting for basic training.

Texas was a place that surprised me because of its size. It was huge and desert-like. Riding a bus to get from one point to another took long hours. New recruits were transported in groups. We were in civilian clothing. The very first thing we had to do was to check in. The process was demeaning. We had to strip down to our underwear and walk among people we did not know until we were given military haircuts, uniforms, and bedding. The next morning we were greeted with "Reveille." It was the sounding of a horn, the wake-up call. We were then instructed on how to make up our bunks, tucking sheets and blankets tightly using military corners such that a quarter could bounce off the bed. We then lined up and ran everywhere we went. We raced double time, double time from the barracks to the mess hall. There we waited. We left the mess hall running to basic training. There we waited. Likewise, we were expected to run to the hospital to see the doctor. There we waited. Everywhere we went we had to hurry. New recruits labeled the process "Hurry up and Wait."

In San Antonio, I was engulfed by loneliness. I was far from home. I knew no one. I was scared to death of the demands that would be placed upon me, especially by drill sergeants. I was only allowed off the base to do some sightseeing a couple of times. I began to write letters as a way of keeping some sort of inner balance. Some I sent, others I wrote and never got around to mailing. In some cases, I did not have the money for postage. All in all, however, letter writing helped me tolerate the loneliness and feelings of loss caused by being so many miles from my family, from anything that was familiar to me.

At the close of basic training I was given a few days' leave to go back home. I had one little stripe that the military gave me in addition to a red ribbon that meant that I was Airman Third Class. I went home feeling excited, pleased with my little stripe and ribbon. My family was thrilled and happy, proud of their son in his air force uniform. I don't think they understood the dangers I faced being in the military. So they were quite pleased with me. I had now a steady income, $97 a month. I was guaranteed a place to stay, clothing, all the necessities. Ultimately, I would make Airman Second and First Class and my pay would improve. I could then be helpful to my parents and would make an allocation from my paycheck so that a portion went regularly to my mother to do with as she pleased. Before being discharged from the air force, I was made staff sergeant.

When I came home on furlough, I thought everyone in the community of Waynesboro, Georgia, would look up and notice, would accord me due consideration. Here I was, France A. Davis, now a member of the United States military, getting ready to go off to war! Well, my bubble was soon burst. I was still called "boy," I still was expected to defer to shopkeepers, and as I walked down the main street of town, I had to scoot to keep from being run over by a white driver. I was not recognized as I felt I ought to have been and thus retreated into my intimate community, spending time only with family and friends. The racial situation had not changed!

32

Texas

The military was in a hurry to get people ready for service in Southeast Asia. Basic training lasted only one month, after which I was transferred to the Amarillo Aircraft Technical Training School. In my case, it was to learn the skills of an aircraft mechanic, to service the 431 fighter-bombers. I was being groomed for a crew chief, one who was ultimately held responsible for the flight-worthiness of a particular airplane. Training was conducted half in the classroom and the other half on the job—OJT. What we learned in the morning, we were expected to practice in the afternoon. Amarillo, being at the top of the state of Texas, was a long way from San Antonio. To reach our destination we had driven hours and hours and hours, it seemed, arriving at midnight. I thought to myself, "This has to be the biggest state in the world!"

In Amarillo I felt heat the likes of which I had never experienced, even in Georgia. We took salt pills daily to insure that our bodies would not be depleted of moisture. It was June, July, and August of that year. The temperatures were unimaginable. It was desert, barren, in the middle of nowhere. Flags flew on the base to indicate whether or not it was safe to be outside at any given time: Green meant you could be safely outside; yellow meant you needed to be cautious; red indicated that if you were caught outside you could receive a court-martial for "destruction of government property." For the first time, I realized that a member of the United States military was no longer a human being. I was a piece of property, a reminder of slavery. Getting back and forth in that climate was therefore a challenge. We went to class in the morning, stayed out of the sun in the middle of the day, and did on-the-job training in the late afternoon.

I stayed in Amarillo for about three months, during which time I preached my second sermon, at Mount Zion Baptist Church, where Reverend Louis B. George was pastor. He was an older man and did not have much help. He was kind and invited me as a boy, so to speak, to help him lead the worship service. I pointed out to him that I was restricted to the military base and did not have freedom to come and go as I pleased. He said, "Come with me." We went into his office and he wrote a letter to my commanding officer asking that I be allowed to leave the base in order to come preach for him from time to time and share in the leadership of the worship services. Permission was granted. I found out later that the commanding officer was a friend of the pastor. I was able to attend Mount Zion every Sunday.

Mount Zion had a large congregation and the members expected to hear their own preacher at the pulpit on Sundays. Reverend George shared with me about other, smaller congregations in the area where I could more frequently have an opportunity to preach. That was a time of trying to find my way, trying to figure out what it meant to deliver a sermon. Reverend George was helpful in giving me a little notebook that had the sermons of famous preachers (about 20 or so) outlined. These included some of his own outlines as well as those of Reverend Tim M. Chambers Sr., a well-known preacher. I studied them. I compared them to passages in the Bible. I tried to see how these preachers had come to a given subject and outline for a given sermon. I thought long and hard about where examples and illustrations for sermons came from. Reverend George told me to keep the little book of outlines and I got some of my early ideas from it. Adding to a skeleton outline, I fleshed it out and developed my own sermons. The guidance I received was invaluable, a foundation upon which I could build, in a sense, my first formal training for the preaching ministry. Later, Reverend Louis B. George did one of the first preaching revivals at Calvary. He was indeed for this pastor, my pastor.

When I was posted from Texas to Nellis AFB in Las Vegas, Nevada, others put their arms around me as mentors and friends, some adopting me as one of the family. In an environment as potentially treacherous to a young man as was Las Vegas, it was good to be accompanied!

33

Las Vegas, Nevada

At graduation from technical school in Amarillo, members of my class received a second ribbon indicating we were now fully certified jet aircraft mechanics, and I was transferred to Nellis Air Force Base in Las Vegas, Nevada, for my first tour of duty. At Nellis, I was a crew member assigned the task of maintaining the giant F105 aircraft, a "workhorse." These fighter planes had one huge engine and could carry a large payload, the greatest number of weapons that any fighter could hold at that time. The F105 crews worked in eight-hour shifts. We reported for duty at eight in the morning, or, if we worked the second shift, we reported at three in the afternoon.

The base was about seven miles from downtown. I decided to purchase a bicycle and was able, along with a couple of other young men, to explore the area off base after work. My pals and I got to know Las Vegas like the backs of our hands, discovering over time that this city was actually two cities. Downtown and on the east side was "the strip," an exciting place with lots of people, bright lights that made walking down Main Street at night like walking down any other city street in broad daylight. Although Las Vegas was a relatively small place at the time, the streets were lined with casinos and wedding chapels where you could throw away your resources as well as your life in the blink of an eye. Ads and billboards promised that by gambling you could double, triple, quadruple your paycheck, and hence these casinos presented a challenge to young men in the military coming into town. Ofttimes, they walked in, put down their monthly paycheck of $117 or $234, and came out with nothing. My father had taught his children that "get rich" schemes were likely designed to take what you had. Early in our lives, we learned not to risk what we had in hopes of getting more, remembering his lessons about hard work. I recall playing the slot machines only twice, losing no more than a dollar. I clung to my paycheck and searched for the "other" Las Vegas.

On the west side of town I soon discovered a world I would never have guessed was there. I saw family homes, apartment complexes, places where ordinary people lived, many times the people who serviced the strip. It seemed to me that there was a church on the west side for every casino on the east side, and that most of those who lived on the west side were African Americans. I got to know a lot of good people there, interacted with them, and was invited to their homes, sleeping at their houses when they worried about my going back to the base after dark.

In Las Vegas I had several "fathers" and "mothers," including Reverend and Mrs. Sylvester Parks, Reverend and Mrs. Simmons, Mrs. Parker, and Mrs. O'Neil, among others. For the most part, I met at various churches the folks who welcomed me into their hearts and their homes, the families whom I came to claim as my own while in Las Vegas.

One of the lessons I learned from the very first time I left home, was to look for and associate with one or more of the local churches as soon as I arrived in a new town. Church for a young man away from home and family was a blessing. Church provided spiritual sustenance, instant community, a shield against loneliness, a place to serve and be with like-minded people, a harbor when fears of being set adrift loomed like heavy weather.

When I landed in Las Vegas, I began by visiting the Saint James Baptist Church, which was right next to Mount Calvary, behind New Jerusalem, not far from Victory Missionary Baptist, and down the street from the Second Baptist. Reverend Simmons, pastor of Saint James, had great wisdom. He was an older man, feeble and eager to have a young man around to help him. He welcomed me very warmly, threw his arms around me, and drew me into the community where I met the Parkers and the O'Neils, whose homes I visited regularly after church. Mrs. O'Neil was the organist and had trained Junior Parker to play the piano at Saint James. Soon I became a member of this church, spending time with those I called Mom and Dad when I was in town. I learned that by making friends with older people in any community, one gained a sense of connectedness, a sense of belonging, especially when everything else seemed to be failing or fading. Plus, you could always get a meal. Various young people from Saint James invited me to their houses to eat or visit. Girls in particular were interested in my company. I went, but spent more time with the older folks, appreciating their warmth and wisdom.

That same year I enrolled in the American Baptist Theological Seminary (extension division) where Reverend Simmons was dean and Reverend Wilson of Bethel Baptist Church was president. Classes were held at Bethel, a block and a half from Saint James. Reverend Simmons took every opportunity to remind me of the importance of getting as much formal education as possible in order to be the best minister that I could be. Up until then, although I had been preaching, teaching, leading, and learning from watching, I had not been exposed to the "craft" of ministry in a classroom setting.

My life in Las Vegas began to assume a certain rhythm. I worked on the base during the day and in the evening came into town either on my bicycle or riding in with someone who had an automobile. At the seminary, I took courses in English from Mrs. Hall, who volunteered her time in the evening and was a teacher in the public schools during the day. In fact, all of our teachers had other jobs, taking time at night to instruct ten or twelve of us young, African American ministers. The group was all male. I was younger than most of my fellow students, had completed high school and a year of college, and probably had more energy and also more education than some. I enrolled in a class in preaching and one on the Bible given by Reverend Marion Bennett, perhaps the best formally educated minister in town. I studied psychology and Bible interpretation, all classes which benefited me enormously. Perhaps the most helpful aspect of my training at the seminary, however, was the opportunity to participate in preaching contests: preparing sermons and listening to others give them.

The preaching contests were something like Olympic events. Seated before us were experienced teachers and pastors who judged and ranked our sermons. At the end we were awarded some sort of financial prize— $10, $20, or $25. Those who won first, second, and third places were invited to compete again. Again, these contestants would be judged by professionals and awarded a prize. This meant we had to do our best. The audience may have been people of all sorts gathered there to listen to us preach, but those judging our sermons were our teachers. After the contests, these same teachers were likely to come to class on Monday or Tuesday night and talk about the content, organization, structure, delivery, and indeed even the application that our sermons had. I learned a great deal from these preaching contests.

Once when I took first place in one of the preaching contests, the elders decided to have a runoff. The runoff was to be held between the Reverend Raymond Harris and myself and take place at his church. We were assigned to preach on the topic of the resurrection of Jesus. As I was the guest, I was invited to go first. I stood up and delivered a sermon enti-tled "Looking in the Wrong Place," based on a passage of scripture that describes people coming to look for Jesus and being told: "He's not here." When I was done, the Reverend Raymond Harris got up, announced that I had preached his sermon, and sat down. Amazingly, the judges (includ-ing his own pastor) awarded him first place. He was so contrite that he gave me the award money and apologized profusely. The judges were our elders over us in school. We were fearful of repercussions if we questioned them and thus were never able to find out why they did what they did. Reverend Harris and I laugh about that incident whenever we see each other!

I learned a great deal from other pastors in Las Vegas, most of whom became my friends. They gave me frequent opportunities to preach on their youth days, to visit their congregations. I observed what they were doing, saw how they delivered their sermons, how they carried out their roles as pastors of churches. Based on these observations and the academic training I was receiving at the American Baptist Seminary, I began to shape my own sense of ministry and a distinct preaching style. Also, very importantly, a love of people began to emerge echoing Reverend Sim-mons, explicit statement: "You really have to love people in order to effec-tively pastor a church." I had no idea at the time that I would one day become pastor of a church myself, much less one in Salt Lake City, Utah!

The American Baptist College is physically located in Nashville, Ten-nessee, sponsored by the National Baptist Convention, U.S.A., Incorpo-rated, and has extension programs in various cities, some on school cam-puses. These, such as the one I attended in Las Vegas, are designed to serve young, African American men trying to get themselves qualified and also certified for the work of ministry. That year in Las Vegas, like my fellow students, I took courses, learned a lot, applied what I learned in preaching contests and made myself available as a young minister to preach at vari-ous local churches in the absence of their pastors. Along with a few others, I became popular and was thus given the opportunity to preach on numer-ous occasions, traveling to such places as Henderson, Nevada, to preach for Reverend Sylvester Parks at his church. I preached for my pastor, for Reverend Simmons, for Reverend Wilson, and for Reverend C. C. Smith in a trailer court where he held worship services as he had no church facil-ity. I also went to the prisons and the nursing homes and hospitals. I learned on the job, actually doing what we were learning in classroom theory and preaching. As youth ministers, we had as a goal to live a life that could be repeated, to be role models and to render service to those who were standing in special need. We, in fact, helped to serve different groups of people, groups we identified as "the least," "the last," and "the lost." The least were those in prison, the last those everyone had forgotten—people in hospitals and nursing homes, the orphans and widows, the homeless. We took seriously the last verse in the first chapter of the Book of James, which directed us to visit the widow and the orphan in their affliction! As to the lost, they were individuals who had no faith at all, those who did not know who God was. We did our utmost to bring the lost back into the Lord's loving embrace.

The year spent in Las Vegas was for me a milestone year. When I received transfer orders for a tour of duty in Southeast Asia and the Air Force shipped me out to Thailand, my calling was firmly in place and my operating instructions clear.

34

Southeast Asia

In July of 1967, I was shipped out to Korat Air Force Base, Thailand, and assigned to serve on the flight line as a jet fighter mechanic. I was not responsible for specialty work such as hydraulics, sheet metal, and oxygen, nor at first loading of weapons; my task was to make sure that this work had been done, that there were no leaks, as it were, before the planes took off. Loading live ammunition on fighters flying missions into Vietnam, however, eventually became another responsibility of the mechanics. My boss was Chief Master Sergeant Watson.

A few months after my arrival at Korat, Chief Master Sergeant Watson asked me if I would consider leaving the flight line to run one of the shops, the tire shop. This meant I could be out of the weather and away from the dangers of snakes and other animals in the field, as our base was on the edge of the jungle. A snake in that jungle was referred to by the men as a "two-stepper" because if he bit you, you took two steps and died. I was only too eager to begin my duties running the shop.

I took charge of the tire shop and the Thai men who were hired locally. We insured that tires were repaired or replaced as needed, that the planes were safe to fly. These men wanted to learn English as a tool toward a better life, some dreaming of coming to America. I wanted to learn Thai. I issued a friendly order that Thai would be spoken in the shop. When I returned home in December of 1968, I was mingling words of Thai in my conversation. Frequently, I was reminded: "Say it in English!"

When I first arrived in Thailand, like other members of the military, I was exposed to an indoctrination speech I shall never forget: "Never drink the water, eat the food or fraternize with the locals, especially the females." We were warned that to do so would result in untold illnesses. Being obedient, I followed orders until one day I came down with a stomach infection so severe that I questioned the cleanliness of the food we were being served on the base. For the remainder of the 18 months I spent in service in Thailand, I ate local food with local people. I drank the water they drank, interacted with them, got to know them personally. I walked through the rice paddies to get to their homes, ate on a mat on the floor with their families, and was sometimes invited to stay overnight, sleeping under their mosquito nets, as bugs were abundant. Thai food was wholesome and agreed with me. I was introduced to local merchants in the area where I was stationed. I remember how they called out my name as I walked by and always sold me fruit at local prices. They did not consider me an "ugly American," but took me in as one of their own, so much so that one day I had the most unimaginable experience of my stay in Thailand.

A man I had befriended in the shop and visited at home suggested we rent a car and driver to explore places where Americans rarely went. I had a great day with him and his family and the next week he invited me to a special dinner. His parents and his wife's parents and their children were going to be present for the meal. I was looking forward to this time of meeting them. They put the mat on the floor and the food was more abundant than usual, a feast of sorts. Lots of people came. We ate and had a great time. The food was good and well prepared, the people friendly, and the family appreciated my attempts to hold my own in Thai. After dinner my friend began to translate what the elders of the family were saying, as it was beyond my grasp: "They would like to give you their daughter in marriage." I was blown away! I liked the family, enjoyed their company, appreciated their hospitality, but I was 20 years old and didn't know how to respond or what to do. The girl was 14. I was shocked but my friend did not notice. He said, "She's already going to school and if she's your wife then she can go with you to America and go to college." He explained that the family was offering me a dowry of $500, adding that the girl was a virgin. I didn't feel right about any of this. Thoughts raced through my mind as my friend listed the many virtues of a Thai wife: I was an American, a minister of the Gospel, and had no idea if I married this girl how I would get her back to America. I was not even ready to get married! I decided on the most direct approach. I thanked the family and declined their offer. My relationship with my friend became strained after that night though he continued to work for me. He was courteous, but did not invite me to his home again until just before I got my transfer papers and was about to leave Thailand for an assignment in the United States.

This experience was unusual, unexpected, and scary for me at the time. I found out later that marriages were arranged as a matter of course in that part of the world, that parents customarily offered dowries consisting of money, or sometimes a buffalo or two, and that men usually had the upper hand. Had I understood the customs better and been willing to run the risk, upping the ante might have been a more acceptable way out, more diplomatic. But I didn't know. I sometimes wonder what happened to that young lady. I remember how sharp and good looking she was in addition to being the best formally educated member of her family. To me, however, she was a child, certainly too young to marry. Some American servicemen did marry young Thai women, however. When I got back to the United States and was stationed in Mountain Home, Idaho, I got to know a training officer well enough to visit him at home. His wife was a young woman much like the 14-year-old girl who had been offered to me. She was really his servant, meeting him at the door, removing his shoes, drawing a bath of water for him, preparing his food, waiting on his every need. She served to remind me of what I personally did not want in a wife. I knew even then what I was looking for was a helpmeet, an equal, someone who would be there beside me, not behind or in front of me. I would find that person in Willene Witt and fulfill my dreams.

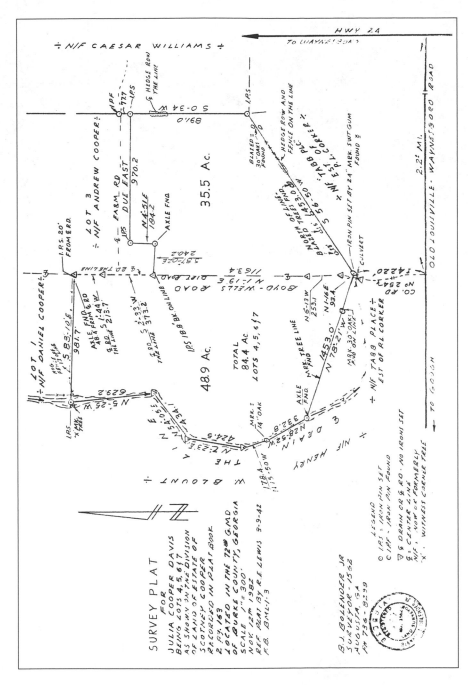

Map of Cooper's Town

Grandma Scoatney Cooper is the only female in this photo taken in an unidentified location in Georgia, early 1900s. It hung behind the altar of the Roberson Grove Baptist Church until the church burned down. The man standing apart is Grandpa July Cooper. Fourth man from the left in the wrinkled hat is Cousin Tommy Cooper.

Mrs. Scoatney Cooper's grandson, France Albert Davis, in one of the earliest pictures of me, late 1940s, with my signature head gear.

Not a photo, this "likeness" of Grandpa July, Mother Julia at age 14 (about 1921), and Grandma Scoatney appears to have been "lightened."

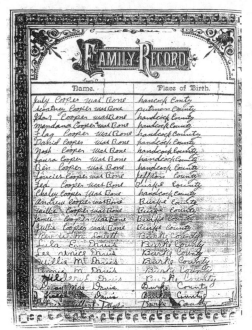
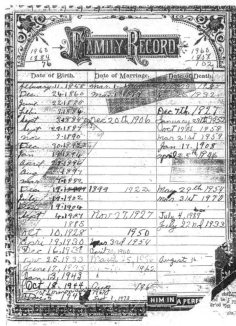
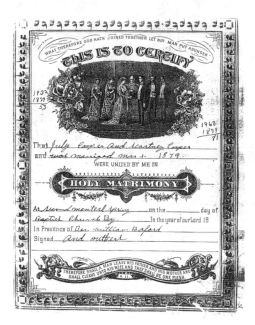
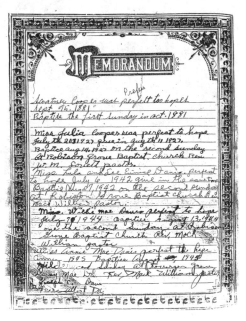

"This is to Certify…"—my grandparents' 1849 marriage certificate and the family record my mother kept in the middle of her Bible.

Our family home with "God Bless This House" painted on the wall behind the front porch where we sat when we had guests.

Davis barn and pump house in a photo by Mary Megalli, taken in 2002.

Bryant Place store, beside Bryant Grove Baptist Church, 1998, is not unlike the "little store" belonging to Uncle Andrew Cooper, which I so vividly described from memory (or perhaps imagined!).

Dad as he looked when I was
growing up, age 37.

Daddy John, near bank in Waynesboro,
about 1975.

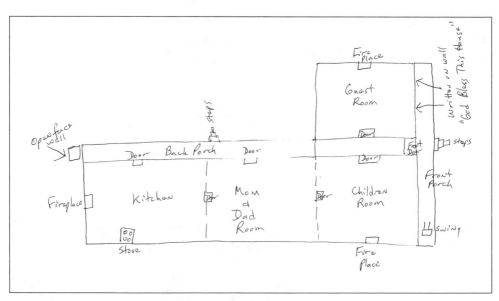

Pastor's floor plan of the old house.

Julia Davis, 1940s.

Mother Julia, on block house porch, holding straw broom used to sweep the floor. Fall 1965.

Cousin Lula Hatcher who named me France, studio photo, early 1950s.

Mother and Cousin Lila Reeves in the living room of the Davis house, possibly 1960s. They appear to be dressed in black for a funeral. Likeness of Grandpa July, Grandma Scoatney, and Mother at age 14 hangs behind them to the left of the window.

Uncles Noah and James Cooper, 1940s or 1950s.

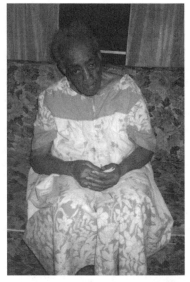

Uncle Noah and Aunt Nancy Cooper in their home in Washington, D.C., where two of my sisters were sent to complete high school. Possibly in the 1950s.

With my uncle, James Cooper, then blind, on a visit to him in 1995. He died two years later.

In old age, Aunt Hattie Cooper, wife of Andrew Cooper. Andrew Cooper's personality and skills as a brick and stone mason are still remembered in Burke County today. The Cooper family graveyard sits on Aunt Hattie's property.

An example of Uncle Andrew Cooper's handiwork, a barbecue pit, by mill, past Bryant Grove Church, is still standing.

The cemetery with Mother Julia's headstone in the shape of a heart beside Dad's.

Left to right, Daisy, France, and Joe standing beside our black, 1941, 4-door Chevrolet, in front of the garage.

Young family members. Top, left to right: brothers Joe and Clarence, Sister Daisy, France. Kneeling, left to right: Nephew Earl (Sister Annie Mae's son, now Captain in Burke County Fire Department, raised by his grandparents John and Julia after his mother's death in 1967), and Niece Carol Doreetha (sister Lula's daughter, died young of sickle cell anemia in 1969).

I am attending Gough Elementary School at the time of this picture.

Gough Elementary School, as it looked in 1998, was the four-room school house I attended. In my time it had two teachers per room.

White pump house and white baptismal pool where I was baptized ("buried in the water") is all that remained of the Roberson Grove Baptist Church after it was burned. This photo was taken in February 2003.

Public speaking photo, 1963, just before graduation.

About age 12, at home, dressed for church around the time of my baptism.

Tuskegee student, 1964, living away from home for the first time.

When I returned from Tuskegee, I went for guidance to Reverend John R. Tarver (holding his Bible), Pastor of Noah's Ark Baptist Church.

The Reverend Tarver beside tractor on his farm, 1940s or 1950s.

In front of Bethel, after my trial sermon, April 1966.

Aunt Rena Davis, who always dressed in multiple layers, captured in a photo taken in February 1975 in Waynesboro.

The bicycle I rode to town. Las Vegas, 1967.

And then there was the United States Air Force…In uniform for basic training, Lackland AFB, Texas, 1966.

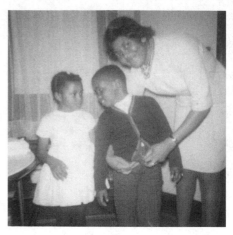

With "Champa" family in Thailand, summer 1967.

Sister Annie, "Miss Beautiful," with Nephew Barney (son of Sister Willie Mae) and Niece Laverne (daughter of Sister Eunice), 1960.

Home on leave from Southeast Asia for my sister Annie's funeral, August 1967. This is the oldest total family photo. Standing: Daisy, Eunice, Clarence, Mom, Dad, James. Below: Willie Mae, Joe, Lulu, France, in front of the new house, beside the old one.

"We didn't give her the respect we should have..." Sister Daisy as a teenager, at the time she was left to "mind" her brothers.

Home from Southeast Asia, I become a member of the St. Paul Baptist Church in Boise, Idaho. Here seen shaking hands with Pastor James Hubbard of St. Paul's.

I am standing with my Volkswagen beetle in front of Brother Joe's house in Oakland, 1972.

As a student at Berkeley, 1972.

In Utah. I was visiting the BYU campus and was escorted off by security, November 1972.

Willene and I are married at the Center Street Baptist Church in Oakland, September 1, 1973. On the right is my brother and best man Joe, on the left is groomsman Roy Robinson, who invited me to go bowling. On the right is maid of honor, Patricia Dandridge. On the left is bridesmaid and Willene's sister, Frances Witt. Carolyn is in front, looking up at Joe. Other children include flower girls Chelita Stewart and Angie Caldwell, ring bearers little Joe Davis and Billy Richardson, and young groomsman Raymond Jenkins.

The Calvary Baptist Church at 532 East 700 South was dedicated in 1966.

Before Commencement prayer at the University of Utah, 1974. Carolyn sports mortar board.

Mrs. E. Louise DeBies' "Boy Pastor," about 1975.

Complete family with France II as baby in front of Calvary
sanctuary, 1978.

Reverend visiting home with
Dad, 1979.

Speaking for February Black History event at Dugway Army Depot, 1979.

Fifth anniversary as pastor of Calvary, April 1979.

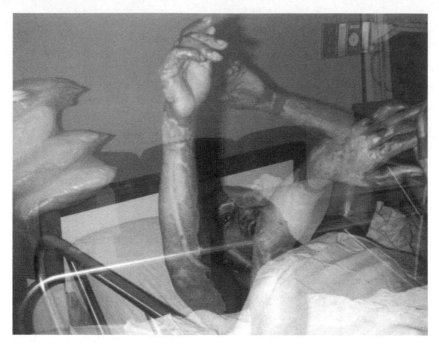

"Burn Profiling," July 1980, in an Augusta, Georgia, hospital bed.

Summer of my burns, 1980.

Recovered from burns, 1982.

After the burns, Mrs. Willene and Pastor France Davis.

France and France II in recliner chair at home, 1984.

A rare moment of relaxation with my family, Fort Lauderdale, 1983. I am holding Willene's hands, Carolyn in front, back turned, Grace with headband, France II apart, looking out to sea.

Reverend France A. Davis, holding Bible, 1985. I begin to cast a vision...

Grace.

Carolyn celebrates graduation after her bone marrow treatment for leukemia.

Groundbreaking and 1987 completed Calvary Tower Housing at 516 East 700 South.

Mother Julia Davis and Mother E. Louise DeBies (white-haired), Deaconess Rose Singleton (standing), Christmas 1989 at old Calvary.

Mom Julia visits her Utah family, January 1988. Carolyn is holding baby Cedric, France II kneels beside his grandmother.

Honorary Doctorate
from the University of
Utah, 1993.

With brother James Hildery in
his Fort Lauderdale front yard,
2001.

France II holding Georgetown
University degree, May 27, 2000,
with his mother, Willene.

Discussion of starting new church construction, February 21, 2001. Left to right: Pastor Davis, Finance Secretary Rick Humbert, Trustee Chairman, the late Edward Miller.

The visible church...1090 S. State Street.

Singing as we march to our new church, October 2001.

Congregation at first service.

Cruising Alaska with Mrs. Davis, trip for Pastor's anniversary from the congregation, 2003.

Pastor at home, 2005.

My siblings, in Washington, D.C., en route to Salt Lake City, spring 2005. Left to right, standing: Daisy, James, Willie. Seated: Lulu and Eunice.

2005 Pastors' Summit in Rock Springs, Wyoming. Left to right: Reverends James Wilson, Lamar Jackson, Charles Petty, France Davis, H. J. Lilly, William Beard, Bobby Ashley, Michael Ross, and President Harold Fields.

The quiet life. Who would have thought of picking up pecans in a suit! Cooper's Town in the 21st century.

"It's what we expect heaven to be like." Reverend Davis delivers a thunderous sermon at the National Cathedral in Washington, D.C., February 2006. "We have more in common than we have differences…" (Photo: Christopher Anderson).

Gough railroad tracks are the same ones that stirred us to dreaming: "We were going somewhere!" (Photo, Mary Megalli, 2002)

35

DREAMING AND SHARING

ONE OF THE TRADEMARKS of the African American rural community was a principle of sharing. Everybody assumed responsibility for everybody else. That assumption of responsibility was particularly present within immediate and extended family units. Each person felt responsible not only for their own success, but for the progress and development of others.

People talked about their dreams much in the same way that Langston Hughes wrote about dreaming: "Hold fast to dreams, for if dreams die life is like a broken-winged bird that cannot fly." Dr. Martin Luther King Jr.'s "I Have a Dream" speech (perhaps identified and made famous because of its expressions about dreaming) truly resonated. We children were encouraged to dream and imagine, imagination being simply gathering facts and ordering them so that they move us to where we are trying to get. Our elders urged us to remember that there was something beyond our immediate world to hope and reach for, saying, "Shoot for the sky and if you fall short, you'll still fall among the stars." Their language was poetic, their lessons illustrated with little proverbs and sayings, making them unforgettable.

Mom and Dad ofttimes said, "If you can imagine it, you can achieve it; if you can dream it, you can reach it." What makes life exciting is knowing that while you may be in the fields, mud and dirt getting in between your toes, you are going somewhere.

Dad taught us how to plow and while doing so taught us a lesson that would help us make sense of life, ever looking toward a higher calling. He would patiently explain: "What you do to make a straight line, boys, is you start where you are and find a landmark, a tree, a pole way ahead. Train your eyes on it, keep your eyes on it as you plow. Don't keep your eyes on the plow, or look down at the dirt. Don't keep them on the mule. Look ahead, look ahead!"

Older folk sat around in the evening, imagining, telling stories, sharing their hopes, dreams, and expectations, especially for their children. Often those dreams were hard to realize, slow in coming, but they were an integral part of interactions between family members. My parents, for example, sought out my mother's brother and his wife to see if they would be willing to help provide an opportunity for my older sisters to go on to higher education. There was a sense within families that "doubling up" was okay.

Doubling up was a way whereby one person would move to better themselves. They would get a house, get a job, save money until they got enough to send for another person. The two of them would then work, then send for a third person who would move in with them. It was common practice to find lots of people living in a small space, pooling resources, then making provisions for other family members or even friends to participate in the better life. When one person found it, they were always eager to share, to make it available as best they could to as many others as possible. I would suggest that many African Americans who moved to Utah in the 1940s moved here by invitation of somebody who was already here. As they got on their feet, they sent back for the rest of the family to come.

In my family, dreams were followed by a plan frequently agreed upon by letter. Letters would be posted in Gough and a response eagerly awaited. Sometimes weeks or months passed before one arrived. However, it did come. Uncle Noah and Aunt Nancy thus provided Lulu and Eunice a place in their home and a high school education. They also took in Willie Mae after she graduated from Boggs Academy in the 1940s. I do not remember my sister Willie Mae prior to her moving to D.C. Also, when my brother Joseph left home before the end of high school, Cousin Lula Hatcher took him in and saw to it that he registered at Lucy Laney High School and got a part-time job. I believe Joe left Cooper's Town walking to Gough, then from there took a bus to Augusta, some 50 miles away. He lived with cousin Lula and her family until he graduated. He and Dad could not bridge the differences between them. Mom helped Joe from a discreet distance.

In 1963, when I turned 16, my sister Annie Mae invited me to spend the summer in New Jersey with her and her boyfriend. They provided me with a place to stay, helped me find a job, made sure I was taken care of. I lived in a little room with a curtain and no door, at the back of a boarding house run by an old lady. My rent was $25 a week. For the time I was in her home, the old lady became as a mother to me during the week, my sister a weekend mom. In each case, the women had authority to challenge my behavior, to offer discipline and correction. As there was no door on my room, I came home from work and went through my routine of searching through the dresser drawers to see if anything was missing. One day, the old lady saw me in action and asked what I was doing, what I had that she might want. That was perhaps my first major lesson in trusting someone who was not my family.

That summer I had a job with Penn furniture store for three months, delivering high-end furniture in New York, New Jersey, and Connecticut. It was my first experience away from my parents. When I returned home I had resources saved for myself, some that would be helpful to the family, also putting aside enough to buy a high school ring upon graduation.

Joe always shared whatever he had and always was concerned about whether I had what I needed. When Clarence went to college, Joe and I were making money, I in the military and Joe as a civilian. It was the two of us who often sent Clarence what he needed so that he might continue his studies at Fort Valley State College.

My older brother James Hildery, whom everyone called Hildery, always took care of his younger siblings in a variety of ways. He made sure we had an opportunity to do some of the things that otherwise might not have been an option given us by Mom and Dad. He took me, my brothers Joseph and Clarence, sister Daisy, and niece Doreetha to our first movie, a musical featuring Fats Domino, at a drive-in theater. It was 1957. We were excited not only to be at the movies but to hear such music being sung—"worldly music," the sort our parents would not have approved of. It was he who first took me fishing and he who gave Joe and me our first vehicle, his old automobile.

Hildery, his wife, Carrie, and their newborn daughter Julia welcomed me into their one-bedroom apartment in Fort Lauderdale, Florida, in 1965. Julia Mae, named after my mother and Carrie's mother, is mother to her own college-aged daughter, Victoria. Julia has worked some 20 years in a managerial position for an insurance company. Both Julia Mae and Victoria attended Bethune-Cookman College, founded by the African American, Dr. Mary McLeod Bethune.

When I moved to Florida, I was in a period of transition, looking for a job that would allow me to eventually return to school. While I was living under their roof, I was expected to live according to the standards set by my brother and his family. This meant going to church, not using foul language, holding down a job, being accountable for the money I made. I was expected to share a portion of my earnings for expenses at home and for tithing at church. My brother worked and his wife took in work or did things for people in the neighborhood. Doubling up gave us an opportunity to get a little further ahead, leaving me enough money to take care of myself, purchase a new automobile, get a place of my own if I wanted it. I chose to live with Hildery and Carrie instead and helped with chores and tending little Julia. They had one of those typical Florida apartments with windows that closed only part way, slats overlapping one another. In such a warm climate, however, one hardly ever needed a sweater. We did not have heaters, though if it did get a little cool we simply turned on the oven to break the chill. I slept on the couch, just inside the front door.

Hildery and I looked so much alike, as I said earlier, that even little Julia sometimes mistook me for her father. Shopkeepers and people in the neighborhood also confused us. As Hildery loved bananas and stopped at our local grocery store to buy them almost daily, when I went in the first time I was astonished to hear the shopkeeper ask me, "How many today?" My brother and I were alike in other ways, too. We were both churchgoers, we sang in the choir, and frequently visited churches other than our own. We had both dropped out of Tuskegee, but worked on bettering ourselves. We were hard workers.

Hildery and Carrie looked upon me as a son, having a son of their own only later on. They were protective and caring, doing all of the things that one would have expected a parent to do even though I was a young man then, one old enough to be on his own perhaps. Hildery, being a decade my senior, took it upon himself to pass on to me family stories and history as did my other older siblings, aunts, uncles, and cousins.

Carrie took me under her wing in her own way. She was an excellent cook and took it upon herself to make sure I was well fed. She did not know how to put a little food on a plate! When Hildery and I came home from work, she fixed our plates and set them before us, piled high. I ate everything as I had been taught to do at home. I still tease Carrie, saying, "You can take credit for fattening me up!"

Hildery and I walked many places together. I confided in my brother, discussed personal matters, and turned to him for answers to any questions I had. He also encouraged my interest in writing. Perhaps he understood that it was for me a way of dealing with feelings. It did in fact help me overcome loneliness, first at Tuskegee, then in the military where I understood what Mom and Dad meant when they talked about feeling alone in a crowd. I wrote poetry that talked about my feelings in relationship to my parents, to experiences that I had dealing with local whites in communities where I was stationed, about incidents that occurred where I was told that maybe I ought to "wash the dirt" off my face. I remember one poem I wrote about the real shame that was upon us as a nation laboring under burdens of hate and racial tensions. To deal with feelings of loneliness and isolation, with feelings of nonexistence, I wrote essays as well as articles for the school newspaper. I wrote about Malcolm X, his assassination, the shame of it all. I grappled with Dr. Martin Luther King's philosophy. I think that until today, it has been Dr. King's approach that most influenced me and helped me to move forward and get as much done as I have in the Utah community where I currently live. So, as a young man, it was in part through writing both poetry and prose that I gradually came to grips with who I was.

In Florida, though living with a cherished brother, I still felt homesick, particularly for my mother. I wrote a poem that expressed what I thought were her feelings for her son, and how her love for me was expressed.

My Mother Prays for Me

As I walk through this life
Today
I can hear the echoing of
Mother as she starts to
Pray.
No matter how far my
Friend's affections for me
Go, My mother's go a little
Further; because she prays for me.
I can see her trembling lips.
As she declares her prayerful words.
I see the first tear as it drips,
I know my Jesus must have heard.
She wants my life built

From above,
And she prays that God
Can be seen
Through my care, tenderness, and love,
Through my hopes, desires, and dreams.
A sincere prayer to God,
I can hear her whispering
Words,
That her toil may not be
In vain,
That her prayer for me be
Heard.
The thoughts of what my
Mother does,
On my mind it shall always be.
To think how much a mother
Really cares
Is to think how my mother
Prays for me.

When I shared this poem with Hildery, he suggested I try to get it published to get "exposure," as he called it. Hildery was positive in his interactions with me and with others, positive in all he tried to do in his lifestyle. I wanted to pattern myself after him. To that end I became an observer, a "studier" of what he said and did. He was a young man out on his own. He seemed to have his "act" together. I saw him as committed to being whatever he thought and said that any human being ought to want to be. We were always great friends. Whatever one needed, the other did what he could to help. When I went to see my brother, it was as if I was going home. His wife and children still treat me as if I belonged there, extending their welcome to my spouse and children as well. In fact, when my daughter Grace decided to move to Florida, she stayed with her uncle and aunt before striking out on her own.

"When are you coming home?" Hildery and Carrie always asked. My family and I make it our business to get there as regularly as we possibly can. Though Hildery was my full-blood brother, he and I became both family and friends in the truest sense of the word by doing things together.

My brother Joe and I were also very close. We did a lot together as we were growing up, and as adults we traveled together. It was Joe who was with me when I was burned over 30 percent of my body on that fateful trip home to Georgia one year. Interestingly, I remember Mom saying that had she been there that day, she would have jumped into the fire behind me. So it is with mothers! Luckily, she and Joe were out visiting relatives in the area.

Of course, when Joe got established in California, I lived with him for two years. Here again, doubling up with Joe, his wife, and their three boys made this time of study and further preparation for ministry possible for me, his younger brother. Those were great days!

In the African American community we dealt with all sorts of situations through family strength. Whether it was a young lady who was "in trouble" being taken in by someone "up North" to spare her embarrassment and provide for (and ofttimes raise) the blameless infant; a sister who wanted to get more education; a brother in conflict with the family; a young man seeking to improve his lot in life, we were "glued" together by circumstance and by family love. All sorts of situations demanded togetherness. We cooperated constantly in coming up with strategies not only for security, but literally for survival. We knew the power of Psalm 133, verse 1: "Behold how good and pleasant it is for brethren to dwell together in unity."

The extended family was our hub. Certainly, not one of us felt that he or she was an "island." Dad told the story of a man and his sons: "A man had seven sons. He took seven switches and asked each son to take his turn and break one. They each did the chore with ease. Then, the man bound seven switches together and asked each son to take his turn and break the bunch. None could break the switches tied together." Of course, the moral was that "Together we stand, divided we fall."

36

SOME SIBLINGS AND OUR OLD HOUSE

MY SISTER WILLIE MAE ALLEN CURRENTLY LIVES just outside of Washington, D.C., and is the archivist and communicator of the family. She is working on a family tree and can answer any question you might have about anyone. If you want to know someone's address, telephone number, anniversary, or birth date, you can count on Willie Mae. She is the one who religiously sends cards on birthdays and holidays, always including a dollar bill, her signature. Now she has raised the amount to five dollars, however, to meet inflation.

Willie Mae has a fig tree growing beside her house. She says it reminds her of home. On the farm we had two. I remember them well. One was about 15 feet tall and eight feet around and seemed to have figs on it most of the year, some ripe, some not so ripe. The other one was smaller. We dubbed it the "public tree" as it grew beside the road and people coming and going helped themselves while the birds ate their share. Willie Mae's fig tree has become an "institution." Countless folk have received starts from it. Some will even travel when Willie signals that the figs are ripe. She is willing to share her fruit, makes sure that visitors have a taste, and even ships some to family and friends. Recently, while on sabbatical, we visited Daisy's daughter Regina and found her front door hidden behind a much larger fig tree.

Willie Mae is the walker of the family. While my late sister Annie Mae was known as "Miss Beautiful," young men on her trail from the time she was a teenager, Willie was famous for walking everywhere she went. It was hard to keep up with her and still is. She is swift and accustomed to getting where she is going without delay. Annie Mae, two years younger than Willie Mae, grew into a proud-looking lady, one who seemed in charge, who appeared to know just where she was going and why. In 1968, only in her late 30s, she died of heart problems, leaving behind a young son, my youngest nephew. Earl was then raised by his grandparents, Julia

Cooper Davis and Deacon John Davis. Today, this stately man serves as a captain in the Burke County Fire Department and looks after family property. We generally turn to Earl when we want to get something done back in Georgia.

My brother Joe was an independent thinker who made his own way. While he and Dad did not see eye to eye, Joe did for himself what he needed to do to survive. He was able to get ahead so that by the time he died he was a businessman, owned several different businesses, had a family, and owned property in various locations. Family members took to calling him their "rich cousin" because Joe always seemed to have extra resources. Or, if he did not have extra, he always seemed willing to share what he did have. He was liberal and kind. Joe was known for saying, "Don't be half stepping now, don't be half stepping," when he wanted to encourage someone to do their best or if he saw anyone doing things half-heartedly. These were also his last words. Mom used to say it another way. In fact, she recited a little poem, all the words of which I no longer recollect. However, it went something like, "If you can't be a pine on the top of a hill, if you can't be a shrub in the valley, be the best of whatever you are."

My brother Clarence was the first of our family to attend an integrated school. He was also the first to graduate from college, and went on to receive a Master's Degree from Fort Valley State College, in Fort Valley, Georgia. He was elected and served as student body president while there and later taught and was a student counselor at Boggs Academy. In the year 2000, Clarence was the only resident left in Cooper's Town, living in Aunt Hattie Cooper's house. Our block house, the one Mom and Dad built just up the road from the old, unpainted one where I was born, is in disrepair. But our old house, the pillars it stood on, the shutters and the tin roof, the porches, all of it is gone! Had it been standing, however, would Clarence have wanted to live there? I doubt it. In fact, I know that my family and African Americans in the rural South in general did their utmost to get away from these wooden houses with no electricity and no plumbing, these unpainted structures that reminded them far too poignantly of hardships! When our old house began to crumble, we did not consider repairing it. We pulled it down. Today, only the stone steps, overgrown with weeds and shrubs, mark the spot where it once was.

For me, the site of the old house does remain a little place of pilgrimage. When I am home, I go there and stand awhile thinking of the comings and goings. I imagine the voices who spoke from the porch, spoke words of wisdom.

37

EDUCATE THE HEAD AND THE HEART

MY PARENTS BELIEVED that experience and exposure as well as spiritual growth were essential to a good education.

"There are some things that you learn just by being in certain places," they used to say. I tell my children nowadays that the education that I received from the travel during my military years was probably as valuable, if not more valuable, than that which I received in a college classroom. I try to encourage them to go and see, not just sit around in one place. Dad had minimal formal training, but great common sense—"horse sense," as we called it—and a great calm about him. His calm nature was, I think, in many ways natural. In many other ways it was nurtured. Out of it sprang his philosophy. He came from a family situation where he was a child born out of wedlock. His mother depended upon him as she did with the other children to carry on the affairs of life. In fact, Dad talked many, many times about how he was only able to go to the third grade because he had to help his mother take care of his sisters and brother. He had a demeanor, he had an attitude that allowed him to be able to interact with other people without being hostile or angry. I think he learned how to survive and nurtured this survival instinct by going to church and becoming a strong Christian and a believer who practiced what the Bible taught. He established good relationships with his family as well as with his community. He was a master at holding his peace and taught us (as did our mother) to count to ten before speaking if we were upset. If you allowed yourself to calm down before speaking, then you spoke more adequately. He said, "Let your nays be nays and your yeas be yeas." In other words, mean what you say, be what you say you are, but also think before speaking out of turn or out of anger. The night my brother and I rolled Dad's car, he made sure he did not come into our room until he had regained his composure. He later said he was afraid of what he might do to us. He was always trying to be what he was, never representing himself as what he was not, determined to be a role model for the family at home and the extended family. Out of that determination he was what he believed.

When my father talked about a well-educated person he meant not only one with experience and book learning, but one who had a sense of "Godly" knowledge, who could make sense out of the interactions between human beings and God. I remember many a day when Dad reflected on the subject of education and spirituality. I heard him say, "Just to go to school and sit in a classroom is to become an educated fool if you don't at the same time balance your knowledge with what's in your heart." He firmly believed (and frequently expressed) that you had to educate the head and the heart. "You know *what* to do if you have head knowledge, but you don't have any reason to do it if your heart's not playin' a part. You miss the mark," I remember him saying. His philosophy left a deep, lasting impression and indeed I believe that you need a little horse sense and a little book sense to stand in balance. When one educates the heart as well, one stands a chance of becoming "whole." Life is not all it can be in terms of fulfillment and joy if the scales are tipped!

Personally I have found my life's balance in Christian ministry, aiming for the head and the heart, to inform and to inspire. Only to the degree that the minister meets his goals, does the community respect him.

38

A MINISTER'S REPUTATION

PRIOR TO MY BEING CALLED TO THE MINISTRY, Reverend J. R. Tarver, pastor of the rural Noah's Ark Baptist Church, was an example of what I thought a minister ought to be. He lived above Keysville, Georgia, between Keysville and Augusta. I sought him out as he had something about him that made him appealing to me. I had dropped out of Tuskegee, or been forced out to be exact. I was searching for myself, for direction.

One day, I decided to drive to Reverend Tarver's house. I found him sitting on the front porch, which was sheltered by a row of trees. Like ours, his house had no paint. He was rocking back and forth. He was an older man, greying now. He had a presence that filled a room, music in his strong, roaring voice, a rhythm to his movements. When he preached people got excited. He was always well dressed and always seemed accessible, easy for people to talk to and get along with. I wanted to have a conversation with him without indicating that I was considering the ministry. I asked about his ministry, how he had been able to develop the reputation and name he had. I think he must have known I was beating about the bush, but he gave me advice—good advice. He said that whatever a minister is, all he has is his name. Whatever else he may have in terms of charisma or training, without a good name he would have little or no effect on his congregation. Proverbs 22, verse 1 says: "A good name is rather to be chosen than great riches, and loving favour rather than silver and gold."

"People will hear the words a minister utters," Reverend Tarver explained, "but unless he has a good name, they will fall on deaf ears and hollow ground." That's a good Georgia comment! Reverend Tarver put me on the right track. Although I didn't know it at the time and continued to search, and search, and search, the advice he gave me was what I needed in order to go forward and accept my call to the ministry. Of course, that call was confirmed by the Reverend George Houston and the members of the Bethel Baptist Church in Fort Lauderdale, Florida, where I announced my call to ministry, where I preached my first sermon, and where I was called a son. My brother Hildery reported that the current pastor of Bethel, though he has been a preacher less time than I, still talks about me in terms of being his "son in the ministry" because I was a member of that church when I started.

This business of ministry is, for me, very, very serious. I approached it by accepting my call and then by taking advantage of every opportunity that came my way to share in ministry. What, for example, does a young man in Thailand do when he is an aircraft mechanic in the Air Force and a minister as well? Well, I discovered that there were missionaries who were running, among other things, leper colonies. I was able to work and share with them, be part of their team, working with lepers. This was my first exposure to a disease very commonly referred to in the Bible, leprosy. I also worked with the chaplain on the military base while there in Korat and took extension courses in communication and sociology, courses offered by the University of Maryland. I did my utmost to develop my skills, preparing myself to be a better minister.

In any event, many years after my conversation with Reverend Tarver, after I had become pastor of the Calvary Baptist Church in Salt Lake City, one of Reverend Tarver's grandsons came to the area from California to play on the University of Utah football team. Another was studying business at Salt Lake Community College, and a third was a policeman in Murray, Utah. I met them all and sensed they had about them the same "we are available, what can we do to help" approach as their grandfather. One with his family is a member of Calvary, always ready to lend a hand. I appreciate that. The Tarver influence is alive and well and I am the better for the experience and exposure. Like my father, Reverend Tarver operated his own farm. Imagine the impact of Reverend Tarver and Deacon Davis in their churches and on their respective farms!

39

Sharecropping Neighbors

Dad could do anything that needed to be done with numbers. Nonetheless, he and Mother reminded us that we would have to do better than they did if we wanted to "get along." They sacrificed and sent us to school even when extra hands were needed in the fields. On our way we saw others working, children of sharecroppers along with their parents. They were ofttimes barefoot, picking cotton, pulling corn, gathering crops, thrashing peanuts. Some of them were my friends. I am ashamed of the way we made fun of them, teasing them. Their plight was dismal and they could do little about it, but to have their peers comment on it must have caused them unbearable suffering and humiliation.

The sharecropping system was one where a man (usually a white man) owned land. He lived in the main house, usually on the hill, and allowed sharecroppers to live in the houses scattered on the plantation. These sharecroppers were usually African American families. Ideally, each family had a certain amount of land they were expected to work, dividing the expenses and the profits with the plantation owner. It rarely worked that way. It seemed to me that the expenses far exceeded the profits for the sharecropping families, throwing them into a perpetual cycle of debt. Their lives were controlled by their limited economics, their limited knowledge and understanding of the system, their fear of what might happen to them and their families should they challenge that system, often by their own lack of inspiration to move along. Some understood, however. They were the ones who made the best of their circumstances as long as they needed to, eventually getting themselves and their families out "by any means necessary," as Malcolm X became famous for saying. My parents said, "By hook or by crook." Sometimes one person would slip away, go up North, out West, or not so far, to south Florida. Opportunities anywhere else were bound to be greater! Once one person was established, he or she eventually sent back for the others. No matter how many left, however, there was always another family waiting to replace them, to move into the house they had vacated, to work the land they had relinquished. There was never any move to organize in the way Cesar Chávez and the California farmers did.

Sharecropping may well be the cruelest form of labor since physical slavery ended. Few sharecroppers could make decisions because they knew only one way of life and had few alternatives. Mom and Dad, on the other hand, owned their land and made their own decisions about what crops to plant and when to plant them, ofttimes based on whatever allotments the government paid. This meant rotating between crops in order to receive the government subsidies to refrain from planting crops that were in surplus. Farming, my parents were always able to grow enough to take care of family needs and obligations. Many of the sharecroppers produced more than my parents did in terms of crops, but because they were working for someone else they were rarely able to get out from under. Often the person keeping the books was dishonest, seeing to it that these families stayed poor, providing plantation owners with cheap labor.

I knew many of these sharecropper families personally. Their children played with us. The Jake Adams family was one we interacted with frequently, probably because they were churchgoers. Their youngest (Morris) was my age. The next one (George) was my brother Joe's age. They also had a daughter (Rosa) my sister Daisy's age. Dad ofttimes picked up their father, who did not drive, to take him to church or to a Masonic Lodge meeting.

Speaking of Masonic lodges, both my mother and father were active members and leaders. Dad was the "Worshipful Master" and Mom the "Matron." The Masons were fraternal orders established all over the country by Prince Hall. There are several of them in Utah. They render community service such as housing assistance, burial and sick aid, and offer scholarships for young people. When I went to college they gave me a fifty-dollar scholarship and when my parents died they helped to pay their burial expenses. As the Masonic orders were secret orders, my parents, like other members, refrained from sharing details.

Another sharecropping family in our community was the family of Horace Simpson, better known as "Mr. Horace." He was the best tractor driver on the Johnson plantation, which was next door to our farm. He worked long hours both as a sharecropper and hiring out to plow other people's fields. It seemed to us that he made enough money at the end of each year to clear his debts with some left over. All too frequently, however, he bought an automobile from the plantation owner with the extra money from his crops, usually in October. It invariably ran until just around Christmastime and then broke down. He parked it and the family used the seats to sit or sleep on, while their chickens appropriated the body, roosting and laying their eggs inside that car. It became a chicken coop.

These families had so little that they transformed whatever they did have into something useful to them or to their animals. In fact, we all did. We called it "making do."

40

Responsibilities and Roles

When it was time to plant or harvest on our farm, it was the same on all the farms around us. Ofttimes only we Davis children were present at the elementary school. When we returned home during such seasons, we found the meal our mother had left us covered by a cloth on the kitchen table as she would go to the fields in the afternoon. After eating, we were also expected to and did join our parents in the fields to pick cotton, pull fodder, or deal with whatever crops were in season.

At dusk we all returned home to do evening chores, eat supper, and catch up on homework before turning in for the night. We used to joke when given our daily or weekly chore assignments by our parents that we worked before we went to work and we worked after we returned from work. My father would chuckle, declaring many times, "Hard work never hurt anybody!" My grandson, Cedric, as I mentioned, went to Kenya on a work mission after his 2005 graduation from high school. When asked what he learned, he said, "That you can work hard without complaining."

For us children, the division of labor was on a rotating basis, giving us the opportunity to do every chore. "Today is your day to do the yard," Mom would say. Our yard had no lawn or grass, but was all dirt. It had to be swept. We kept it tidy of trash and leaves that blew in by using brush brooms made from the branches of a slender bush growing wild in the woods. We cut and tied together a bunch for brooms and everyone bragged a little about who had the best swept yard.

Another time Dad might say, "Today is your week to milk the cows, chop and bring in the wood," or "This is your turn to put up the chickens," which meant catching chickens in the yard, putting them in pens above the ground, and feeding them clean corn and meal for a week. On Saturday we slaughtered three or four of our hundred or so chickens for Sunday's dinner. Mom kept an eye on the chickens and picked those she wanted killed. The first to go were ones that pecked the others bloody, roosters that acted like hens, followed by that striped one, the one with dots on its wings, and so on.

One of the chores none of us relished was wringing or cutting off the heads of the chickens. We didn't much like preparing them, either, which meant dipping them in boiling water, plucking the feathers, cleaning out the cavity, removing heart and livers, removing the bile (which if it burst would make the meat bitter), and slicing open the gizzard, scraping out what grain was left sticking to its tough, corrugated, slick membrane. This offal was then cleaned and cooked along with the legs, necks, and heads to make soup for chicken and dumplings. We threw nothing away. Even the feathers were used in making soap for washing clothes. I wish I had paid more attention and could recollect how this was done.

As to the distribution of chores we looked forward to hearing Mom say, "Next week you work inside fixing breakfast, supper, or helping with the cleaning." Inside chores were traditionally reserved for girls, although Mom insisted on teaching them to boys as well. She said we might one day need to cook, clean, wash, and iron for ourselves and that she might as well prepare us. Her lessons served us well. While feeding the chickens was usually girls' and women's work, as was gathering their eggs, feeding mules and hogs was work for boys and men. Also feeding and milking cows and taking them to pasture. Girls went to the fields but were not expected to do as much. Whatever our assignments or tasks, Mom and Dad counted on us to carry them out without being reminded. With every person doing their share, the load was lighter for all.

Roles were clearly defined in our home and there was a division between men and women, what was expected of each, where they sat at church. At Roberson Grove women and girls sat on the right side, men and boys on the left. The men and women who were more responsive and participatory in the worship service sat in front, again the women on the right, the men on the left. They were, by and large, older men and women, deacons and deaconesses. Their section was called the "Amen Corner." Clearly, they were the ones who verbally responded to the prayers and preaching. While the separate seating does not exist at Calvary today, the participatory behavior is common and expected. It is, in fact, required of deacons and deaconesses. When there is a lull, I will ofttimes ask where my "Amen corner" has gone. Ours is a call-responsive, participatory worship experience. No spectators here!

Roles were just as clear in everyday activities. For example, girls played sing-songy, gentle games; boys played more physical games. In our community some parents did not feel it was appropriate for girls to play baseball or games where there was hitting, swinging, running, stretching, or wrestling.

Christmas gifts also reflected different roles. Boys were given cap pistols, reflecting outdoor activities; girls were given dolls, indicating family responsibilities. Roles were meant to define girls as caring and boys as providers.

There was a difference in how we were disciplined, as well. Dad never disciplined the girls. Mom could discipline both the boys and girls to a certain age. In our house, girls were dealt with more leniently than boys, rarely disciplined physically.

In our high school curriculum, there was an unspoken division as well. Boys or young men studied agriculture; girls and young women studied home economics. Once in a while a boy would pop up in a home economics class, and a girl in agriculture, but seldom did this happen. When one of my classmates enrolled in home economics, he was laughed at and called a sissy. He went, after graduation, to successfully own and operate his own hospitality business.

Interestingly, when it came down to times when there had to be a choice made between who would go to school and who would be kept behind to work, the boys were the ones who for the most part stayed home. The girls were sent to school. There was a sense that girls would grow up to get a better job with education, that boys could always do farm work with less formal education.

Ultimately, as I look back at the way we were reared, the distinctions in our roles, the clarity of our parents' expectations, I think their approach was sound, certainly practical insofar as how to handle a number of children growing up at the same time. We always knew what was required of us and what the consequences of not complying were. Most of my siblings and I grew up with a marked sense of stability as a result, one that sustains us to this day. I wonder about the fate of this modern generation: unclear, uncertain, waffling! The only time I was ever "booed" in giving a speech was when I challenged college students, "Don't just learn something, learn how to do something with your hands!"

41

CRAFTS

Our family included basket weavers and leather workers on my father's side and woodworkers and carvers on my mother's side. My mother's brother, Uncle Andrew Cooper, was such a one, though a stone mason and bricklayer by profession. He was also an inventor of sorts, an unusual personality who was little understood in his community during his day. I will tell you about that later.

As a weaver, my father wove baskets at two times during the year. In winter he did so sitting by the kitchen fireplace. In summer, he sat on the back porch, which ran the length of the kitchen and my parents' bedroom. Summer weaving usually took place in July or early August after the crops had been laid by, the plowing and hoeing done. We children went with our father to gather "straw," which grew five or six feet tall on the edge of the woods some miles from our farm, sometimes right on our own land. Dad showed us how to cut and soak this straw, but we never learned to weave, although I remember watching him closely. When the straw became pliable, he started weaving the bottom of a basket with a tight weave. He secured the straw with twine. He then worked his way up with a looser weave. Close to the top, he twisted the straw into a pair of handles and finished the basket with a coiled rim. These baskets were large and sturdy, used for carrying cotton and corn. He also used baskets to "winter" wheat, that is to separate the grain from the chaff. I can still see him standing with the wind to his back, holding the basket above his head, pouring the grain in the middle of four cotton sheets, spread on the ground in the backyard. Once he was done, he stored the grain in what was once Uncle Ben Cooper's old store, known to some in the community as "the little store."

Throughout the year, Dad made belts, harnesses for the mules, whatever items of this nature were needed on the farm. I still have at home some of his tools, including the hole punches. But none of us children ever learned how to make any of these things. Weaving, leather work, and basket weaving are unfortunately lost arts with our family today.

When we were very young, Mom made toys for us and we learned to make toys for ourselves as we grew older. We had very few store-bought items and were encouraged to use our imaginations and our hands. We made cars using cans for wheels. Some of these were big enough for the smallest of us to ride in. We used barrel rims as hoops to push along with a stick. We made baseball bats with tree limbs. We cobbled swings with chains, ropes, and old tires. We made all sorts of games with wood and twine, games like Cat's Cradle. In fact, I still have in my possession one such game that Uncle Andrew Cooper once made for us children.

In weaving baskets, carving wood, piecing together quilts, or knitting wool caps, my parents always took available materials and created something needed on the farm, something functional, something useful in the home, something to wear, as well as something for us to play with. That, too, was "making do."

As a boy I was "famous" for my cap with ear flaps. There are still a few black and white photographs of me wearing such a cap. I was the butt of many jokes and I can still hear ringing in my ears the taunts and laughter of other children. I didn't pay them any mind. I was warm while everyone else was laughing in the cold. I have one just like it that I wear even today. At a recent Pastor's Anniversary, my wife's slide show included one of my childhood pictures wearing those favorite, precious flaps. I suppose in some respects I was as different as is my given name, France.

42

Mom

Our mother was principally a homemaker. With few exceptions, she stayed home to wash, sew or mend, clean, and cook, preparing our main meal of the day, the noonday meal, which we called dinner. When chores were done and as needed, she sewed sheets and pillow cases from soft, cotton flour sacks. She washed and saved them until she had enough to cut and piece together. In fact, my parents sometimes bought flour in order to get the sacks just for pillow cases.

My mother also made quilts, as did all the women in the countryside at that time. Family members, friends, and neighbors gathered at someone's home for quilting bees, which were also a time to socialize while creating something that would make a difference in the household. These quilts were made from any fabric scraps including shirt and pant parts. Although sometimes rough, they kept us warm, especially in the late hours of night in winter, after the fires that Dad had stoked before bedtime had gone out.

As we were growing up, Mom taught us skills of the homemaker, saying, "You may one day have to do this for yourselves, so you might as well learn now." Eventually, when we had mastered certain skills, she asked us to make breakfast or supper. I learned to make biscuits from scratch at my mother's side. Today, I make them when I want to please my wife.

Interestingly, our sister Daisy Mae, the oldest of my parents' second crop of children, did not seem to have a lot of demands placed upon her. We always thought that she had some kind of advantage over us because she had more time to sit around, read, and study without being called upon to do housework. She didn't see it that way.

There were three of us boys under Daisy Mae. Joe was two years younger, I was four years younger, and Clarence, the baby of the family, was six years younger than Daisy. Perhaps Mom and Dad felt she had responsibility enough in helping tend her younger siblings. She was put in charge of us if they were not present and was, in fact, held accountable for our actions. She handled her role with style.

One night, when my sister Eunice came to visit from up North, she and her husband took Mom and Dad in their car to call on family living a few miles away. While they were gone, Joe and I decided to test Dad's newly remodeled 1949 Ford automobile. Neither of us had a driver's license. Daisy pleaded with us to stop, but we went anyway. Joe was daring and would try just about anything. This intrepid nature of his, his unwillingness to take punishment, and his "sassing" is what finally caused the rift between him and Dad. That night, setting out at breakneck speed in Dad's automobile, Joe and I ended up hitting a sand bed on the dirt road. Joe lost control of the vehicle and rolled it. We were pinned underneath until local people, hearing the ruckus, came and helped us get out. As soon as we got home, we crept into our bed. Mom and Dad were still out. We listened for their footsteps, but they never came into our room. Dad told me years later that he was afraid if he did, he might kill us. We were in trouble and were later punished after our parents' fury cooled. Daisy was in trouble, too, as she had been in charge.

My brothers and I did not treat Daisy with the regard and respect brothers should have. We teased and tormented her. She was pretty sensitive and squeamish. At the table, we prodded her. She got up and left her food. We ate it. Once, we threw her hat behind the porch swing where there was a nest of wasps. She got up in a huff, went to retrieve it, and was stung. Even as adults, when the subject came up in conversation, Daisy was not amused. I have sometimes wondered if she ever forgave us, and on a recent visit to her in Texas she said she was glad we were finally owning up to our mischief.

In any event, once we were old enough to do chores, our first assignments were to sweep the bedroom and make up our bed. Mother did the bulk of the washing and ironing though we were called to help from time to time. She boiled the "whites" in a big, black iron pot, scrubbed everything clean on a "rub board," and hung it out to dry in the sun. She ironed with a flatiron heated on the stove and patched our clothes until they were no longer fit to be handed down. She taught us that there was no shame in patches as long as we were clean. "Cleanliness is next to Godliness," she ofttimes repeated.

Our knees and elbows may have been textured with corduroy or denim, our shirts two-toned, our jeans or coveralls exhibiting a rainbow of colors, but we were always clean. On Sunday we exchanged our "patches" for dress clothes. The boys wore white shirts and dark pants or a suit like Dad. The girls, like Mother, wore crisp dresses, homemade or purchased at Goldbergs. Our shoes were like mirrors, polished to a high shine on Saturday night, which was also bath night.

The weekly bath was sacrosanct. It was conducted in the kitchen, a fire made up in the fireplace when it was cold. Water was drawn from the well, heated on the wood stove, poured into a No. 10 galvanized metal washtub, and refreshed after each batch of children was done. The girls went first, followed by the boys, and lastly our parents. We were not allowed to go to bed until we passed Mom's "squeaky clean" inspection and were declared ready for Sunday.

If we were walking to Bryant Grove or First Baptist, we ofttimes carried our shoes to keep them clean. Wiping our feet when we got to church, we put on our shoes, shined the night before.

Dressing up is a way African Americans give honor to God when going to worship in His house. It is an unspoken tradition to wear "Sunday-go-to-meetin'" clothes and polished shoes (even if they are polished with tallow), to look our best at church. My clothes were many times hand-me-downs, but we wore our best and we were always clean. Mom made sure of that and Dad insisted on it!

43

DAD

My father had a built-in "time machine." Without the benefit of a timepiece, he knew when the hour had come to quit the fields and start home for dinner. When we got within earshot of our house we heard Mother ringing the dinner bell, one with a high-pitched tone, a little glass chicken decorating the handle. On each side of that bell was a salt or pepper shaker. In the kitchen the table would be laid and our noonday meal ready.

Dad knew when it was time to go back to work, to leave the cool shade of the pecan trees where we relaxed a half hour or so after dinner. He could tell quite accurately by a look toward the sun and by the shadows on the ground what time it was. Nature was his guide in everything. He knew when putting a seed in the ground would prove most productive. Watching when the moon was full, failing, or gaining, he planted according to the lunar cycle. He studied the sky, the elements. He could tell if a storm was brewing before there was ever any sign of it. He would point out the playful activity of the animals as indication that the weather was about to change. We saw them heading for higher ground. In fact, with the sky above still clear, he'd announce, "Get your hoe and your sack and let's head back to the house. It's gonna rain." And, sure enough, by the time we got home the clouds had gathered and the skies opened up. Dad said he could smell the rain and could tell by the way the sun sat in the sky the day before if the weather would be rough. I don't know if he could predict ice storms. Sometimes they descended on us with a vengeance. One that I remember vividly destroyed our crops, beat them down so hard that Dad had us go out and plow them under. Nothing was going to come from them after that storm. He talked about that time as "the year of the great hail storm."

Dad identified periods of time saying this or that happened "the year of the boll weevil," or "the year of the grasshoppers…"

He studied the night sky, naming planets. He could point to the Big Dipper, the Little Dipper, and other stellar configurations. Perhaps he came by it through his parents or his ancestors, slaves who found their way to freedom guided by the arrangement of the stars.

John Davis was also known in our community as one who went into the woods with a gun and always came home with rabbit, coon, possum, and sometimes squirrel without ever having fired a shot. He had sharp eyes. He was very quiet. People said that he walked up to a nest and captured whatever animal was there by hitting it over the head with the butt of his gun. We ate wild animals at least once a week and also raised cows, pigs, chickens, and sometimes turkeys, domesticated animals to supply us with milk and eggs as well as meat. We harvested vegetables we grew in the "truck patch" and in the garden as well as fruit from our own trees, both for our use and to sell.

My parents had about 50 peach trees, three orchards of pecans, apple and mulberry trees, two fig trees, and a number of pear trees, which bore very sweet fruit. We ofttimes ate wild blackberries, huckleberries, dewberries, and wild grapes we called muscadines.

In season, people from all over the community (some driving for miles) came to pick and buy pears by the bushel right off our trees, which grew up the road from us, on our land but in front of Aunt Hattie and Uncle Andrew Cooper's house. Aunt Hattie, Cousin Solomon's grandmother, died at the age of 100. Her daughter, Allie Mae Cooper Turner, Solomon's mother, lives near Wrens, Georgia. She is the oldest living member of our family today.

44

THE FRUITS OF SUMMER

GROWING UP, I SPENT HALF OF EVERY SUMMER picking fruit and harvesting vegetables, helping to prepare them for canning or for sale. We
harvested watermelon from Dad's watermelon patch, shelled butter beans
on the back porch or in the shade of the pecan trees, hauling our produce
to Gough on the wagon or in the trunk of our automobile. We sold door
to door, generally to white families who did not have their own gardens,
though it was African American women in their employ who actually did
the buying. And we had to go to the back door to transact our business, as
black folk could not go to the front door. We used a quart cup with a lip
on it to measure, charging 50 cents a quart or 25 cents a quart, depending
on the produce: okra, butter beans, peas. Corn, watermelon, and other
vegetables and fruit, we sold by the bushel, by the item, or by the bag.

When we were done with our rounds, Dad ofttimes took us to the
local store for an ice cream cone or a five-cent soda. Returning our empty
bottle, we got a penny back, which Dad let us keep.

Although we made ice cream at home using a hand-cranked ice cream
maker, we relished anything that was store-bought. Instead of homemade
bread or biscuits, Mom made my sandwich for the trip to Tuskegee on
store-bought light bread. That was meant to be special.

Sometimes, Mother went into town with us. I can still hear her laughter when telling the story of "Mr. Tightwad," a fellow whose reputation for
being unusually stingy had earned him his name. She had dropped her ice
cream off the cone on the floor of the store one day. "Let me throw this out
for you," Mr. T had said, scooping up what was left of her ice cream and
going out the door. Mother had noticed him wiping his lips as he
returned.

We always drove home in time for evening chores. We brought the
cows in from pasture and milked them. We fed the mules and hogs. We
got the chickens into the chicken house to keep them safe from night

predators. Daisy Mae gathered the eggs and Mom made sure supper was on the table when we were done, usually just after dusk. As we had no electricity or running water, we took turns cleaning the glass globes of the kerosene lamps and making sure the wicks were trimmed before lighting them. We were expected to keep the water bucket by the kitchen door full, and the dipper clean and in place. We drew water from an open-faced well at the west end of the back porch and were instructed never to use the dipper (at times a hollowed-out gourd, other times a tin cup) to drink. Each of us had our own glass, jar, or can with ragged edges smoothed. Needless to say, as children, we could not resist drinking from that dipper, however. It was so handy and the water seemed sweeter somehow.

After chores and before sitting down to eat, Mom or Dad raised the question: "Did you wash your hands? Let me see them." When they were satisfied, Dad sat at the head of the table and said Grace: "Good Lord, help us to be 'umble and thankful for what we are about to receive for the nourishment of our bodies. Amen." Each child then recited a verse from the Bible. The youngest ones clung to short verses such as "Jesus wept," or "The Lord is my shepherd." As we got older, we were encouraged to learn longer verses. We sometimes held contests to see who would find and say the most interesting or longest ones. One I recited frequently warned not to put your trust in an unfaithful man: "Confidence in an unfaithful man in time of trouble is like a broken tooth, or a foot out of joint" (Proverbs, chapter 25, verse 19).

With the opening ritual completed, Mom or Dad said, "Help yourselves," which we did, taking a portion of what was on the plate closest to us and passing the dishes of food around.

Mom always placed the bread dish beside our father as he was the most dedicated bread eater in our family. In fact, Dad did not feel he had eaten unless cornbread or biscuits were served up. The same was true of grits at breakfast. He had to have them! Mom usually ate standing, a plate in her hand, looking after the rest of us, handing us a pitcher of Kool Aid, or making sure our plates were clean before we asked to be excused from the table. My parents expected us to leave the table only after each one of us reported loudly and clearly, "Please excuse me, I had a plenty."

Every summer, I peeled more peaches than I care to remember and my mother spent a lot of time canning them. She also canned vegetables and meat. What meat was not canned or eaten fresh, however, was cured by my father in a one-room smokehouse, a building about 20 feet behind our house, between our house and the barn. A few pens attached to the barn were for our milk cows. The barn itself was used to store corn, wheat, and other grain. It also housed the wagon and our mules, Mag and Queen. Old Cora had died and Mag had replaced her.

The wagon was generally used to haul cotton to the gin, wood for heating the house, produce, and supplies. From time to time it served to transport children to and from school. At such times, we, the Davis children, jumped off before getting to the schoolhouse and hurried out after school, hoping to meet our father halfway up the road. I remember that we were a little shy, even ashamed, that he drove a wagon pulled by mules. We were always told not to dangle our feet off the side so as to avoid getting them caught in the spokes of the wheels.

Our mules, long-suffering, were principally beasts of burden used to plow. Once a year, Dad hitched them to a press used to extract pale green juice from sugar cane. So, Mag and Queen were blindfolded and hitched to a long pole, which they activated by going around and around. The blindfold kept them from getting dizzy. Sugar cane season was also a time to make molasses. Mom cooked the juice in the black cauldron of many uses, bottled it, and stored it in the smokehouse. When we had nothing else to eat, we ate it with cornbread. Later, I found out that this rich syrup is loaded with minerals and iron, healthy and energizing. After Mag and Queen were done, all that remained of the sugar cane was the pulp, which Dad plowed under.

Well, wherever we were, and whatever the season or the work, Mag and Queen were practically jubilant when released from the plow or the press. At the end of the day, they were once again hitched to the wagon that carried us home. They made for the barn at lightning speed, kicking up dirt as red as the setting sun, no doubt motivated by the prospect of their evening meal. We had to hold on fast to the sides to avoid being bounced off, but were equally glad when our long day of labor in the fields was done. A good supper awaited us at home. We ate and soon went to bed, cradled by the sounds of nature and secure in the knowledge that God and our parents were watching over us.

All was well.

45

Body and the Soul

I was the next to youngest of the second crop of my parents' children. By the time I came along, my father had given up smoking meat much. He salt-cured it instead, rubbing pork quarters with coarse salt, burying the meat for two or three days in bins four feet deep and six feet wide, filled with the same salt. Salt, which we bought in bulk from a supplier in Waynesboro, served to pull the moisture from the meat and protect the flesh from rot and maggots. This meat was then hung to dry from the rough beams spanning the width of the smokehouse.

Our smokehouse had a second function. Shelves were stacked with food bottled in the pressure cooker, stored there for winter use. We always had plenty of fruit, vegetables, and meat during the off seasons. We also had juice and bottles of wine made from green Scuppernongs that grew on an arbor beside our house, or from the wild purple Muscadines. As Mom was a "Mother of the Church," the wine she made was primarily to be used by the church for the Lord's Supper, for communion. We would always get to taste it before it fermented. Today, in our churches, we use grape juice.

We cured pork in late November or early December. It was always cold. Pork would spoil quickly if it was hot. Sometimes, however, we killed a hog in the summertime for the Fourth of July celebration or for family reunions. On such occasions, the men cooked it promptly as barbecue, making pulled pork hash and ribs.

Dad killed four or five hogs at once during hog-killing time, distributing pieces of meat to our neighbors and family before preserving the rest. We always knew it was "hog-killing time" when everyone had fresh meat to eat. As children, we favored the tongue and the liver. My mother made sausage from portions of the hog, mincing the meat in a metal hand-grinder attached to the kitchen table with screws. Not a single part of the animal went to waste, as my parents were masters at taking what we had and stretching it. Mom was famous for saying, "We may not have enough meat to go around but as long as there's water we'll have plenty of soup." Even the intestines of the hogs were utilized. Some people liked to cook "Chitterlings." My mother, however, favored the use of them as casings for sausage, having washed them repeatedly and cleaned them thoroughly. We children cranked the meat grinder and Mom stuffed the casings with ground pork and spices. These sausage links were then hung to dry in the smokehouse along with the hog quarters Dad had prepared. He later used the hog hairs and hooves mixed with potash to make soap. In the backyard, over a wood fire that had to be carefully stoked, my father simmered this mixture in the three-legged iron cauldron also used to boil water for cleaning the slaughtered hogs. Extra fat and skins from the animals were fried for "cracklins" and "meat skins," salty snacks that we all enjoyed.

The smokehouse was a favorite hangout, especially for us children. It smelled good and suggested the possibility of a tasty meal. We knew that once the meat hanging there was cured, Mother would fry up sausage links or ham for breakfast along with eggs, grits, and biscuits, except on Saturdays when we had pancakes to eat with our eggs and meat. Sundays we had the very best food, mostly prepared on Saturday as Sunday was a day of rest. Mom served fried chicken, fresh corn, collard greens, and black-eyed peas seasoned with chunks of salt pork or fatback. We always had warm cornbread, fruit, cakes, and pies. Mom, being a master baker, made these desserts with our own fresh butter. She cooked them in the oven of the wood-burning stove, baking as many as eight or ten cakes and pies. I remember how we had to bring in extra wood on such occasions and to this day I wonder how Mom ever controlled the temperature in the old oven! She never once (that I can remember) burned or undercooked a cake or a pie. As to our drink of choice, it was red Kool Aid, or sometimes lemonade sweetened with lots of sugar.

Sunday was the Lord's Day and every other Sunday we held worship services at Roberson Grove Baptist Church. Roberson Grove was a "second Sunday" church and when we had no service there, we attended other churches as guests. Some of our ministers came from miles away and ours, the Reverend Mack C. Williams, lived in Waynesboro.

It was my grandmother, Scoatney Scott Cooper, who helped to found Roberson Grove. My mother, who followed in her mother's footsteps, was a "Mother of the Church," one who was expected to be a role model, an example of the best of womanhood, someone to whom ladies came for advice, especially young ladies. Dad was chairman of the deacons and superintendent of the Sunday school, in charge of the church and all of its activities in the absence of the minister, that is, until he decided to move to another church. But, that's a story for another time.

Because the ministers who served our communities sometimes lived many miles away, they were ofttimes invited home after church for Sunday dinner with members of their congregations. When they came to our house, it was customary for them to sit at the table with Mom and Dad while we children waited. Of course, they had first pick of the food, sometimes eating all the good bits, leaving nothing but undesirable pieces of chicken for the family to have. In some cases, they ate it all! I remember a story that circulated in our community about just such a minister. After the table grace, the wife invited the minister to eat, saying, "Help yourself, Reverend." The minister took his knife, cut off the end of a stick of butter, then proceeded to slice off the other end. As these were the days before refrigeration, the host had apparently said, "We don't cut off both ends of the butter, Reverend; that'll make it spoil." I remember how my parents laughed when mimicking this minister's reply: "Well, it don't matter, brother, I'm gonna eat it all anyway!"

I had a number of experiences of this nature, observing ministers taking the best of what a host family had to offer, be it meat, watermelons, peaches...They sometimes departed with a basket full of whatever was growing in the garden. After a time, when ministers were invited to our house, my mother made a point of "putting back"—that is, putting some food aside for us, keeping a few of our favorite pieces of chicken or meat hidden in the stove. She put only as much food on the table as she wanted a guest to eat, thus making sure there was always something for us, enough for her children. Mom told a story about Grand Mama Scoatney, one her mother used to tell about a man who made a habit of dropping by at mealtimes.

"A man always came around at meal times. If I offered something to eat, he never said no. One day, I saw him coming down the road just as I was sitting down to eat my apple pie. I was holding one of you children. What did I do? Just as this man came in the door, I placed the baby's feet in the middle of the pie. The man said, 'You just put that baby's feet in that pie to keep me from getting any!'"

Speaking of food, I remember Dad guiding our eating habits and to this day I reflect on his teachings. "Collards are great for dinner," he would say, "but they're too heavy for supper." Or, "A light meal and a little relaxation before bedtime makes for restful sleep." For Dad, relaxation (which was very rare) could simply be spending a little time reading from the Bible or singing a spiritual: "Try Jesus, try Jesus, he's alright. I done tried him and he's alright…" Singing was a way of talking about his faith, of easing his tired body or aching heart. Favorites of his were "Come ye that love the Lord," a short-metered hymn, and "Faaaather I stretch myyyyy haaaaands to theeeeee, no oooooother help I knoooow," a common-metered hymn.

If Dad sat down for more than a few minutes, if he was not busy doing something, he would invariably fall asleep in his chair. I wondered at times if maybe he was just saying, "I don't want to be bothered." When he opened his eyes, however, he would know everything that had been said. I have carried on the tradition.

Although they themselves drank coffee from time to time, my parents discouraged their children from doing so. I have sometimes wondered why. Was it a precious commodity that they wanted to keep for themselves? The reason they gave was, "It will make you black!" I recall that *Jet* and *Ebony* magazines were chock full of ads for skin whiteners, bleaching agents, and hair straighteners. It was not until the 1950s and 60s that James Brown, Richard Wright, and Dr. Martin Luther King Jr. began to say things like "Black is beautiful," "I'm Black and I'm proud."

Early training dies hard, as do old habits. To this day, I do not drink coffee, or tea for that matter. I refresh myself with fruits, nuts, and from time to time a hard candy or a Tropical Bar, my old-time Georgia favorite. Sometimes I'll eat a handful of raisins before preaching a sermon. Fruit gives me energy and my love of fruit may go back to the days when I was a teething infant. My older sisters tell me that my mother applied fruit juice to my baby gums to soothe me. The taste has remained.

Through all the good times and the difficult times growing up, I know that I was guided and nurtured by the regular rhythm of our lives, shared faith, the loving commitment of my family, the concern of my teachers and community, and certainly by the unwavering clarity of my parents' values and expectations. Of course, the meals Mother prepared provided sustenance for the body and spiritual training guided the soul.

46

Born Again

I was 12. It was an unusually hot summer, a Thursday night in August. I was at church for revival meeting with my family. Roberson Grove was on the edge of the woods. The windows were wide open. Bugs buzzed around the lights, dropping into our hair, sometimes stinging and biting. Everyone had a hand fan from Carter's, Phinazee's, or some other mortuary, fanning themselves. I was sitting on the "mourners' bench" along with 18 or so children. I was minding my own business and my business was at the other end of the mourners' bench; she had good looks and pretty legs. I was on the mourners' bench because she was on the mourners' bench and because my parents said I ought to be there. I was not paying any mind to what the preacher was talking about, what the deacons were saying, nor was I listening too intently to the singing. Pretty soon a breeze came through the window, the sermon ended, and the invitation was extended. I didn't know it just then, but I was about to be moved from a life principally motivated by physical concerns to one empowered by God and the Holy Spirit.

All of us on the mourners' bench were instructed to get on our knees. We did. Deacons and mothers of the church joined us. I shall always remember the old country deacon who came and knelt beside me. He was unlearned, untaught. Formal education had escaped him, yet he was effective in his communion and communication with God. He knew how to do it.

He asked: "Boy, have you been prayin'?"

I said, "Yessah."

He said, "Well, what you say?"

I told him, "Now I lay me down to sleep, I pray the Lord…"

"No, not that prayah," he stopped me.

I said, "Good Lawd help us to be 'umble and thankful for what we are about to receive…"

He said, "No, not that."

I said, "Our Father which art in heaven, hallowed be Thy name, Thy…"

He said, "No, son, you don't have to do all that. All you have to say is 'Lawd have mercy on me, a sinnah.'"

I knew the old man was there for the duration. I knew that he was not going to leave. He was going to stay on my case until I gave him what he thought was the right answer. So, I prayed as he had instructed me to do. All at once, moving through me and within me, I felt an extraordinary warmth. A sense of great caring and power dawned on me. I believed it to be God taking over my life. I yielded. It was not the sermon that had touched my heart. It was not the voices singing, "Run, sinner, run, you gotta fin' yoa hidin' place." The shift had come through prayer. The change came in the course of dealing with this old, unlearned, persistent deacon, when I actually uttered the words of his simple prayer. The pastor was winding down the sermon. He began to sing, "What you gonna do when the world's on fire? What you gonna do?" He cast his eyes in my direction. When the invitation was extended I made up my mind to join the church and felt ready to accept God's gift of grace.

I had heard the stories from the Book of Genesis of how the world would never again be destroyed by floods, but by fire. The congregation was singing about it, some clapping, some witnessing, arms raised, hands waving. Many had tears running down their faces as they lifted their voices: "You run to the rock and the rock is rolling, you run to the water and the water is boiling…What you gonna do when the world's on fire?" When the song tapered off, I knew I wanted to be saved. I made my commitment to accept the message, to take Christ into my heart. As I did, a sense of peace and happiness settled over me, and the words of the song, "A change has come over me…I looked at my hands and my hands were new. I looked at my feet and they did too" made more sense to me. It was not that I had grown new hands or feet, but the perspective from which I now started to look at life was fresh and new. I was excited, knowing baptism would follow. My focus was no longer my business seated at the other end of the mourners' bench. When I walked out of the church that night my footsteps seemed lighter, I felt a freshness in the air, an excitement among the people. Voices seemed pitched a little higher. "None but the righteous shall see God, none but the righteous shall see God," they sang. Eyes seemed aglow, the stars above brighter somehow. As I watched the moon rise that Thursday night, full and nearly golden, I was full of expectation.

On the Friday night of baptism, the cement pool a few feet from the church was filled with water using the hand pump to which a pipe was attached. This pool was not much more than 12 feet by six feet, just big enough for the preacher, a deacon, and the one being baptized. It was deep enough for immersion.

I shall never forget that night! I can still hear the sound of the water gushing, now fast, now slow, as 15 of us youngsters, all dressed in white, stood bathed in moonlight and the glow of a bare bulb attached to an extension cord plugged in a socket inside the church. Beetles, candle flies, all kinds of insects circled. A faint buzzing was followed by a dull thud now and then as a bug hit the bulb and fell into the water. Pastor M. C. Williams said some words and buried me in the liquid grave. I felt suspended, waiting for something to happen. I felt like the crippled man in the Biblical passage who sat at the edge of the pool for 38 years. When the angel came to trouble the water for healing, no one would help him get in. Finally, the Master told him to simply "rise, take up thy bed, and walk" (John 5, verses 1–9). I remember how the crowd made up of friends and family stood around leaning over the edge of the pool, singing, "Since I laid my burden down, since I laid my burden down…" When they struck up the old spiritual "Waaaade in the waaaater, waaade in the waateeer, waaade in the waaater, children; God's gonna touble the waaater," that was our signal to descend into the pool, one at a time. "I stepped in the water and the water was cold. It chilled my body but not my soul…" they sang, their voices rising with excitement. While supported by the minister on one side and the deacon on the other, I was thrice "buried" in the water, baptized in the name of the Father, the Son, and the Holy Spirit. When I emerged I felt as if an invisible entity had picked me up and set me down on a brighter path.

So, baptism…My wife, Willene, was baptized before I met her. I baptized our children Carolyn, Grace, and France II, and Carolyn's son, Cedric, along with hundreds more. My children and grandson remain active participants and leaders in church. What had been my hope was fulfilled and my shoulders lifted with joy.

I can still hear the congregational "Amens" as each came forward.

47

It Takes a Village

Cooper's Town, although small, still functioned as a town, and because it was small, everyone knew everyone. Folks knew each other's business. This was both good and bad. Dad used to say, "It takes fifty percent of my time to mind my own business and fifty percent to leave the other fellow's alone." People were not just meddlesome, however, they genuinely looked out for one another, putting aside their differences when needs arose. Adults particularly kept a close eye on children. Everybody (whether related or not) was our "parent." Our uncles and aunts, our older sisters and brothers, our teachers, even adults we knew only by name, all were charged with looking out for us and disciplining us. My mother and father ofttimes repeated, "If we don't do it, the Man will." Everyone was concerned with our safety. In fact, I can still hear the voices of community elders saying, "That's Deacon Davis' boy. He ought not to be there" or, "He's in danger doing that." My reputation as a "good child" had nothing to do with me, but everything to do with my parents' names and reputations. I even got by in school as everyone knew the Davises to be education-minded and keen on insuring that their children were the best that they could be.

When we were old enough to drive the wagon, and later the automobile, Dad sometimes let us take them to run an errand. He also let us drive his car when we were old enough to date, "go courtin'." If an adult caught one of us spinning the wheels of the automobile, speeding along the country road kicking up dust, they stopped us and gave us a stern lecture, and news of our misbehavior reached Mom and Dad sometimes before we ourselves made it home. We were issued a warning or punished: "If I don't correct you now, then the police will; better me get you straight than them get you straight," our parents and elders repeated more times than I can count. They were concerned and wanted us to avoid getting in trouble with the authorities, as they would likely treat us more harshly. With the disparate numbers in the jails and prisons, home discipline is still rather emphasized (in fact rather heavy-handedly) among African Americans to this day.

As I was saying, if we got home before our deeds had been reported, we knew we were well served to tell Mom or Dad that Mr. Jones or Ms. Blaylock did this or that to put us in our place. Ofttimes, we might get away with a "talkin' to" and a warning. If we persisted our parents resorted to the belt, applying it to the "fatty" parts of our anatomy. About the worst thing we could do was to lie about what had happened. I remember many times lying across my father's lap for discipline and hearing his speech, "I'm not gettin' you for what you did, but for not tellin' the truth!"

Our teachers were particularly helpful in coming to our rescue during times of fear and worry. For example, the first time I went to a Halloween party at Gough Elementary School, when I opened the door and saw the scary costumes, I let out a yell and my teacher, Mrs. Davis, came running to my rescue. She picked me up in her arms and I quieted down. I was in the first grade.

Teachers always had a word of calm to offer, a word of reassurance. And they also made sure our parents were informed of our behavior, good or bad. Once, my mathematics teacher came to church to tell my parents that I had been fighting. In fact, I was being a bully. I knew I had the protection of my brothers and sisters as we walked to and from school, and made it my business to "beat up" on James Cunningham, a classmate who had no siblings walking with him to protect him. The Cunninghams moved away from our community without my ever having had the opportunity to say, "I am sorry, please forgive me." To this day I am filled with regret. I have tried to tell my own children that while it is alright to defend themselves, they ought not to start a fight. By and large, they have accepted my advice.

Growing up, if we ran into trouble, particularly with a white man or woman, a black elder came to our rescue. They would do what was necessary to extricate us, offering excuses, making us apologize, whatever it took to save our skins as it were. Our misdeeds would be promptly reported to our parents and we would again be disciplined.

My parents' method of discipline covered a wide range. They disciplined us with their tongue, their eyes, or as a last resort with a switch or a belt. If we were in public, they warned us with a twitch of their nose, by moving their lips, lifting an eyebrow, looking at us in a way we well understood meant we were in trouble. At home, if talking worked, they stopped there. If it didn't, they took drastic measures, never in the heat of anger, however. We were summoned, generally, by our father, who always seemed to be calm and collected. He confronted us with what we had said or done. He then proceeded to explain (for what seemed like hours) why he was going to do what he was about to do, always stressing that it would hurt him and our mother more than it would hurt us.

Discipline was not applied in the same way to girls and boys. Girls were treated more gently. When I had my own girls and boys, my father recommended that I be "tender" with the girls. He believed that boys were more rugged and could tolerate a higher level of discipline. So the rule was to expose girls to the more loving approach, boys to the more rugged, physical approach. Our folks believed they were preparing us for what we could expect when we got out into the world. Joe eventually refused to submit to discipline and said, "Rather than take any more whippings, I'm leaving." He did, as I said earlier. Dad frequently warned us: "He who sits on a red hot stove is bound to rise," but Joe came through fine. Still, he was looked upon as the prodigal son and even referred to himself as "the seventh child." I am not certain just what he meant by it. Mom thought Dad had been too harsh and never quite got over being upset with him.

Some of us children responded more to talk, others less. The latter were disciplined with the switch or the belt. The offender ofttimes had to fetch the instrument of discipline after listening to Dad or Mom's long lecture. All of us received our share of both talk and whippings. My parents' approach to rearing children was based on the Biblical model, primarily the Book of Proverbs. They took literally the teaching that if you train up your children in the way that they should go, when they're older they will not depart from it. They would say, "You will not always have a flowery bed of ease." They did their best to guide and direct us, however, and were clear with us as to what they expected. If they promised us a dime, we got it. If it was a whipping, there was no escape.

At church, if Mom and Dad were not present, the deacons, mothers of the church, and members of the congregation all kept us in line, sometimes with nothing more than a look. Any adult under the sound of whose voice we happened to be was expected and prepared to teach us right from wrong, to discipline us when necessary, sometimes harshly. To us children some of them seemed cruel. As I got older, however, I realized that they acted as they understood to insure our behaviors or decisions would not cost us life or limb later. Like the hens in our yard, clucking for their chickens to gather beneath their wings for protection when they saw the hawk circling above, our elders did all that they could to keep us out of harm's way. Mr. Aaron Ellison and his wife, Elnora, were two elders of our church who did this for us. In fact, they considered me as a son to them, so much so that they requested at the time of their death that I be the one to conduct their funerals. And, indeed, I did both.

As a boy, my father saw a hen and her chicks caught in a burning grass field. He told the story of how the hen saved her babies by calling them to her and sitting on them. When the flames subsided, the "biddies" scampered out from beneath their mother's dead body, scattered across the charred landscape, and went about their business. Our parents and the adults of our community exemplified the African saying, "It takes a village to raise a child." They acted as one body, nurturing us both physically and spiritually, and correcting our behavior. Even those who frequented the juke joints spoke up to remind us of our reputations.

Dad used to say, "Silence gives consent." In fact, the folks who drank, gambled, consorted with "ladies of the night," and behaved in ways Mom and Dad called "rough" did not hesitate to speak up if they saw us where they knew we ought not to be. "You ought not to be hea!" one might declare. Another might say: "You're Deacon Davis' boy…You're Miss Julia's boy… Don't you be hangin' round here now. Go on home! Go on home!"

If we talked about going someplace, our parents always asked who we were going with. If they did not recognize the name, they asked who the parents or the grandparents were. They were very careful in teaching us that the company you keep determines your reputation. If you hung around people who were what my parents called "midnight ramblers," you got that reputation whether or not you rambled at midnight. As long as we lived in my dad's house, our curfew time was nine-thirty. If we came in at ten, we had better be with an adult or have some pretty good excuse. When we started driving, we knew if we wanted to use the car again we needed to respect the family-imposed curfew. Later, when I had my own family, Mrs. Davis and I used to joke with my dad that our children never went out until nine-thirty or later! However, we, the children of John and Julia Davis, grew up hearing Dad say: "What you do in the dark will come to the light, so you might as well do what you are goin' to do during the daytime." In fact, Mom and Dad believed that anyone going about late at night was up to "no good" except when it was revival time, which took place after dark in the warm months of the year. During this season of renewal, each of the one-Sunday churches took their designated weeks for revival during July, August, and September. Everyone attended all of them, going to each other's churches. The whole summer was committed to revival, in fact. Those were special times when guest preachers were invited in and spirits were high. Non-believers ("sinners," they were called) were always seated on the front row, the mourners' bench.

Although the word *revival* suggests starting again, these revival meetings were really focused on those people who never started. Nonbelievers ofttimes came just for something to do. Others, still living in their parents' homes, were "drug" there. In fact, I was a "drugged" child! All of my siblings and I were "drug" to revival and wherever else Mom and Dad wanted to drag us. Revivals at Calvary and other churches in this new century are primarily to reinvigorate the already saved. A guest preacher comes and the best hymns are sung. In years gone by, people joined church and were baptized during revival season. Today, they come all along anytime.

When we got old enough to go off on our own, we tried our wings, of course. We stopped in juke joints and hung around people we ought not to have befriended. In my case, however, I quickly turned my back on them. In such places, people drank, smoked, and gambled. The atmosphere was always charged and fights broke out regularly. The music from the juke box went "Boompetty, boompety, boom," adding noise to the mayhem of the dark, smoke-filled room. I found nothing there for me. I made the same choice my father had, to stay away.

I am convinced that the manner in which I was reared contributed to my becoming the person I have become. Dad was certainly my chief role model and I took seriously his warning: "A guilty conscience is a person's own load." I have endeavored to the best of my ability to stay out from under it and move on.

48

Neighbors and Mutual Aid Societies

As early as I can remember, the Cooper land had four houses on it for my grandmother and her descendants. A few other houses in the area were occupied by non-family members. Mr. Caesar Glover and his wife lived in one. I remember that they always had a car. An automobile was a rarity in our community, which is why the fact that Mr. Glover had one stands out in my memory. My father and Mr. Caesar Glover were in fact the only two people in our immediate neighborhood who owned a vehicle. Cousin Horace Cooper, on the other hand, had a pickup. All three were called upon to transport people to town or the sick to places they needed to go. As a boy, I remember thinking that Dad's 1941 Chevrolet was huge. Of course, it was not, much less so once children piled in for a drive to Gough on Saturday or to visit friends and family on Sundays after church. Of my father's automobiles, I clearly remember only four: the Chevy, a 1949 Ford, a 1951 Mercury, and his first pickup, also a Chevrolet.

Another one of the houses adjoining the Cooper land was occupied by Mrs. Josie Evans, Mr. Glover's sister, who by the time I came along was a single mother of two adult children, Mr. Johnny Evans and Mrs. Sarah Harvey. All of us were like family to each other, sharing and sharing alike. What one family did not have, if the other did, it was shared. Some emergency needs, like sickness and death, were met through funds paid monthly by members into mutual aid societies. Others were covered by small insurance policies purchased locally. The Willing Workers' Penny Club was a mutual aid society where each family paid dues from one to 10 cents each month. The club always met at Mrs. Josie Evans' home. If someone was sick or there was a death among the club members, the family would receive flowers, a plant, a spray of greens, or a cash benefit, usually not exceeding $30.

My parents were members of a number of other societies. The UB and A was a secret order, now called Gough United. Bryant Grove, Walker Grove, and Junior Star were other mutual aid societies in the area. As I said, these societies, along with inexpensive insurance policies, were a hedge against bad times, one of our ways of helping cover costs if someone became seriously ill, or when someone died. Our family insurance policies were purchased from Pilgrim Insurance Company. As a reminder of the need to prepare for the future and when the subject of sickness or death came up, Mom or Dad ofttimes simply said: "I have a policy."

A number of my siblings and I are still members of some of the societies to which our parents belonged. One is the Junior Star Mutual Aid Society, based in Vidette, Georgia. Another is the Walker Grove Mutual Aid Society. We pay a few dollars into these each year to maintain a commitment honoring our parents and expressing loyalty to our heritage. I expect when I die, my wife will collect about a hundred dollars from Walker Grove Mutual Aid Society. She'll use it to pay for my funeral!

49

The Little Store

There had been two stores in Cooper's Town once. By the time I came up, I recalled only one, owned and operated by my mother's brother, Uncle Ben Cooper. Uncle Ben's store was situated in a small structure right beside my parents' house, the house where I was born. Constructed of wooden slats, it was perhaps 10 by 20 feet in size, had a tin top that was somewhat weather-worn and rusty, and a single window and door. It was a sort of convenience store, or so I thought. I remembered it as a place where people met, gossiped, bought small items, and where children bought treats. I remember Mom saying that it was more a pastime than a business. I can still to this day see myself as a little boy running in and out, as all that separated our house and the store was the wide dirt drive used by our animals on their way to the fields, to move our wagon out of the barn, and our automobile out of its shed. In fact, my recollections are so vivid and detailed that I was certain for years that I had been an active participant in the life of the little store. I remembered it as our first stop for everyday items. I remembered going there for snacks and candy, purchasing a five-cent bag of roasted peanuts and a bottle of soda pop. I remember even now the taste of pop and peanuts, as I liked to pour the peanuts into the pop and in this way eat and drink at the same time. I remember eating a Johnny Cake with a slice of bologna on top, purchasing a few pennies' worth of chocolate kisses or my favorite candy, a colorful Georgia specialty called Tropical Coconut Bar. It is just the same today as it was then—red on one side, yellow on the other, and white in the middle. It was also a favorite of my sister Daisy, by the way. Now, Daisy remembers Uncle Ben's store being called "the little store" and says that people could buy homegrown eggs there if they had no chickens of their own. Mom spoke of it as the Cooper's Town store. My oldest siblings (born starting around 1928) maintain that they do not remember this store at all. Willie Mae, Lula, Eunice, and Hildery all chuckled when I described it. They said, "Why, Reverend, you weren't even born then! But then a good preacher has to have imagination!" I agree, while clearly keeping in mind the fine line between a good imagination and childhood exaggeration. Mom, however, frequently told stories about her brother's store and it could be that I simply made her recollections my own. All the stuff Daisy and I remember getting from that store must have been gotten someplace else.

The physical structure that had indeed once housed Uncle Ben's little store existed until just a few years ago and was pulled down along with our old house. My father used it to store fertilizers, seed, and cotton by the croaker full. In fact, I can still see him at daybreak, backing up to the door of that shed, putting up the tin sides of our wagon, and packing in a bale of cotton to take to the gin. This memory, I know, is not a figment of my imagination!

50

ANDREW COOPER AND FAMILY

UNCLE ANDREW COOPER, another of Mom's brothers, was a brick mason by profession and a successful one at that. In fact, if you travel through Burke County today, you can still see houses, chimneys, barbecue pits, walls of now derelict structures that he built over the years. I can remember people pointing and saying, "Andrew Cooper built that." He obviously had a distinct style.

Uncle Andrew was ofttimes referred to as an "original," adventuresome and curious. It is said that he was always creating something, doing something that no one else dared to do. My mother told the story of how her brother, as a boy, built a flying machine before anyone had heard of the Wright bothers. It was a contraption with flapping wings, which he even tested one day. Taking it up to the top of a tall haystack, he had evidently called his mother and siblings to come watch him fly. Mom later said, "He nearly killed himself!" She was wistful when remembering her brother, even while chuckling about his antics.

Andrew Cooper had a wife and two children who were older than I as well as a grandson, Solomon Cooper, who was the age of my youngest sister, Daisy. He lived with his grandparents, in the next house down the road from us. Unlike the rest of us children, however, he seemed to have some money in his pockets pretty much all the time. Dad explained that Uncle Andrew could indulge his grandson because he had a "public job," a job off the farm, an income that did not depend on weather or crops. In fact, Cousin Solomon was the first of our generation to own his own car. Although we went to school together and played together, my parents were reluctant to let us hang around with Solomon outside family gatherings or off family property. The Davis children looked upon him with some awe as he had liberties we just did not have. He seemed to come and go pretty much as he pleased, always seemed to have a way to get to where he wanted to go, was not obligated to attend church, and could shoot marbles. Our parents considered playing with marbles a form of gambling, as you were out to win the other fellow's stash. We were forbidden, in fact, from playing anything that approximated a "game of chance." We "snuck" in a game of marbles now and then despite our parents' admonitions, but certainly never on Sunday!

Our cousin Solomon met a tragic end as a relatively young man. His wife and mother stepped in to bring up his children and eventually his grandchildren. This was not a time for playing games.

51

GAMES

As we were growing up, we had plenty to do and plenty of space to run around. We were never bored. We climbed trees and slid off the tin roof of the barn despite our parents' warnings and our mother's repeatedly expressed fear for our safety. We borrowed chains used to harness the mules, cobbled bits of discarded rope together to attach to the limbs of the pecan trees. Swinging full gate, when the chain or ropes broke, we sometimes went flying, coming down with a thud, cracking our heads on the hard ground. We ofttimes made tree houses and played in the leafy green haze between the limbs. Or, we sat in the shade of the trees—especially the pecans—ate watermelon, relaxed in the evening after chores, and watched nature take its course. We saw the ant trying to carry something twice its size—a twig or a peanut. Another ant and still another came to help. From the ants we learned a lesson in cooperation. From the birds we learned about freedom, daydreaming as we saw them soar. We watched the woodpecker peck a hole in a stump or a rotten trunk, making its home there. We observed the robin, the sparrow, the blue jay, the pigeon, and the dove build nests among the branches. Sometimes, we robbed a pigeon's nest and ate the eggs, however. So, we learned from observing nature, from living close to the earth, and certainly from Dad's stories, many of which revolved around animals. One I remember vividly had the moral that if you give folks enough rope when they are misbehaving, they will eventually hang themselves. Remember the story Dad told a jury about the woodpecker?

As children, we played all sorts of games. We used the metal rims from broken barrels. We pushed them along with sticks, pretending we were driving a car. Or we set up competitions to see who could keep his hoop balanced longest. We also rolled rubber tires, running and getting exercise. If our parents were gone, we "snuck" one of the mules out of the barn to go "sledding." Harnessing it to the flatbed sleigh (we called it sled) used to transport water in barrels when our open-faced well was dry, we went for a thrill ride across the fields. The barrels bumped and the water splashed. Keep in mind that for us, water was scarce and too precious to waste in playing. In winter our well had water, but in summer it was dry. We had to haul water for ourselves and our animals daily from someone else's well. In our community, whoever had water made it available to those who had none. Perhaps the scarcity of water was why we had a full bath only once a week. In any event, we were young and full of mischief and often would not think of the consequences of our actions. There was no way to hide the ruts we made in the fields. Our joy ride was likely to earn us a "talkin' to" and more likely we would be punished.

Since there were a number of us children growing up together, we had a lot of group games such as Ring Around the Rosies, singing "Ring around the rosies, pocket full of tosies," and "She'll be comin' round the mountain when she comes..." The girls particularly liked these games as well as jump rope games they played while singing other jingles. Hide and Go Seek was another favorite. It was one of the games that taught us important lessons in communication and cooperation. It was also a game that gave us opportunity to explore boy-girl things, when we could hide with the "right" person. I remember as a very young boy that when I could not find a place to hide, I stood stock still in the open and squeezed my eyes shut. I denied having been "found" when my brother Clarence, Cousin Solomon, sister Daisy Mae, or any other child grabbed me. I could not see them and hence insisted that they had not found me. We were creative, made up our own rules. And certainly, we stretched our imaginations.

Mom taught us other games intended to bring home a lesson. One of them was called Peanut Grabbing, meant to demonstrate the consequences of greed and the importance of sharing. She poured a row of peanuts on the ground or on a table. We hurried to grab as many as we could as soon as she gave the signal, discovering that the wider we stretched our arms trying to get every peanut within reach, the fewer we were able to grab. Other players got in between our outstretched arms before we had a chance to close in on the bounty. Mom was teaching us to set our goals realistically and not be greedy.

Mom also led us in a game she called "How a Blind Mule Eats Corn." One of the children playing was blindfolded. He or she searched for food, trying to locate the arm, leg, face, or head of another child who played the part of the food. When the child playing the part of the blind mule found food by moving around and feeling, it pinched the child who was the food and "ate" it. This game was intended as a lesson about pain and triumph, about adversity and limitations, about how you can compensate. We learned that by being patient, by persevering, by enduring, we could reach our goal and overcome our limitations. This game continues to come to mind when facing the devastation of my trials by fire.

52

MONEY

AFRICAN AMERICAN FARMERS were people who did not have access to money of any kind on a regular basis. However, growing up, I never thought of our family as being poor, for we always had shelter and plenty to eat. Yet, I can seldom recall my father having more than a few dollars in his pocket at one time, certainly never hundreds of dollars! If my father needed to get seed or fertilizer, he went into town to the general store and said "Charge it" and the merchant would put it on the books, or "take it up," as we called it. That was true of food as well. Business was transacted on the honor system. Interestingly, when Dad had money to cancel his debts (normally after harvest and the sale of his crops), he never got an itemized bill, but simply paid what he was told. Honesty was one of the values Mom and Dad emphasized, though they may not have been treated the same.

My parents did not believe in banks, having come through the hard times of the great financial crash and depression. Whatever they had, they kept at home. In fact, if we children wanted a nickel or a dime for a soda or a snack, we learned to ask our mother. From time to time, she had a little extra to give us. Dad paid the large bills and kept a little money tied in a handkerchief somewhere known only to himself. The rest he gave to Mother. He considered it her due as our farm came to us through her side of the family. She could do with it whatever she wanted. In many cases she kept it on her person, often in her bra.

My parents gave our church the earnings from the sale of their first harvested crops, their first bale of cotton, their first bushel of wheat or corn, as they believed in the Biblical principle of the "first fruits" as indicated in Proverbs 3, verse 9: "Honor the Lord with thy substance, and with the first fruits of all thine increase: So shall thy barns be filled with plenty and thy presses shall burst out with new wines." In fact, we learned that you cannot hold on to God's money as it does not belong to you. People here at Calvary have been heard to state the same principle when they said, "I didn't give as I ought, and the car broke down, or Junior got sick, or I lost my wallet…"

The churches in our communities literally depended on "first fruit givers" and were most prosperous in August, September, and October—harvest season. The rest of the year people gave as they could. Most often it was change and never more than a dollar.

My experience regarding money was not much different from that of my older siblings, to hear them tell it. If we, the second crop of Davis children, asked Dad for a coin to buy a treat, he could justifiably answer, "I don't have any money to give you," since he kept no money. However, on Saturdays whatever work we did for our father in the morning, he paid us for. Saturday we worked half-day. If we picked 100 pounds of cotton that morning, Dad paid us the going rate, say, two cents a pound. We then had money to spend in Gough or Waynesboro on Saturday afternoon. Annie Mae and Joe were the big cotton-pickers, ofttimes scoring 100-plus pounds a day. I could never seem to catch up to them and that is one of the reasons I left the farm for higher education.

Mom used to laugh when telling the story of a trip to Gough with their first crop of children. My oldest brother was then the only boy. Something spooked the mules and they bolted, overturning the wagon. Everyone was concerned about who might be hurt except my brother Hildery, who could only think to ask: "Where's Mama's pocketbook? Where's Mama's pocketbook?" She had promised him a nickel when they got into town.

While Mother was famous for having some money tucked away inside her bra or pocketbook, we knew she had another, personal stash. This money she kept hidden for those times when the spirit moved her to travel. And indeed, Mom was a traveler! She would say to Dad, whom she always referred to as H: "H, I want to go to New Jersey, to Florida, to Washington, D.C." His reply was always the same: "It's alright with me, J, if you got some money." Mom was always sure she had enough to get on the bus or the train to go where she wanted. She never worried about how she would get back, but she always did!

53

LET YOUR WORD BE YOUR BOND

WE DID NOT HAVE TELEPHONES WHEN I WAS GROWING UP. We communicated by letter with those who were far away. In fact, my mother made a habit of writing to her family once a week. Her letters always started: "Dear Brother Noah," or "Dear Daughter Eunice," then, "We are fine and hope you are the same..." There was invariably a line or two about what was happening with the family, Dad's health, the crops, some news of the community, possibly a request for opportunities for children still at home. She always concluded: "God bless you. Yours truly, your sister Julia" or "God bless you. Yours truly, Mother."

As we got older, Mom encouraged us to write these letters, dictating to us. "Come," she would say, "I need to send a letter to your aunt...to your sister...to your brother..." Most of the time, we wrote exactly what she said, sometimes adding a word here or there, but we were careful as she checked the letters before sending them. We were also called upon to read the ones she received.

Mom and Dad taught us by example, through word, and by letting us "do." Thus, to learn to write letters, we wrote them, at the same time learning about the importance of family solidarity. To learn about church, we went. To learn about honesty, we practiced it. We also heard about it: "If a person will steal, he will lie."

Even though they maintained that there was no guidebook to raising children, my parents' approach depended on the Biblical model, on their common sense, and on the dream they nurtured that their children would go on to do better than they did. They certainly made their share of mistakes, but their approach was far from haphazard.

Dad might say, "Come, let's repair this fence." We took all day to do the job he could have done in an hour, doing, redoing, undoing and doing again, hearing him say, "If at first you don't succeed, try and try again." If we were instructed to plow and made a snaking swatch in the field, he encouraged us to keep trying. Everything we did was meant to help us aim higher, be the best we could be. Saying things like, "If a task is first begun, never quit until it's done" or "Be the labor great or small, do it well or not at all," Dad encouraged us until we got it right. And he spent time with us.

"He who says it can't be done is he who never tries" was another of his favorite sayings. When we tried, he acknowledged our effort, all the while teaching us steadfastness, perseverance, the value of hard work, keeping your word, and controlling your tongue.

"If you won't work, you will steal," he would say. Or, "Let your word be your bond." "Actions speak louder than words," both he and Mother would remind us. Or, "Don't let your mouth overload your behind." These were sayings they used, almost like flash cards. Dad lived by proverbs and stories!

We learned about the facts of life by observing, although my brother Hildery did take me aside as I became a teenager and taught me some of what he thought a boy should know. Mom and Dad did not talk about sex. However, Dad took us with him when he would breed his animals and when they gave birth to their young. We also watched the hens lay eggs, the roosters do their part, chicks hatch and grow. In fact, there was nothing happening on the farm that we were not allowed to watch and experience. "Experience is not the only, but the best teacher," he reminded his children. Dad was a philosopher!

My parents believed that the way out of the predicament of being African American in the days of "separate but equal" was by getting an education. And education, as they understood it, consisted of what they called "book learning," but was also part experience, part good sense, and part spiritual growth. Dad used to say, "Get something between your ears and under your hat." Mom would add, "Empty wagons make a lot of noise."

Despite their own limitations, at great sacrifice, and armed with unusual wisdom and good sense, our parents set down a foundation that prepared their children for a world beyond their rural roots and black community. To that end, they taught us that effective communication and control were essential tools for survival first, and for advancement second. Dad was ofttimes heard saying, sternly, "Control yourself!" W. E. B. DuBois explained very effectively that African Americans have to figure out how to live in two worlds, learning to say one thing in one community, refraining from doing so in another. Even though Dad had minimal book learning, he was a master at the skills of survival. He made a point of passing them on. I remember him saying, "Bend the twig, or break the tree." While flexibility was a strategy for survival, however, he stressed that one must know oneself, be oneself, and be true to oneself. In fact, another of his favorite sayings, which I'll mention again, was, "Be what you is and not what you ain't 'cause if you ain't what you is, you is what you ain't." My favorite quote!

We were taught early that control was developed in part by knowing who you were, and also by thinking things through before acting. It was a key in the survival equation. Mom used to say, "God gave us two ears and one mouth. Listen twice as much as you speak." Our elders drilled into us that to lose control of your emotions to a degree where you are willing to lash out with your tongue or to physically destroy something or someone was a sign that your education was not complete. I learned the hard way and often remind our congregation, "When you lose your cool, you lose the game." That is to say, "Let not the sun go down upon your wrath" (Ephesians chapter 4, verse 26). We were also encouraged to safeguard one another's reputations. Dad said, "If you dig one ditch for another, dig two." To hate was another sign of losing control. Dr. Martin Luther King Jr. said it best: "Let no man pull you so low that you hate him."

Young people today ask me, "What can I do to make this world a better place?" I give them two recommendations: Learn as much as you can about yourself so that you know what your tendencies are, what your behavior is like, what your heritage is, where the lines are drawn. Then, once you have a good grasp of self, learn about others who are different from you. When you put the two together then life can be thrilling albeit controlled, whole.

54

Aunt Rena, Folklore, and Home Remedies

When my mother took her long trips, my father invariably invited one of his sisters to stay with us and help out. Aunt Rena McFadden arrived dressed, as always, in double of everything. She wore a hat and a scarf on top of it; she wore two tops; two skirts…Everything was in twos, and even her handbag had two visible pockets. As she had no children of her own, she was the auntie most often called upon.

Aunt Rena was superstitious and used old wives' tales to keep us children in line as well as entertained. She had dramatic flair when she told stories and her repeated warnings reflected folk beliefs that came down through time and from another place. She guided our behavior and left a lasting sense of heritage and creativity. She would tell my sisters that if the hems of their dresses were turned up, they would catch a butterfly. The color of the wings would indicate the color of a new dress they would get. If you named the four corners of your bedroom after people you loved, the name that came to you in your dreams would be the one you would marry. Or, if you swept the feet of one you loved with a broom, they would become your intended. To this day, I remember her also warning: "Don't you carry that broom over your shoulder now, chial, it's bad luck." Or, "Don't you be walking backward in this house, now, it's bad luck." And again, "Stop sweeping that dirt outa hea, you be sweeping blessings from this house!" She frightened us with the consequences of using each other's cups to drink, and worse yet, the dipper. Might she have instinctively known something about passing germs around that we are still trying to figure out today?

Aunt Rena told the story of Brer Fox and Brer Rabbit. I can still hear her high-pitched voice twanging as she began: "Brer Fox was chasing Brer Rabbit. Brer Rabbit jumped into an empty bucket above an open-faced well and disappeared right out of sight. Brer Fox caught up with him and asked: 'How d' you get down thea?' The rabbit said, 'You see that bucket up thea? Just hop in and come on down!' Brer Fox took a leaping jump into the bucket and sailed on down. Halfway down, though, he met Brer Rabbit on his way up, who said, as they passed each other: 'That's the way the world goes, Brer Fox! That's the way the world goes! Some go up and some go down!'" Isn't that the truth? I sat mesmerized when she spun tales, creating unforgettable images.

Without ever laying a hand on us, Aunt Rena got us to behave. She warned against walking under a ladder, letting a black cat cross our path, opening an umbrella inside the house. She said that if you put your hand on your head with the fingers joined you were praying for your father to die; if you buried certain things in the yard or threw dishwater out of a window, someone could work their magic against you. She certainly kept control over a gaggle of sometimes unruly children and literally had us under her spell!

As I grew up, I carefully considered these tales and superstitions, weighing their merits as they were frequently taken to extremes. Many of the people I grew up with believed in magic and practiced witchcraft. Aunt Rena talked about "putting the fix" on someone (the "mojo"), a way of getting even (the "jemma"), getting back at someone, causing them to have bad luck.

Many years later, when Dad was diagnosed with terminal cancer, I went to bring him to Salt Lake City to live with my family. There were coins in every window of my Aunt Eva's house where he had been living. These were intended to reverse the evil that brought about his illness. Coins placed on window sills were also thought to bring good luck. Aunt Eva, like Aunt Rena, also called in the "spiritualists" and the "root workers," whose business it was to administer a variety of concoctions to cure some illness or keep away bad luck. They created poultices to apply to ailing parts of the body to bring down swelling, compresses to draw out pus, and all kinds of remedies to bring relief. They used salt peter, turpentine, plants collected in the woods that were cooked, steeped in alcohol, or infused with hot water, to be drunk or inhaled. While some of these might have been helpful with minor injuries, none had any effect on the cancer from which Dad suffered.

One of the infusions I remember from the time of my childhood was "cow chip tea." Mom made it with cow dung that had been dried, then steeped in boiling water. The steam was inhaled to unstop a stuffy nose.

Another cure for the common cold was a few drops of kerosene mixed with sugar and placed beneath the tongue. This was usually given to children. We were also bathed, our bodies rubbed with tallow (the fat from cows), and we were sent to bed, buried under quilts to sweat it out. Once, when I stepped on a nail in the yard, Dad wrapped a piece of fat pork meat in a cloth and tied this poultice to my foot, saying it would draw out the poison. Indeed, a few days later the swelling in my foot went down and it began to heal, leaving no scar where the puncture wound had been. Of course, Dad was always ready with warmed castor oil, Black Drought syrup, or Three Sixes, all used to ward off colds and chills. These were most frequently purchased from the Watkins man or the Watkins woman who peddled remedies door to door. I am reminded of Psalm 133, verse 1, which speaks of brethren dwelling together like the ointment that runs down on the head, pleasant and good. Castor oil may have been good for us, but it was far from pleasant!

Until I was out of my father's home, until I went to college, I never once saw a medical doctor for a check-up or when I was sick. I was born at home, my mother having been assisted by a midwife, not a medical doctor. Any ailment or childhood disease was addressed at home, treated with a number of the home remedies and medicines I just mentioned, which my parents had come to depend upon. We made do and never expected any other treatments.

I believe medicine is one of the signs of a cultured place. It should be dispensed liberally and without regard to race or creed. It is one of the measures of whether a people or a place is "civilized." Certainly, for African Americans in the time I was a boy, there was little medical care, even fewer, if any, preventative or palliative measures offered to us by the medical professions, be it doctors or dentists. Even today, scores of African Americans of my generation and older have no teeth as a result of dentists doing nothing but extracting teeth. In many ways, you could say that in the rural Georgia of my youth, there was not a whole lot of civilization in that respect.

55

MEDICAL CARE

MY UNCLE ANDREW COOPER, I AM TOLD, WAS A BELIEVER IN MAGIC. His beliefs did not set him apart, however, nor were they the reason why members of our community called him an "original." Rather, it was probably because he was not understood. Some of what he did was chalked up to eccentricity. However, as an old man (sometime in the 1950s), he is reputed to have literally taken leave of his senses—he lost his mind along with his sense of person.

When Uncle Andrew was one day found standing naked in the middle of the road, his family tied him to his bed to keep him from harming himself. He was a strong man, popped the plow lines, and escaped. Four or five men were summoned to get him out of the road, but could no more budge him than move an oak tree until a noisy tractor literally startled him into submission. When they caught him, the family hauled him off to the Milligeville Insane Asylum and committed him. He remained there for the rest of his life, warehoused as it were. I am told that from time to time the adults of the family visited him until he finally died. Once committed, he never again came home.

As for regular medical care, doctors did not treat African Americans, as I mentioned earlier. Dentists only extracted our teeth, never filling them, cleaning them, or giving us any instruction in oral hygiene. Again, as I was growing up, these doctors and dentists were by and large members of the dominant race. In fact, it was not until I had left home that an African American doctor moved into our community and began to provide preventative care and treatment for the young and old. I still remember my dad bragging about his skills and bedside manner.

If you had a problem at that time, your first line of defense, as I mentioned earlier, was home remedies. Second line of defense was to take the advice of the root workers. And thirdly, if you were an adult or an elder, you went to see the doctor if you could. My parents went from time to time, which meant driving 13 or 14 miles to get there. By and large, however, they learned to diagnose pretty accurately, treating their children for flu, croup, whatever childhood diseases came up. As to the doctor in Waynesboro, he scheduled appointments for members of our community only twice a week, all at nine o'clock in the morning. African Americans waited in a room set apart, sometimes all day. In fact, they knew to pack their lunch. At best they saw the doctor in the afternoon, though often they never made it in to see him at all. I believe that is one of the reasons my daddy may have been reluctant to go to the doctor. Perhaps his eventually refusing to go at all slowed down his recovery from a serious illness the year I was born. Mom told me that he had to stay in bed, unable to work for an entire growing season and when harvest time came as well. The neighbors chipped in to keep the farm going. They were a community of sharers.

56

Peddlers and Storekeepers

As I was growing up, there was a bus called the "Blue Goose" that traveled up and down our country roads, stopping in Cooper's Town. We waited for candy and soda pop when this rolling store came by. It also had food items, snacks, notions, soaps, candles, and a limited selection of medical supplies. It came by faithfully each week just as the insurance man and the ice man came. Much of the time these three were the only regular visitors other than nearby neighbors and family. What we did not buy in town, we bought from the "Blue Goose" or from the Watkins man or the Watkins woman who peddled liniments, droughts, ointments and oils, folk and other remedies, door to door.

The Blue Goose and the Watkins team provided us with some of the necessities we did not grow, raise, hunt, or gather. However, when we needed gasoline, farm equipment, or certain food items, we got them in Gough or Waynesboro, driving there on Saturday afternoons after our work was done. Waynesboro was where we went primarily for yearly supplies, as well as shoes and clothing.

The post office and general store that serviced our community was located in Gough, Georgia, three miles from Cooper's Town. The postmaster was also the storekeeper. Like most storekeepers and business owners in Gough, he was Caucasian American. Only a small number of African Americans had businesses in the area. They included two stores in Gough and a mortuary as well as several juke joints where people went to drink, dance, and carouse. These nightspots often had a little establishment attached that operated somewhat like a convenience store, selling tobacco, soda pop, and snacks. The smaller of the stores was owned by Mr. Melvin Evans. Mr. Homer Smith owned the other as well as one of the nightspots. Both men drove school buses during the day. Mr. Evans was active in his church (a deacon), and a member of the Masons. He had the reputation of being a good family man. Mr. Smith was better known as a business man, owning a fairly large farm outside of Gough. He always drove the newest car and pickup and lived in the best house in town. I remember his home as being large, painted white, and about a block from his store. When I was a senior in high school, I used to take his place driving the school bus if other duties called him away. Both men were very friendly and had a love for children. Dad always did business with these establishments when he had cash and they had what he wanted. By and large, however, what these stores offered was limited.

With the exception of these few African American-owned businesses, Caucasian Americans owned and operated the bank, the filling station, the lumber mill, the cotton gins, and the grocery stores. They also owned the clothing and furniture stores used by blacks and whites. Whatever we needed to buy, we mostly bought from "white-owned" businesses, usually on credit, no money ever passing hands until after harvest when my father sold his crops and announced, "I'm going to get my word," or "I'm going to get my name."

My father's reputation meant everything to him. He would say, "My word is my bond," or "You have to match your walk to your talk." He pointed out to his children that a good reputation opens doors that neither money nor power can budge and invariably illustrated his point through stories and certainly by example. I never knew him to fail on a debt or a promise, teaching my brothers and sisters and me that if we had nothing else, we wanted to have a good name. "A good name is more precious than silver and gold," he said, quoting from Proverbs.

When all was said and done, however, Dad's good name did not deter white merchants or shopkeepers with whom he did business from addressing Deacon Davis as John, nor did it give him license to park his car or the wagon on the main street. He parked behind the store, behind the bank, in the "backyard." These were still the days of the "separate, but equal" doctrine established in 1896 by the Plessy vs. Ferguson case. Although it was overturned by Brown vs. Board of Education in 1954, it remained very much a reality in our daily lives and interactions for years to come.

Years earlier, crossing certain lines could mean death. Mom once told the story of a great aunt who refused to step off the sidewalk to make way for a white woman coming in the other direction. That evening the Klansmen called, presumably to give her a whipping and remind her of her place. When her husband came to her defense, the Klansmen dragged him off to the local African American church, locked him inside, and set the building on fire. The church burned to the ground and he went down with it. Mom also told us how when she was a little girl, the Klansmen came after my grandfather, July Cooper. While they waited on the porch for him to come home, her mother whispered to one of the children to slip out the back door, meet him up the road, and give him the message to stay away. As she had 16 children, one was not missed and grandfather's life was saved. Mother chuckled when recounting her own mother's presence of mind, but I can only imagine all of their terror at that time!

When I came home the summer after my first year at Tuskegee, I was all fired up by the civil rights movement. I was tired of hearing my dad and mom called by their first names. I was tired of hearing grown men called "boy." I was determined that I would no longer allow myself to be addressed in this way because of the color of my skin. A fire burned in me to work to change being considered "less than." One day, having borrowed Dad's car to drive into Gough, I went to the gasoline station. The owner came out and asked, "Boy, what d'ya want?" I shot from the hip: "Nothing, John," I said, using his first name with no title. I had crossed a line. He ran back into the station and came out with his gun. I knew enough to drive off in a hurry!

Had my parents found out what I had done, they would have reprimanded me and attempted to made amends, all the while making sure I was sent as far away from danger as possible. In fact, it was not uncommon for African American families at that time to ship north children or family members of any age should they ever be labeled "uppity." Many who found themselves in danger and facing death had to crawl their way out of sight, hop the rails, leave town by any means they could find. Next time they were heard from they might be living in D.C., New Jersey, New York, or some other place where that "attitude" would not be the sentence of certain death.

57

GOLDBERG'S

ONCE A YEAR, AFTER THE COTTON HARVEST, when the crops were sold and my father had paid his grocery bills and covered his farming expenses, my parents took the children into Waynesboro, to Goldberg's, to be outfitted for the year. That was an exciting trip because we got new clothes and also could look forward to a treat after our shopping expedition. That treat was a fried fish sandwich on white bread, something like Wonder Bread. We called it "light bread." We picked out our own fish, the storekeeper cleaned it, dipped it in meal, and dropped it in hot oil. We ate it, hot and crispy, between two slices of that store-bought bread that we thought was the best thing this side of heaven. In fact, one Saturday, I was so hungry that I ate it too hurriedly and got a bone stuck in my throat. My parents tried to dislodge it, but nothing worked until Dad literally put his hand down my throat and pulled it out. Mom rebuked me for eating without first checking the fish for bones.

Goldberg's department store sold furniture and clothing. Mr. Goldberg was of Jewish American descent. A jovial, round-faced, balding man, he was short and spry, always well dressed. I don't recollect ever seeing him wearing a tie, however. Mr. Goldberg always greeted Dad with these words: "Bring those boys in hea now, John, and lets get 'em somethin' to wayah!" It seemed to me at the time that Mr. Goldberg carried summer suits in winter and winter suits in summer, last year's models as it were. It could be, however, that my parents bought winter clothes in summer and summer clothes in winter, on sale, to help make ends meet. It was surely another way of "making do."

At Goldberg's you could buy work clothes, the sort farmers wore; boots (Brogans to be exact), which we wore to work or to school if we wore shoes at all; jeans; bib overalls with two pockets in front and two in back, with a patch pocket across the chest where old men stashed tobacco and matches, children their little treasures or candy. Mom and Dad always tried to buy us something we could wear to church as well. For the girls it might be a fancy dress, white socks, dress shoes, hair ribbons, and a hat. For the boys it was suits, white shirts, sometimes a bow tie, a pair of loafers or low-cut string shoes. My father measured our feet, carried pieces of string to reflect his measurements, and did his utmost to get us shoes or boots that fit. Ofttimes, however, they were long enough but too narrow. On one occasion, when I was in high school, pointed dress shoes were in style and everybody wanted them. Of course, I wanted a pair, too. What I did not realize at the time was that you had to buy them a size bigger than you would normally wear. Today, my toes are stacked thanks to those narrow, pointed shoes I insisted my father get for me at Goldberg's, trying to be in style.

When shopping for clothes or shoes, one of the difficulties we faced was that we could not go into a fitting room or try anything on; not clothes, certainly not shoes. If by chance you did slip your feet into a pair of shoes only to discover they did not fit, you had to buy them. If you bought them without trying them on and they did not fit, you wore them anyway. When I was growing up, and certainly for years before, that was an unwritten rule applied to and understood by African Americans. It would be years before this rule melted into the shadows. The scars remain and my stacked toes are the evidence.

58

COMPANY

My family lived at the southernmost part of Cooper's Town and our house was beside a dirt road with two ruts running the length of it, the work of buggies and cars going back and forth year after year. When it rained this road was muddy, slushy. When it was dry, it was dusty. Either way the soil was sandy and avoiding getting stuck when driving this road took some experience. The road was also a winding road, snaking between the four houses occupied by our families, then branching into a spur that led to the family graveyard. When we would be going to the society meeting at Mrs. Josie Evans' house on a Thursday night, we always had to pass that graveyard. Having learned about "haints" (ghosts), we were always afraid as we went by. My father would take us by the hand and everything would be alright.

We always knew before they arrived when company was coming by a telltale cloud of dust in the distance, rising off that two-rut road. Ofttimes, we had just enough time to sweep the porch, set up chairs, make whatever preparations were needed to welcome friends or family. Mom would say, "Company's a comin' and you're all expected to be on your best behavior." If a child misbehaved, Mom did not wait for guests to leave to show her displeasure. At best, she "looked" you into your right place, narrowing her eyes, lifting an eyebrow, displaying a frown. If we did not read her face, we then experienced her hand and heard her declare, "A hard head makes for a soft behind!"

Lots of things were considered "misbehavior." One was to listen in on conversations between adults without being invited to do so. If we lingered, someone said, "Grown folk are talkin' in here. Go play!" To fight or argue with siblings, especially when guests were present, was another. To make extraneous noise while our elders were socializing was likely to draw the ire, the looks, and result in punishment if we did not promptly mend our ways. The rules were clear, as were the consequences. One of the house rules was "no singing at the table." When we gathered for meals, we were encouraged to converse. We talked about family matters. We talked about school, church, guests who were expected to visit. We talked about work to be done in the fields. It was around the family table, while we ate, that we had the greatest conversations and talked in the greatest of detail about everything.

We seldom used the front porch unless we had guests. Adults sat on the rocking chairs or the porch swing, and children sat on the steps when permission was given for them to stay. If subjects of conversation were not "suitable" for children's ears (talk of someone getting pregnant out of wedlock, for example) we were told to go play. There were lots of things adults did not talk to young people about. If we were inquisitive, they might say, "When you get old enough we'll talk to you about that..." Or, "One of these days we'll tell you about that..." However, even among themselves, adults I grew up around rarely talked about sex, childbirth, or unusual relationships. Conversation usually revolved around children, community and church, health, crops, the weather.

"God Bless this House," painted in big, white letters on a wall near the front door was the first thing visitors saw when stepping onto our porch. The message was like a protective amulet as well as a way of conveying to all that ours was a God-centered home. It was also the only paint anywhere on the house. This fact was significant because in those days, in rural Georgia, paint was one way to distinguish the houses of African Americans from those of white folks. Theirs were painted. Ours were not. As a matter of fact, when people from our community improved their lot they often left behind those unpainted houses, building block or brick homes that were painted. It was their way perhaps of shedding a mantle of pain, a way to indicate they were moving on, moving up.

My mother claimed she could sense guests were on their way by an itch on the side of her nose. In fact, she said that if her left nostril itched, a woman was coming. If it was the right, the visitor would be a man. Of course both sides itching meant mixed company. My mother, as I said, always had a room ready for visitors who came from a distance, often one or more of her 15 siblings. I don't recollect ever spending more than a few minutes in what we called the "front room." Certainly, none of us slept there. It was reserved as a guest room.

Though my mother has been dead many years now, I still hear her relatives talk about visiting Aunt Julia's house, or spending time with Cousin

Julia. John and Julia Davis' house was a kind of center in the Cooper's Town community, a gathering place. They genuinely felt that "the time of day is due to everybody." Visitors, if they made it there, were sure of a warm welcome, a comfortable bed, and a good meal. They knew their needs would be met.

God had blessed this house.

59

BE STILL, GOD IS AT WORK

THE HOUSE WE LIVED IN WAS L-SHAPED, made of wood, of boards that were weather worn. It was mounted on pillars about 18 inches off the ground. The crawl space under the house was sandy, a good place to play, a good place for the dogs and chickens to shelter from rain and intense summer heat. The dogs, in fact, bedded down there year-round. We had no locks on our doors, but wooden bars kept the house more or less secure. The back door had a latch with a string threaded through a rough-hewn hole; when pulled, it released the door. If no one was home, we pushed that string inside. To unlatch the door when we came home, we worked the string back up with a knife. We had no glass in the windows, but wooden shutters that gave us some privacy and protection, though not from bugs, rodents, and other small creatures who made themselves quite at home in every part of the house. We slept on mattresses piled high to avoid them and had to get to bed by climbing up on a chair or a stool. On stormy nights, when it thundered and lightning streaked across the heavens, my parents said, "Be still, God is at work." At such times we were told to stop whatever it was we were doing, sit quietly, or go to bed. I was glad to do so as the storms ofttimes frightened me when I was a little boy. I remember snuggling beneath the quilts with my brothers and listening to the rain on the tin roof above our heads. Eventually, its melody lulled me to sleep. Mom and Dad had a healthy awe for the workings of God in nature!

As I grew older, I came to truly appreciate the storms and all of the sounds around us. In the country, you could listen to the silence, clearly hear the song of the cricket, the bird, the frog, the rooster calling us to rise, the music of the rain and the clapping of the thunder. I came to understand that all these were some of God's many voices, speaking through his creations. I listened and felt his almighty power.

For ministry, of course, silence is a primary tool for meditation, for thought, and for creative imagination. When one spends time in silent prayer, in preparation for a sermon, for example, those are times when great power seems to come forth, subsequently reflected in the speaking part of ministry. Meditation itself is a way of focusing inward, turning to one's inner strength, finding the strength from within to do what needs to be done. In the country we likened it to a cow chewing its cud. Years later, as I studied the Scriptures, I reflected on a story in First Kings 19, verses 11 and 12. It talks about how God was a still, small voice: "And behold, the Lord passed by, and a great and strong wind rent the mountains and brake in pieces the rocks before the Lord: But the Lord was not in the wind; and after the wind an earthquake: but the Lord was not in the earthquake: and after the earthquake a fire; but the Lord was not in the fire: and after the fire a still small voice." Dr. Howard Thurman related the following story. He was asked to say a prayer at the bedside of a dying man. He struggled, searching for words, finally uttering, "Amen!" The man whispered, "That's the greatest prayer." Moments later he closed his eyes and died. Out of the silence, out of the hush of the hour, Dr. Thurman said that he was able to sense God's workings in his life.

"Hush, hush, somebody's calling my name…" For me, this spiritual conveys the essence of that still, small voice, silence's overtone, if you will.

O Lord my God,
when I in awesome wonder
consider all the worlds Thy hands have made,
I see the stars, I hear the rolling thunder,
Thy power throughout the universe displayed.
Then sings my soul, my Savior God, to thee…

Listening to the silence, listening for God's voice in the thunder, in the song of the rain, one can hear the call of one's life. And one is able to respond. Perhaps in urging us to be still when "God is at work," my parents taught a first lesson in being attentive, in listening to what it is that is speaking from within, and from within, having stilled our hearts, then sing His praises.

60

Medicine for the Soul

Music held an important place in our lives. Music was a means to communicate and also to deal with life's issues. Certainly, it kept despair from our door.

Dr. Howard Thurman said, "The songs my parents sang came from their faith, from their book (the Bible), from their experiences…, and from nature." I doubt that my parents thought of their songs in terms of categories, but they sang about the "green trees a tremblin', the lightnin' a flashin'…" They sang "Nobody knows the trouble I seen…" They sang lines from the Scriptures: "A charge to keep I have, God to glorify…" Raising their voices to express their faith, they sang "My hope is built on nothing less than Jesus' blood and righteousness…" They sang with fervor, with feeling, with power, their voices at their best, designed to invite others to join in even if they did not know what a song was about. Their music was inclusive. They sang to keep cadence while working in the fields, while doing chores, to alleviate drudgery. They sang when alone to cradle an aching heart or to express jubilation. They sang…

On Sundays, after we moved to the block house, Mom and Dad sometimes listened to church music on the radio, a Philco from Sears, one with two or three flat knobs. As a family, we also listened to sports events. The radio was a means of keeping up with Jackie Robinson, a way of knowing about the great boxers, a way to listen to the fights. Sometimes, we listened to "Amos and Andy." By and large, the radio was our contact with a world beyond the farm and Burke County. It was a center of attraction around which people gathered, however, only after chores were completed, homework done, responsibilities met. Listening to the radio (unlike watching television) required us to use our imaginations to make sense of a lot of what we heard, what was going on. The Bible says, "Where there's no vision, the people perish." The radio entertained us. It also gave us a chance to look beyond what was on the surface, imagine possibilities, dream. On our phonograph we played old 78 and 45 rpm records of comedy routines, sermons, and gospel music. I never heard my parents listen to anything else, certainly not the blues! When I asked about this, they said, "Son, what you feed your mind is what you become!" However, when television came along, Mom's favorite program was the Lawrence Welk Show. She watched it religiously on Saturday nights. I can still remember the words of the theme song: "You go to your church and I'll go to mine." I wonder if Mom gave any thought to the meaning. I never asked her.

Mom and Dad sang without notes or words on a page, the choice of song often reflecting their moods. They sang from Psalms: "The Lord is my fortress, the Lord is my strength…" They sang one way when happy, another when sad, another when the spirit caught them in its whirling embrace. A particular song signaled a particular kind of feeling, place, circumstance, situation that one would find oneself in. Ofttimes, coming home from school and from the fields, we heard our mother singing. Even from a distance, we could tell the "temperature" of the house by the song wafting out to meet us. If things were not going well, Mother might be singing, "Nobody knows the trouble I see, nobody knows but Jesus and me…" If, on the other hand, she was cheerful and things were going well, we heard her singing "Amazing Grace" or "Swing Low Sweet Chariot." These songs were signals to come in quiet as a cloud, or swing into the house full gate. Indeed, music was a way of dealing with many of the less desirable curves life threw in our direction as we were growing up.

Everybody had a song they were known for even if they couldn't carry a tune. Mom was known for "Be Ready When He Comes." Folks at church and in the community knew it as "Miss Julia's song." She sang it with a little tingle in her voice, the sincerity of her feelings shining through. Dad, on the other hand, was a metered hymn singer. "Come Ye that Love the Lord" was one he sang. Deacon Davis' signature song, however, went, "Father I stretch my hands to Thee no other help I know. If Thou withdraw Thyself from me, oh whither shall I go?" He sang this hymn with a depth of feeling that brought tears to every eye.

Of course, there was always music at church, uplifting singing. We heard it as we walked up the road on our way to prayer meeting on Sundays. We heard those who had arrived before us, singing and praising the Lord. Our pulses would quicken, our hearts would flutter, and we pressed on, eager to join in. Many of the Negro spirituals we sang talked about where you are and where you are going: "We are climbing Jacob's ladder,

we are climbing Jacob's ladder....Every round goes higher and higher..."
We felt propelled up the "rounds," the steps of this ladder from the Book
of Genesis, a ladder resting on earth, stretching up to heaven. This was a
song about the values of starting where you are and dreaming to move on
up a little higher.

We also sang in call and response, a pattern familiar in the African
American tradition, when one person calls and the background responds.
The call: "Swing loooow sweeeet chaaaariooot." The response: "Cooooom-
ing for to caaaarryyyy me hoooome."

The response, also called the background, plays just as important a
role in choir singing as the solo, the lead. One without the other leaves the
spirit of the song incomplete. When I first sang in a choir—in Fort Lauderdale, Florida, then in Boise, Idaho, and Oakland, California—I had a
great time backing others up. I learned the value of being in the background in singing, echoing the leader. My choice of songs was primarily
based on what they reflected of my experience. In fact, I refused to sing
"Jordan River" in those early days because one verse says, "My mother is
dead and gone..." It had no relevance to me at the time. I could sing it
today. Back then, however, I mostly searched out songs of hope such as
"This Little Light of Mine." The words gave me a lift, bolstered up my
courage: "This little light of mine, I'm gonna let it shine, let it shine, let it
shine, let it shine." I also sang "Shine on me, let the light from the light
house shine on me..." or "Will the circle be unbroken...," songs that
strengthened my faith and mirrored my life experience in the light of my
belief in God and Jesus Christ as my Savior.

Early in my life I learned to sing "What a Friend We Have in Jesus" in
a metered style. That metered style is a way to sing and be of one accord
without the accompaniment of the musical instrument. The tune was set
by the leader and everybody else followed. As I traveled about, became a
teenager, then an adult, going from church to church, I was often requested
to sing it: "What a friend we have in Jesus, all our sins and griefs to bear.
What a privilege to carry everything to God in prayer." That was my song
growing up. It was an irregular meter. Now, my songs are "Amazing Grace"
and "Precious Lord." Both speak of my trust and dependence on God.
They move the heart.

So, music and songs...They make a difference in terms of who we are,
helping us to define our sense of person, anchoring our faith, giving breath
to our dreams.

The folks I grew up with sang from memory. We learned songs by rote, through repetition. There was no "prescription" to follow, if you will. You listened and learned. You sang and learned. The call and response style made it easy and as the spirit moved within you, it gave your voice a life of its own.

Breath control, of course, does play a part in learning to sing the metered hymns. Long meter requires extended breath, one word, one syllable held as one would two words with four syllables: "Goooooooooooooo ooooooooooooo…" Common meter, as in "Aaamaaaziiing graaace," required you to hold your breath for a shorter duration. As to short meter, an example would be: "A chaarge to keep I haave…" Here, the line of a song would be held no longer than would be one word in the long-metered hymn.

Metered hymns were and are a convenient way of setting the tone when the congregation gathers to sing. It was practiced as follows: One person stood up and defined the meter. He said, "We're going to sing Hymn number 408, arranged in the common meter and I would thank some brother or sister for a suitable tune." The "liner" then lined out the hymn. Someone began: "Faaather, I stretch myyy haaands toooo Theeee. No oooother help I know…" The liner then repeated the next two lines, "what pain, what joy," at which point the song was picked up again by the brother or sister who set the "suitable tune." Once the tune was set, the congregation joined in.

Sometimes the diction was not clear, the words imprecise, but the fervor and the spirit, the meaning and the impact of those old songs carried us through the service, even into our day-to-day lives. Good music will carry you in times of despair. It is a way of drawing others to you, a way of understanding them and yourself, a way of getting across certain lines and barriers. Is it any surprise then that our nation has used musicians such as Louis Armstrong as goodwill ambassadors!?

Frederick Douglass in his narrative explained that our people sang as they went, as they moved from place to place, their songs expressing their feelings, telling their stories, preserving their traditions. We, too, sang to express our feelings and our faith, to convey our thoughts, to speak of what was around us, to tell a story. Our singing was a significant expression of our oral tradition. And, just as the stories told to us over and over again had a little different twist at every telling, the music and the songs were also never exactly the same. There was something out of your past that you sang about in the present. In fact, we were taught that you could no more sing the same song twice as tell a story as if it were set in stone. Yet, there was repetition and there was continuity in our lives as in the songs and the stories we grew up with. The outdoors where we labored, played, day-dreamed, and prayed; the homes that sheltered us; the churches that nurtured our faith and gave us community, all these were rooted in a tradition of music and storytelling.

We, like our ancestors, found definition and sustenance in music and in storytelling. Singing songs of experience, songs of faith and hope, songs about nature, songs from the Scriptures, music had great impact and meaning in our lives. So, music and stories were tools for motivation, tools for communication, and tools for insuring that certain actions would occur. Now ofttimes details were hidden in both. So, to sing the song "Go down Moses, way down in Egypt's land, tell old Pharaoh to let my people go" had one meaning in the days of slavery. It had to do with abolitionists helping to free people from bondage. Currently, it refers to something other than physical slavery. It means the efforts of people like Dr. Martin Luther King Jr. helping people gain their rights—voting, being a full citizen.

Of course, music is the key to our survival, medicine for the soul, a universal language. It is such an integral part of our lives that we couldn't think to be without it. Still cannot. My father summed it up: "Everybody can sing but the buzzard!"

61

HOME

AS MY PARENTS HAD TWO CROPS OF CHILDREN with a break in between, the older ones were gone by the time the younger ones came along. Mom and Dad never saw all of their children together at one time. In fact, it was only in 1968, at the funeral of my sister Annie Mae, that our parents and all of their remaining children gathered. Annie Mae was buried in the family graveyard where both Mother and Dad were later laid to rest.

As I was growing up, those of us children living at home slept in one room. There was a bed for the boys and one for our sister, Daisy. Mom and Dad had their own room. The front room, as I said, was always clean with the bed made up for guests. Dad made a fire there for their comfort if they happened to visit during the winter months. Of the three fireplaces in our house, however, the one most frequently used was in the kitchen. On winter mornings, Dad started the fire before we got up and waited for us with the proverbial bottle of castor oil or Black Drought syrup in his hand. Needless to say, we were drawn to the warmth of the kitchen like moths to a flame. A little fruit juice helped the medicine go down.

We had no indoor facilities, but an outhouse just beyond the barn, one with two seats. A Sears and Roebuck catalogue inside the door served as toilet paper and was also reading material. In fact, we referred to that catalogue as the "dream book," as its thin, shiny pages held the promise of a refrigerator to replace our icebox, a radio on which to listen to the ball games and fights, a new pair of shoes, a bicycle, anything we could dream of!

The outhouse was not only a convenience, but a refuge. It was a place to get away, particularly for my father, who frequently retreated to escape tensions mounting in the house, sometimes even in the middle of the night. We kept the outhouse for a number of years after building our new block home with electricity and indoor plumbing, just 100 or so feet away. When the outhouse was later torn down, Dad lost a precious refuge and not long after moved out. He and Mom were going through their own personal trials when my brother Joe and I decided to take a road trip together from California to Georgia to visit them. I had made a habit of going back to see my parents at least once a year, sometimes twice or three times. On that balmy summer day in 1980, when Joe and I set out in the early hours of the morning, feeling the excitement of the road ahead, I never imagined that I would be tried in the fire!

62

Burns: My Side of the Story

I drove my wife and our three children to California to spend some time with my in-laws. My brother and I then drove back to Salt Lake City and spent the weekend. I asked a friend to preach and look after things at the church I pastored until I returned. On Sunday, we picked up two passengers and went on to the National Baptist Congress of Christian Education in St. Louis. The session inspired and instructed. It ended on Friday night with a massive youth rally. My brother and I traveled on to Nashville where we got my sister and her son. Early Monday, June 23, 1980, we reached the family homestead outside of Gough, Georgia.

The trip had been long and tiring. When we pulled into the driveway, we could hardly see the house. It was almost like entering a jungle. There were trees and limbs and oversized rose bushes everywhere. We spent the night and got up the next morning with ideas about visiting friends and relatives. However, the yard needed cleaning and clearing. So, I decided to stay around and clean up. My mother joined the others and they were off visiting. I got some tools for cutting and digging and chopping. I cut down trees, dug up bushes, and chopped back weeds. As evening came it was time to get rid of all the piled trash.

I had cut and piled the bushes with paper underneath in two separate locations. The sun was creeping toward her western resting place. The temperature remained nearly 100 degrees. Tired and sweated, I took a folder of matches from my left front pocket. Pulling one match from the folder with my right hand, I closed the lip and struck the match. Nothing happened! I walked into the house, found an old kerosene can, poured its contents on the pile, and struck a second match. Still nothing happened! Of course, the stuff was green but it seemed the paper would catch fire if nothing else. About that time, my younger brother came in from work. He said, "Hey man, I've got some gasoline." I took what he gave me and poured it on the bushes. For the third time I struck a match and again nothing happened. I borrowed my brother's car, went three miles into the little country town, and bought some more gasoline. I took it back to the farm, poured it on the end mostly, walked around to the other end, struck another match, and this time the air exploded!

I could feel the heat against my arms and face. I saw no flames but something said to me, "You must be on fire." So, I fell to the ground and rolled over and over and over again. By the time I got up from the ground, the heat was all gone but the sting remained. My face felt cool and tight. My polyester pants had melted to nothing but cuffs and belt loops. My short-sleeved, white T-shirt remained intact. I looked down at my arms and saw the skin hanging like wet spaghetti. My flesh was raw and white with particles of dirt clinging to the blood on my arms. There was one small cut on my leg, evidently from rolling over glass and tin on the old house spot.

I walked anxiously around the back of the house to where my brother was tinkering with his car. I said, "Let's go to the hospital." By that time, he saw my hanging skin. He rushed to lock the house doors. We got in the car and drove in haste to the nearest hospital. There, we entered the emergency room door only to find nobody there. My brother walked south down one wing and I walked north down the other.

All the way to the hospital, I kept hoping and praying. I wondered how this thing could have happened. I wondered how it could happen to me. I wondered how it could happen to me so far away from home. I wondered how it could happen to me so far away from home in the midst of my long-overdue vacation. I worried about healing and how I would look and feel in the days and years ahead. What would other people say? My hopes were that the doctors could do something to take care of the burn with minimal time and scarring. Silently I begged God to help me. I prayed simply: "Please, Lord. Please, Lord." About halfway down the hall I came upon two nurses and a man talking in a small room. I poked my head in and asked where I might find a doctor. One nurse looked up, saw me and cried out, "Oh, Lord!" I spoke rather quickly, "Look, Lady, I'm not looking for the Lord, I already know where He is. What I need now is a doctor!" Nobody else knew that I had been talking to the Lord for some 13 miles or more. The nurse said, "I'll find you one. Go back to the emergency room." The other nurse followed me and quickly gathered some supplies to clean my skin.

In the emergency room the nurse took sterile water and started washing the sand and dirt out of my flesh. She asked again and again if she was hurting me. In fact, she cringed for me. I assured her that the pain was bearable. She offered me pain medication several times, but I refused. Soon, a rather young-looking doctor (one who looked like he was still in medical school) came in. He looked me over rather carefully. He looked like he wanted to do some poking, but he didn't. He asked the usual questions and asked about my pain. He offered me something for pain, but again I refused. He then said, "I'm sorry. We can't do anything for you here. What do you want to do?" With shock and amazement, I answered, "I want the very best medical care possible, no matter what."

The doctor left the emergency room section promising to call and see what he could arrange. He called several hospitals in the Augusta area. One hospital that could take burn patients had no space available for me. A second said they did have a room and would be glad to take me. Having made the contact, the ambulance driver was called. He soon arrived to drive me some 40 miles to the other facility. Fortunately, my brother knew the driver. In their conversation the driver mentioned that I would have to sit up all the way. My brother asked if I thought we could make it there just as well in his car. Certainly, we had come this far and we could go the rest of the distance plus avoid the 70 dollars it would cost to ride in the ambulance. (My brother would follow us anyway.) We told the doctor of our choice and he did not argue. I wondered, "Do they want to get rid of me as quickly as possible?" The doctor insisted that I should take some pain medication, but I refused again. The staff helped me into a hospital gown and I walked out.

My brother helped me into the car and made sure that I was in a comfortable position. I had him roll the windows partly down and we were on our way. He had called my other brother and told him of the incident and where we would be going. The trip did not seem very long. When we arrived, my older brother, my oldest sister, her son, and my mother were waiting outside. We pulled up to the emergency room entrance. I waved and smiled to them while walking inside.

When the hospital personnel saw me, several dropped what they were doing and ran here and there. Soon, some orderly rushed in with a gurney. They sat me on it and hurried toward the elevator. We went up to the fourth floor to the burn unit. The nurses wore green. They went about taking my vital signs. Five doctors came almost as if out of nowhere. They asked questions and checked this and that time and time again. My face was burned and peeled. My ears were parched and hard. My hair was singed off my face and head. The nurse simply brushed it off. My lips continued to sting. The skin on my arms was baked off except where I wore a watch. A small part of my chest and back were also burned. In fact, approximately 25 percent of my body was burned. Fortunately, no fire had entered my eyes, or my nose, and I did not swallow any.

The medical people got my situation under control and got me stabilized without delay. I asked the doctor, "How soon can I expect to get out of here?" He answered, "Well, you're going to be here a while." I said to him, "I have to be in Washington, D.C., by Friday." He said, "Well, I don't think you're going to make it." I then pointed out, "I have to be there by Saturday. I've got a wedding to do and a sermon to preach on Sunday." He said, "I don't think you'll make it to either. In fact, you're going to be here at least seven weeks."

With some anxiety, I resigned myself to stay as long as I had to, knowing that God still works miracles. Maybe I didn't have much choice, anyway. My oldest sister came to visit but found the rawness of my flesh hard to bear. She soon returned to her own hometown. I continued there in the burn unit with my brother sleeping either down the hall or in my room. He stayed almost every hour, helping in every way possible. He made the necessary telephone calls to my family and church family. I urged him to go on to my niece's wedding in Washington, but he would not, although my mother and younger brother did go.

The hospital was quite the place. My personal nurse was Bennie. She worked hard, stayed long, and spoke softly. Her patience could not be beat. Bennie was special. Each day, one of my fellow burn patients sat in the hall. He was burned on the foot and had been at the hospital four months. Healing seemed to have been slow for him. Even the doctors were discouraged, but that old gentleman had an untiring faith. Sitting there daily, he sang without shame, "Amazing Grace." I wondered how long I would have to stay. Would the healing be that long in coming? I then remembered that "nobody ever promised skateboards or bicycles!"

Word of my accident and resulting condition reached my wife, Willene, and the children while they were still in California. She wanted to drop everything and fly to Georgia. At one point, she actually made reservations and ordered an airplane ticket. My brother talked her out of the trip time and time again. I told him, "Tell her that there is no need to come. Everything will be alright here. There is nothing she can do but just be here. Tell her to take care of the kids and if anything drive back home where I will see her soon." You see, I had the medical personnel doing what they could. My brother was seeing to the business and other needs. There were lots of times she could not be with me due to various treatments. Plus the expense and inconvenience of finding someone to keep the children and getting a place to stay in Georgia were the excuses I gave. Of course, the real reasons were more personal. I did not want her to see me looking like I was and going through the pain and chills. (Even now, she can hardly stand to look at pictures that were taken several days after my admission to the hospital!) I wanted to shield her from real suffering and true pain. She called or we called her daily. My emotions were mixed. I wanted her near me, but more so I wanted her not there. Honestly, I thought she had enough to deal with without having to look on helplessly during my suffering in the hospital! After much persuasion, she accepted and soon went on home with the children to prepare for my homecoming although I am certain that she will never really understand my decision. My prayers are that I made the right one. Only time and experience will tell, I suppose.

I never realized how many friends I had or how many people were concerned. People called daily to see how I was. They sent flowers, so much so that the hospital finally had to refuse them. All kinds of cards came from all across the country expressing care. The local people learned about my situation and made it their business to visit regularly. Believe it or not, one dear friend rerouted himself from Nashville to New York by way of Augusta just to spend a few hours with me. Even the governor of my home state called to inquire of my condition. The churches went down in prayer like never before. People were praying everywhere, even some whom I had never known to pray before.

The hospital food was excellent. I ate and drank more than I could remember in recent years. "Plenty of protein and calories," they said, "help burns to heal." The nursing care matched the food for the most part. In short, the hospital was not a bad place to be.

My pain was like none I knew or had heard of before. (I still want to talk to some mother about birth pain and burn pain.) The thought alone of the wet to dry debriding bandages causes me to shiver even today. Keeping warm was probably the bigger problem. I sometimes sat an hour or more under the soothing warmth of the shower waters. I lived on a heating pad and under a long electric heater. Without skin, my body temperatures escaped. Further, when I got up to walk, most times, I had to carry my hands up above my head just to maintain balance. Somebody told me that in such situations, the blood rushes to the farthest point from the heart. While in the Intensive Burn Unit, my arms were bandaged. The portions with no burns were also covered. Since no veins in the arm were available for drawing blood, my foot was used to insert intravenous needles and for other needle work. I still feel tingling sensations in my toes from time to time.

One day, a lady came to draw blood and had real difficulty finding a vein. She stuck my foot time and time again with no results. It hurt. It hurt like nothing before. I broke down, cried, and lashed out: "Find somebody who knows what they are doing! Send the doctor in!" Now that I look back, I don't think she intentionally caused me more pain. It must have been my release time. She never returned and the doctor came each day thereafter and drew blood from my groin.

Remember the doctor had said that I would have to be in the hospital at least seven weeks? Time passed and I seldom knew one day from another. The first week was behind me before I knew it. The second week lapsed without delay. One Sunday passed and the second Sunday found me getting ready to leave. The staff wrapped me up well. My brother made airplane reservations. They gave me medicine and supplies, and I started out late that afternoon. On my way, I met the doctor and he said to me, "You must know somebody up there!" My face lit up and I answered, "I've been trying to tell you, doc. I've been trying to tell you."

My brother drove me to the airport and saw to it that I got on safely. I felt kind of bad leaving him to drive back to California all by himself, but he had insisted that I go home. On the airplane, the attendant seemed especially sensitive. The crew checked to make sure I was warm and comfortable and that my change in Atlanta was as smooth as possible. Between Atlanta and Salt Lake City, I got cold. The flight attendant put more blankets on me. Finally, we reached Salt Lake City during the early morning hours. I was the last passenger to leave the airplane. They put me in a wheelchair, gave me the blankets I had used to keep me warm, and pushed me toward the exit. To my great surprise and delight I saw there, along with my wife, many of my friends waiting to greet me. My eyes welled up with tears. I waved, said very little about my feelings, and rode on out. One of our neighbors drove his luxury car for me and my wife to ride home in. There were not very many smiles, but I sure was happy to be home!

At home, the house smelled of cleaning agents. The children were asleep, but I looked in to see each one. Willene pulled out pillows and covers to insure that I was comfortable. I do thank my Heavenly Father for giving me the wife that he knew I really needed.

Indeed, I have been snatched out of the burning by one of God's greatest miracles and I will tell the world that I have been tried in the Fire!

63

Burns: Willene's Side of the Story

"The Fire from the View of a Wife," as told in 1985

Reverend evidently was burned the day before. Nobody notified me until about ten the next morning. I was feeding France II his breakfast. Reverend's brother, Joe, called and said he had something to tell me. I asked what it was. He said, "While France was burning trash, he got burned. The doctors say they're doing everything they can for him. And I'm here with him. Clarence is here too. And Mom is here." When I asked how bad it was, Joe said, "He is burned pretty bad." I was not the first one called because when I said I needed to call someone at home, Joe said he had already talked to Deacon Harding Jones. That upset me. And why wasn't I told until the next day? Plus, I wasn't there and wanted to be there. I couldn't concentrate. My mom said, "Pray."

I started making plans to go to Georgia, but Joe said he was there. I felt I should have been there. But evidently, I wasn't needed for strength. I didn't understand why and still don't. I decided to go anyway. But Joe kept saying, "No, don't come. Everything is under control." Then the phone started ringing with people from Salt Lake City wanting to know what was going on. Here I was in the dark, not knowing anything. Edward Miller [Chairman of the Board of Trustees, Calvary Baptist Church] and family seemed like the only ones who understood the reason why I wanted and needed to go. Brother Miller called and said he would make airplane reservations to get me down there. I told him I would have to call him back and tell him when I made arrangements. Then he would arrange to pay for the tickets.

Joe called again that same day. I told him I was making arrangements to come down to Georgia. He told me no, that France didn't want me to come. He wanted me to stay until he needed me. I yelled out, "Until he needs me!!" Joe said, "He's alright and conscious. Maybe you'll need to come down later if things get worse." When I asked Joe where France was burned, he said, "The arms and a little on the face." He didn't tell me that the ears and hands were also burned.

Brother Miller called again to say he could make the arrangements. I told him to go ahead and make them. My brother-in-law kept calling, saying, "Don't come." But the next morning I started preparing to go anyway. Carolyn would watch France and Grace. They would stay with my sister Betty and my mom and my dad. Carolyn knew how to fix France's special food (to help control acid reflux). Brother Miller made the arrangements for me to leave that evening. Before I was about to leave, France's brother called again and said, "Don't do that." He said to trust him and to do what he asked. He asked if I wanted to talk to France. I said, "Yes." He said he would fix it for the next day so I could know he was "doing alright." I called Brother Miller and had him cancel the flight. He said, "Let me know if you still want to go any time."

The next day Joe called and put France on the phone. France talked and was saying the same as Joe: "Don't come down." He kept asking who was going to take care of my mother [who was ill] and what was I going to do with the kids if I came down there? He said that I needed to get ready to drive back to Utah if I didn't want to stay in California. "Don't come down" was the message I got. Every day I called, I got the same message.

One day I called and they said they had taken France where they were going to do something. It must have been time to get the dead skin off. Then I and the kids got ready to drive back to Utah. My brother Joe came along but was of little help; he can't drive. Finally, the children and I arrived in Utah in the early morning. I took my brother to the airport. Brother Miller offered to use the church's charge card to pay for my brother's ticket back to California. I refused thinking I might still need help myself to go to Georgia. I got my brother off.

Back at home, people were calling. Deacon Willie Hesleph called to see if we wanted to come to his house for the Fourth of July. I wanted to stay home. But, Linda Dowell (church member and neighbor) said, "No, you are not going to stay home today." She packed a lunch and we took my three children and her daughter and another friend, Sharon Carter and her daughter and we drove to Heber City to ride the Heber Creeper train.

I called and talked to France every day. But Reverend seemed upset that I was calling every day. He kept saying it was costing. He told me to call various people, especially Brother Lawrence Wynne. I was to tell him that when they write checks to give me Reverend's so I could pay the bills.

Reverend had already talked to Reverend Isaac Brantley [associate minister and close friend]. Then Pat, a former member of Calvary, called. We were talking about France's condition. She told me his sister Lulu said things were worse than reported to me. He was barely alive, worse, much worse than his brother was saying. That upset me more. But her husband Richard said he would go by and see since he was going that way. Later, France's brother Joe called and I asked him about what Pat had said. I told him it must have been worse since they didn't want me to come down there. He got upset and said Lulu shouldn't have said that.

The next day or so Richard came to visit me in Utah. He told me Reverend wasn't as bad as his sister had said. He said, listening to her, one would think him almost dead. He described to me his condition—his arms, his face, his ears, and the back of his hands. But he said that with the burns he had, he was alright. He said, "I wouldn't tell you a lie. That wouldn't help."

Then Joe and I started trying to get Reverend back to the VA or the University Hospital in Salt Lake City. When we finally got him back, I met him at the airport. Reverend didn't want me to tell anybody when he was coming in. His brother told me to ask Brother Tommie Gant to pick Reverend up. I told Sister Johnnie Wynne and talked to Reverend Theodore Fields. Somehow, when I got to the airport lots of people were there. I kept asking where Reverend was. When is he coming? I was so glad to see him! On the way home, I kept saying to myself, "Lord, thank you. Lord, thank you."

With Brother Gant's help, we got him home and our neighbor, Linda Dowell, had been watching the children.

When he got inside the house, Reverend kept asking, "What is that smell?" I had "Pinesoled" the house, sterilized the room and bath, and changed the bedding. We got him in the bed and tried to make him as comfortable as possible. I gave Brother Gant a hug and thanked him for all his help. I didn't sleep any at all that night. The next morning, I got him ready to go to the VA. We stopped by the copy center to get some copies made of the medical report so we would have one for ourselves and one for the hospital.

At the VA we saw a doctor. He said Reverend didn't need to be in the hospital. He got started with physical therapy that afternoon. Then he went every morning except Saturday and Sunday. For the first month he was very touchy. I kept asking what I could do. He would say, "Nothing."

64

UTAH

UTAH HAS BEEN FOR THE DAVISES A PLACE OF GOOD AND BAD. When I first arrived in Salt Lake City, I was turned down for an apartment where I had paid a deposit and had a telephone installed. Going to public places was sometimes stressful as people stared at us or through us, or made comments about our skin color. In stores we were sometimes followed around as if we were about to take something. In restaurants, we were sometimes ignored. I was determined to do what I could to bring about change. I signed up as a member of the Speakers' Bureau for the Utah Endowment for the Humanities and spoke about Dr. Martin Luther King Jr., about the African American church, about African American culture and the African American experience in general all over the state. I was invited by groups across the state and went. I believe that by speaking I helped to educate and bring about some change.

There were still restrictive covenants in some of the real estate contracts in the 1970s in terms of who could buy what property. I got involved in trying to bring about a fair housing bill. In fact, so much of what we did here in Utah was not just about people of color, but about people who were just poor and had special needs. One of the organizations that I helped to start here in Utah was called UOIC (Utah Opportunities Industrialization Center), a community-based manpower training program. OICA (Opportunities Industrialization Center of America) was started by one Reverend Doctor Leon H. Sullivan of Philadelphia, Pennsylvania, in response to what Dr. Martin Luther King Jr. did there. Dr. King got a company to hire some African Americans to work in Philadelphia. They did, but soon these workers were fired. Dr. Sullivan approached the company and asked why they had hired them only to fire them a short time later. The answer was that they lacked the technical skills or the motivation to handle the job. Dr. Sullivan's response in a meeting was, "Oh, I see." And from that the name of the organization—OIC—was put together. In the middle 1970s the late Dr. Alberta Henry, who already operated a scholarship fund and was an activist in civil rights, invited the organization to come and take a look at Utah. (She set a good example of community leadership and was an active member in Calvary.) They came and decided this was a good place for OIC. I was drafted by the group to become the first chairman of the board of directors of the UOIC movement in the state of Utah. We helped people on welfare, people who were in dead-end jobs, those who were displaced from jobs, housewives who had not worked before. We helped school dropouts get their GEDs, taught people how to fill out a job application, how to dress for work, how to deal with body hygiene, how to participate in an interview. The OIC program was for more than 10 years a major player in the job training and placement business for the state of Utah, as it had been all over the United States. We talked to employers, getting them to work with us, telling us what they needed, giving us necessary equipment so that we could train prospective employees. Thus, when the Kennecott Copper mine shut down and became computerized, and Union Pacific Railroad downsized, we helped retrain workers. Our goal was to make sure that everybody had a fair chance and opportunity at meaningful and gainful employment.

In 1974 I was a member of the governor's Black Advisory Council, a council established by Governor Calvin Rampton as a way of making sure he had input from minority groups in the community. One day while we were talking, I pointed out to the governor that there were no African Americans on the Board of Corrections (a policy board) and none on the Board of Pardons, the most powerful board in the state. There were no African American employees at an institution where some 10 to 16 percent of clients were people of color. Governor Rampton asked, "What can we do about it?" I suggested that we get someone on the board and hire African Americans. He promptly picked up the phone and called the personnel office. The first two hired were good workers and became a success for the program because they were committed to making a difference. One was male, one was female. I suggested a chaplain be appointed and Reverend Douglas A. Washington accepted the assignment. I was appointed to the Board of Corrections and served for 10 years. We made decisions about hiring and firing, appointed members to the Board of Pardons, decided about the location of facilities, housing of inmates, and in major ways we made policies that governed how the prisons would operate.

There came a day in 1986 when the federal government passed a Martin Luther King Jr. holiday bill, signed by President Reagan. A number of states said it did not apply to them. Utah was one. A number of us introduced a bill into the state legislature, which did not pass the first time. The second time, I chaired a committee to lobby and educate legislators and the community at large. There were major objections. There were those who asked what Martin Luther King Jr. had done for Utah, that he had never been to Utah, that he had moral problems and issues. Senator Terry Williams, the only African American in the Utah legislative body, sponsored the bill. We looked for sponsors in the House and got beat up pretty badly. Eventually, Representative Robert Sykes and I debated the issue on "Take Two," a news program on Sunday evenings. He was opposed to the bill, but by the end of the debate, convinced by my argument and responses, he asked, "Reverend, what can I do to make sure that this bill will pass the state legislature?" We were then able to get him to sign on as a co-sponsor of the bill in the House. Eventually it passed, but as a compromise bill that proposed instead a Martin Luther King/Human Rights Day. It was not until the year 2000 that the bill was changed and renamed the Martin Luther King Holiday Bill. Even then objections continued. A year later we petitioned the city and state to designate 600 South as Martin Luther King Jr. Boulevard. They agreed, but required us to raise funds to pay for the sign changes. We have still not raised enough funds to change the big freeway exit signs.

My goal and that of the Calvary congregation was to try to make a positive difference wherever people hurt. When people ask me about what I'm doing, I tell them that I am first and foremost a pastor of the church, concerned about the spiritual welfare and well-being of people in our community. But then, just as much, I am concerned about what it is that causes people to hurt and working on making it better. That has been my goal in terms of my leadership as pastor of the Calvary Baptist Church. So, if you are hungry, there are some people working on it. If you are in prison we render counseling and worship services. We have made it our business to visit men, women, and youth at the Point of the Mountain prison and men at the Gunnison facility. The turnout has always been tremendous, inmates asking what they can do to make our visits more frequent. When I told them of my reluctance to make the drive, one staff member volunteered to pick me up anytime. The inmates were excited to hear my talk about self-esteem, our goodly heritage, everybody having worth, and how to be a meaningful contributor even while locked up. Our most recent visit was a celebration where the inmates said to me, "Let us show you what we are doing about what you've been talking about." Some brought out a quilt. Others had been working on computers.

At Calvary, we focus on the old and the young. We built a 30-unit facility for seniors and run nutrition and day programs for the elderly, providing entertainment, crafts, and a hot meal. And, of course, we have countless reading, science literacy programs, music, and tutoring programs for our youth.

Perhaps our most engaging commitment focused on about 600 victims of the 2005 Katrina hurricane. Governor Jon Huntsman Jr. invited them to find shelter in Utah. We joined his team to meet them at the Air National Guard Base, transport them to Camp Williams for housing, and meet their physical and spiritual needs in every way. We are excited not to call them "refugees," as many did, but "guest" and "friend." We worked to get the Utah Transit Authority bus line to extend service to Camp Williams and issue passes for each rider.

We at Calvary are concerned about a better way of life for all. Personally, I am convinced that only as all move up will we get where we are going.

65

Going Somewhere!

Cooper's Town was mostly flat with lots of fruit trees and trees planted for timber. My parents owned perhaps the most productive parcel of land there. Our property had a stream running through it in the winter months. It widened into a pond that became muddy in the heat of summer. It was there that I ofttimes caught fish as a boy, simply stirring the mud with a hoe. The last time I was home, as my brother and I drove around to the pond, we talked about the fish we used to catch, and how the beautiful birds are now catching and eating them.

In the three-mile radius between Cooper's Town and Gough, there were a number of plantations owned by whites. The bulk of the farm work on these was done by black sharecroppers and their children who were in essence just above being slaves. They worked sun to sun all year long only to be told at the end of each season that they still owed the landowner for supplies they had acquired on credit. So, they were obliged to work another year, and another year, and another year… To escape, some sharecroppers and their families literally had to slip away under cover of night, often hopping a freight train.

Unlike Gough and Waynesboro, Cooper's Town was an all-African American community with landowners. People knew each other and the grapevine was more effective than any telephone today. If anyone did anything they ought not to have done, the word spread at the speed of lightning and the person was confronted by members of the community either at home or at church. People knew each other's business, sharing the good times and the bad.

My mother told the story of how my father took ill shortly after I was born. The crops had been planted. It was time for final plowing, "laying by." My father was bedridden and could not go out to the fields, as I mentioned earlier. When others had done what was needed in their own fields, they came with their animals and plows and did the work for him. Some were neighbors and others were family. They returned to pick his cotton, corn, or whatever crop was ready to be harvested. At such times, even those who did not get along put differences aside and pitched in.

Gough, a bigger community, was "two-toned" and not so tight-knit as Cooper's Town. Of the four churches in Gough, three were African American. One was First Baptist. The other two were Methodist churches. All were located on the east side, the African American side of town. The whites lived on the west side. Separating the black and white communities was the railroad with a station in Gough. That railroad suggested undreamed-of worlds. I thought of it when I went to Israel in January of 1992 to participate with seven other pastors from across the country in a clergy familiarization trip, referred to as a "clergy fam trip." We walked where Jesus walked and could imagine what it was like to have met the woman at the well, to have baptized in the Jordan, walked in the Mount of Olives, been crucified at the rugged skull, and been buried in a garden tomb. My convictions about Jesus Christ, my day-to-day commitment, and my preaching changed as I came away with a new appreciation for the gift of His coming and the price He paid for my guilt. But as a youngster in Georgia, the railroad offered only a glimmer of things to come.

As children, we learned that if we put our ear to the railroad track, we could tell by the vibration off the rails if a train was coming and even how far it might be. We could then decide if we had time to wait to see it pull into the station, or if we needed to go about our business. The mere sound of the train whistle ignited a spark in our hearts. We got excited. We wanted to see who got off and who got on at the station. The railroad was a symbol of opportunity as well as escape when necessary. It offered possibilities for our own future. Growing up in rural Georgia, we were certain that riding behind a pair of mules would not get us very far. Thus, when we heard the train whistle, when we saw the locomotive speed by or slow down as it pulled into the station, that was something we could grasp. It was something we could reach for. We dreamed!

For so many of us, making it to Gough meant we could make it to Waynesboro. And, if we made it to Waynesboro, we knew we could make it to Augusta. And if we reached Augusta, we might be able to go on to Washington D.C., New York, Chicago…

Whether a freight train was being loaded with bales of cotton, peaches, lumber, animals, or for that matter harboring stowaways, or a passenger train was pulling into the station, the iron horse's comings and goings stirred up longings. The railroad was our connection to the outside world, a springboard to a better life.

WE WERE GOING SOMEWHERE!

Acknowledgments

SPECIAL THANKS to the Calvary Baptist Church congregation, to Mrs. Willene Davis, and to Carolyn, Grace, France II, and Cedric. Thanks also to Ms. Donnette Atiyah for first bringing Nayra to Calvary in the 1990s; to Ms. Mary Megalli for traveling to Gough and Cooper's Town, Georgia, in the winter of 2002 and contributing photographs and notes; to Calvary Baptist Church associate minister Anthony Bennett and to Artur Kapriyelov for their help with computer-related matters; and to Ms. Carol Edison for suggesting "short" chapters.

ANN GARRETT

Nayra Atiya lives in Salt Lake City.
This is her sixth book.

"A friend loveth at all times."
PROVERBS 17:17